THE MEDIEVAL HORSE
AND ITS EQUIPMENT

*c.*1150–*c.*1450

Half-title Horseman with horse decorated with a range of harness pendants, *c.* 1300 (*Mappa Mundi* – Dean and Chapter, Hereford Cathedral)

Title page Personal seal of a medieval marshal: seal of Ralph, the marshal of the Bishop of Durham, showing a horseshoe, hammer and nails (after Fleming 1869, 379)

MEDIEVAL FINDS FROM EXCAVATIONS IN LONDON: 5

The Medieval Horse and its Equipment
c.1150 – c.1450

edited by John Clark

with contributions by
John Clark, Blanche M A Ellis, Geoff Egan, Nick Griffiths,
D James Rackham, Brian Spencer and Angela Wardle

Principal Illustrators
Nigel Harriss and Susan Mitford

BOYDELL PRESS
in association with Museum of London

© 1995, 2004 Museum of London

All Rights Reserved. Except as permitted under current legislation
no part of this work may be photocopied, stored in a retrieval system,
published, performed in public, adapted, broadcast,
transmitted, recorded or reproduced in any form or by any means,
without the prior permission of the copyright owner

First published 1995
Her Majesty's Stationery Office

New edition 2004
The Boydell Press, Woodbridge
Reprinted in paperback 2011

ISBN 978-1-84383-679-7

A Museum of London Publication
Museum of London, London Wall,
London EC2Y 5HN
www.museumoflondon.org.uk

The Boydell Press is an imprint of Boydell & Brewer Ltd
PO Box 9, Woodbridge, Suffolk IP12 3DF, UK
and of Boydell & Brewer Inc.
668 Mt Hope Avenue, Rochester, NY 14620, USA
website: www.boydellandbrewer.com

A catalogue record for this book is available
from the British Library

Library of Congress Catalog Card Number: 2004007726

Papers used by Boydell & Brewer Ltd are natural, recyclable products
made from wood grown in sustainable forests

Printed in Great Britain by
CPI Antony Rowe, Chippenham and Eastbourne

Contents

Acknowledgements

In a series entitled *Medieval Finds from Excavations in London* the first acknowledgements must be to many present and former members of the archaeological staff of the Museum of London, and of its predecessor the Guildhall Museum (under whose auspices such sites as Baynard's Castle (1972) and Trig Lane (1974–5) were investigated): to the field staff of the former Department of Urban Archaeology who carried out the excavations and to those whose painstaking interpretation of the results – through the establishment of site sequences and through dendrochronology and ceramic studies in particular – provided the chronological framework for the present study of the finds. We must also thank the members of the Society of Thames Mudlarks whose skill with metal detectors so greatly enhanced the level of finds recovery on sites where conventional archaeological techniques could not be used, particularly at Swan Lane and Billingsgate.

Excavation would not have been possible without the co-operation and in some cases financial support of the landowners or developers of the sites. In particular, of the excavations here considered, the following received sponsorship from the developers:

BIS82	Pontsarn Investments Ltd
BOY86	Morgan Guaranty
EST83	Land Securities (Management) Ltd
IME83	Trollope & Colls (City) Ltd
IRO80	Guardian Royal Exchange Assurance plc
LUD82	Norwich Union Insurance Group
OPT81	Commercial Union Properties Ltd
PDN81	National Provident Institution and English Property Corporation
PET81	Trafalgar House Development/ Wimpey Property Holdings
SUN86	LEP Group plc
SWA81	Edgar Investments Ltd
TAV82	Winglaw Properties Ltd and Maritime Property Investments Ltd

Most of the excavations, however, were funded by the Department of the Environment, which also paid for the bulk of the post-excavation work until this responsibility – including the funding of much of the preparation of this volume – was taken over by its successor body, English Heritage. Thanks are due to the officers of those organisations for their support. Additional grants were received from the Corporation of the City of London and the Manpower Services Commission (Billingsgate) and from the Museum of London Trust Fund and the City of London Archaeological Trust (Swan Lane and Billingsgate). Further grants from the City of London Archaeological Trust allowed the completion of work on this volume, in particular the provision of many of the illustrations.

Although the names of several authors appear on the title page, their research would not have been possible without the support of many others working within the archaeological finds section, under the direction at first of Michael Rhodes and Francis Grew, later of Angela Wardle, Penny MacConnoran and Hedley Swain – both in carrying out initial identifications and recording finds, and later in so efficiently making material available for study. The statistical study of the horseshoes was derived from a computerised database, most of the data being input by Pat Reynolds from measurements by Lynne Keys. Conservation was carried out in the Museum of London Conservation Department, particularly by Rose Johnson and Helen Ganiaris, who also provided the essential identifications of materials. Advice on such identifications also came from English Heritage's Ancient Monuments Laboratory, as is acknowledged in individual cases in the text.

Drawings are chiefly by Nigel Harriss and Sue Mitford, working under the direction of Nick Griffiths and later of Ann Jenner and Alison Hawkins; Nick Griffiths provided drawings for his own chapter on harness pendants. Photographs, except those from outside sources listed below, are the work of Julian Sandiford and of the photographic staff of the Museum of London Archaeology Service (and of its predecessor the

Museum's Department of Urban Archaeology) and of the Museum's Photographic Department.

Angela Wardle assisted with editing the text; John Schofield and Tony Dyson commented on early drafts. Ian Goodall read the text on behalf of English Heritage and provided invaluable comments on matters of both form and content. We are also grateful to Anne Muffett and Frances Maher and staff of HMSO for their meticulous work in the final stages of preparation and production of this volume.

Specific thanks, more fully detailed in the text where appropriate, are due to a number of individuals: Philip Armitage, Mrs J Betts, John Cherry, David Gaimster, Francis Grew, Claudia Hart, Captain David Horn, Malcolm Jones, Arthur MacGregor, Peter Marsden, Patrick Ottaway, Nigel Ramsay, Michael Rhodes, Ian Soden, Brian Spencer and James White. Ann Hyland of Wisbech showed great forbearance in responding to ill-informed questions regarding horses from one of the authors (John Clark) whose first-hand experience had previously been limited to childhood donkey rides at the seaside. She kindly read through a draft of his text; if through her advice he has avoided a fall at the first fence, subsequent faults are his own responsibility. Blanche Ellis wishes to acknowledge the help of Claude Blair and of Sarah Barter-Bailey and former colleagues at the Royal Armouries in providing her with references to spurs from their own researches. John Clark also acknowledges the patience with which his colleagues at the Museum of London viewed his commitment to this project, which was at times at some expense to his museum curatorial work.

Though it is not perhaps normal in Acknowledgements such as this to record a debt to one whose assistance has been largely through published works, a glance at the bibliography will reveal one name that recurs more often than any other: that of Dr Ian Goodall. Without his studies of medieval iron objects from excavations throughout much of Britain, published over many years, the finding of *comparanda* for material from our London sites would have been very difficult and its relationship to forms and chronologies elsewhere impossible to assess. Similarly, frequent reference is made to the pioneering work of John Ward Perkins, published chiefly in the London Museum's *Medieval Catalogue* (1940); 50 years on, the typologies and chronologies he established remain a vital starting point.

Copyright in illustrations, which we gratefully acknowledge permission to reproduce, is as follows: The Bodleian Library, Oxford – Figs 12 and 15; The British Library – front cover, Figs 7, 9, 17 and 114; City of Derby Museums and Art Gallery – Fig 14; Blanche Ellis – Fig 98; English Heritage – Fig 100; Fitzwilliam Museum, Cambridge – Fig 28; Guildhall Library – Fig 5; National Gallery – Fig 105; University of Edinburgh Library – Fig 10. Fig 46 was drawn by Nick Griffiths and is reproduced by kind permission of the Dean and Chapter of Hereford Cathedral.

Permission to adapt the following original drawings is gratefully acknowledged: Figs 56 and 78 John Hickman and Martin Humphrey/J A Allen & Co Ltd.

Other illustrations are copyright of the Board of Governors of the Museum of London.

Conventions

Numerical references

All the items catalogued and described in this volume are given simple consecutive *catalogue numbers*; when discussed in the text they are referred to as '*No 1*', '*No 2*' etc. The catalogue entry for each item normally contains its site reference number, consisting of a *site code* of the form '*BC72*', '*BIG82*' etc. (an abbreviation or mnemonic for the site location with two digits of the year in which work began), followed by an *accession number* or *acc no* (the registered small find number, unique within the site); thus site code and accession number together provide a unique number which will serve to identify the object within the Museum of London archaeological archive. These are followed in the catalogue entry by a site *context* number, in parentheses, and a date (where available) for the context, usually in the form of a *ceramic phase*. The significance of this form of dating is discussed below in the chapter titled 'The excavations'; the location of the sites concerned is also detailed there – both are summarised below. Some finds included in the catalogue have a number of the form '*ER——*'; these are finds from sites recorded in the former Guildhall Museum's 'Excavation Register', usually small salvage excavations carried out by museum staff before 1972. Some items recovered off-site among spoil from sites such as the Billingsgate lorry park (BIG82 and BWB83) were acquired directly by the Museum of London from the finders; these have Museum of London ('*MoL*') accession numbers such as '*86.159/1*'. Comparative material in the Museum of London collections is referred to in the text, and may have accession numbers of a variety of forms.

Abbreviations

acc no	– accession number
AML	– analysis by Ancient Monuments Laboratory (English Heritage)
d	– diameter
DUA	– Museum of London Department of Urban Archaeology
h	– height
l	– length
MLC	– analysis by Museum of London Conservation Department
MoL	– Museum of London
MoLAS	– Museum of London Archaeology Service
nd	– no date
RAK	– X-ray fluorescence analysis at Royal Armouries, HM Tower of London, by Roger Turner of Kevex Ltd
th	– thickness
w	– width
wt	– weight
+	– (as context date) unstratified

Site codes

The following sites are referred to in the text, although not all of them produced material to be included in the catalogue; major sites from which catalogued finds came are marked with an asterisk and discussed in more detail in the chapter titled 'The excavations'. All sites are in the City of London, except where the postcode (e.g. SE1, WC2) indicates otherwise.

ABS86 – St Albans House, 124 Wood Street, 1986
AL74 – 62–4 Aldgate High Street, 1974
AMB87 – 58–63 Aldermanbury, 1987
*BC72 – Baynard House, Queen Victoria Street ('Baynard's Castle'), 1972
*BIG82 – Billingsgate lorry park, Lower Thames Street, 1982
*BIS82 – 76–80 Bishopsgate, 1982
*BOP82 – 28–32 Bishopsgate, 1982
*BOY86 – 5–11 Tudor Street, former City of London Boys' School, 1986
BSF86 – Beddington Sewage Farm, Sutton, 1986
*BWB83 – Billingsgate lorry park, watching brief, 1983
*BYD81 – Baynard's Castle, City of London Boys' School (new site), Upper Thames Street, 1981
CAP86 – Capel House, 54–62 New Broad Street, 1986
CH75 – Chaucer House, Tabard Street, SE1, 1975
*CLE81 – 29–32 Clements Lane, 1981
*CUS73 – Custom House, Wool Quay, Lower Thames Street, 1973
*CUT78 – Harrow Place, 1978
ER872 – finds from Thames foreshore (Ivor Noël-Hume Collection)
ER1279A – Thames at site of Old London Bridge, dredging 1967
*EST83 – 27–9 Eastcheap, 1983
FST85 – 94–7 Fenchurch Street, 1985
GAG87 – Guildhall Art Gallery, 1987
GDH85 – Guildhall House, 81–7 Gresham Street, 1985
*GPO75 – British Telecom Headquarters, formerly GPO site, 76–80 Newgate Street, 1975

HOO88 – Hooper Street/Backchurch Lane, E1, 1988
ILA79 – Miles Lane, 132–7 Upper Thames Street, 1979
*IME83 – 27–30 Lime Street, 1983
*IRO80 – 24–5 Ironmonger Lane, 1980
JUB85 – Jubilee Hall site, Covent Garden, WC2, 1985
LDW84 – 44 London Wall, 1984
LEA84 – 71–7, Leadenhall Street, 32–40 Mitre Street, 1984
LH74 – 44–6 Ludgate Hill/1–5 Old Bailey, 1974
*LLO78 – Lloyds, Leadenhall Place, 1978
LSO88 – 47–57 Gresham Street, 1988
LUD82 – 1–6 Old Bailey/42–6 Ludgate Hill, 1982
*MC73 – St Mildred Bread Street, 84–94 Queen Victoria Street, 1973
MFS76 – finds from modern Thames foreshore, 1976
*MLK76 – 1–6 Milk Street, 1976
MOG86 – 49–53 Moorgate/72–4 Coleman Street, 1986
NEB87 – 35–45 New Broad Street, 1987
OPS88 – 158–64 Bishopsgate, 1988
*OPT81 – 2–3 Cross Keys Court, Copthall Avenue, 1981
ORM88 – Ormond House, 38 Cannon Street/ 62–3 Queen Victoria Street, 1988
*PDN81 – Pudding Lane, 118–27 Lower Thames Street, 1981
PEA87 – Peabody site, Bedfordbury, WC2, 1987
*PET81 – St Peter's Hill/Castle Baynard Street, Upper Thames Street, 1981
PIC87 – 1–3 Pilgrim Street/56–66 Carter Lane, 1987
*POM79 – GPO site, Newgate Street (central area), 1979
SBG87 – St Bartholomew the Great, West Smithfield, 1987
*SH74 – Seal House, 106–8 Upper Thames Street, 1974
SSL84 – 19 St Swithin's Lane, 1984
STO86 – Stothard Place, 284–94 Bishopsgate, 1986
*SUN86 – Sunlight Wharf, Upper Thames Street, 1986

*SWA81 – Swan Lane car park, 95–103 Upper Thames Street, 1981

*TAV82 – 29–31 Knightrider Street, 1982

*THE79 – Mermaid Theatre, Puddle Dock, Upper Thames Street, 1979

TIG84 – Trig Lane/Queen Victoria Street, 1984

*TL74 – Trig Lane, Upper Thames Street, 1974

TR74 – Billingsgate Buildings, 101–10 Lower Thames Street, 1974

*TUD78 – 1–3 Tudor Street, 1978

*UT74 – Upper Thames Street (Baynard House), 1974

VRY89 – Vintry House, 68 Upper Thames Street, 1989

*WAT78 – Watling Court, 41–53 Cannon Street, 1978

175BHS – 175 Borough High Street, SE1, 1976

Ceramic phase dates

phase 1 $c.900 - c.1000$

phase 2 $c.970 - c.1050$

phase 3 $c.1000 - c.1050$

phase 4 $c.1050 - c.1080/1150$

phase 5 $c.1080 - c.1150$

phase 6 $c.1150 - c.1200$

phase 7 $c.1200 - c.1230$

phase 8 $c.1230 - c.1260$

phase 9 $c.1270 - c.1350$

phase 10 $c.1330 - c.1380$

phase 11 $c.1350 - c.1400$

phase 12 $c.1400 - c.1450$

Note: Recent study has suggested that several of the figures given here may be subject to adjustment by 10 or 20 years – see Schofield, Allen & Taylor 1990, 44–5; however, for consistency, the dates used throughout the *Medieval Finds from Excavations in London* series are adopted in this volume and have been used for example to construct the chronological tables in the chapter on horseshoes.

Introduction to the second edition

JOHN CLARK

In the nine years since this book first appeared there has been much interest in the history of the horse and its equipment, mirrored for example in Ann Hyland's recent volumes on *The Warhorse, 1250–1600* (1998) and *The Horse in the Middle Ages* (1999) and in an exhibition in 2003 in Lexington, Kentucky, 'All the Queen's Horses' with its associated catalogue (Kentucky Horse Park 2003) – these and other publications are listed in the Supplementary Bibliography below. However, there have been few published archaeological studies that add to or alter significantly the conclusions reached in the present volume.

Some recent work in various fields should however be noted here.

The sites

The stratigraphic context of the artefacts from several notable waterfront groups from four sites around the bridgehead (Swan Lane, Seal House, New Fresh Wharf and Billingsgate), included in this volume, will be reviewed in a publication in preparation (Schofield & Dyson in prep). This will place the material discussed here in the context of where the pieces were found, and perhaps refine some of the dating of the groups from those sites.

Remains of medieval horses

In an unusual attempt at prognostication I commented in the first edition (p 20) that it might be 'just beyond the City boundaries that we should seek London's horse graveyards'. Although rather further from the City than I suggested, such a 'graveyard' of late medieval to Tudor date came to light in Elverton Street, Westminster, in 1994–6 (Cowie & Pipe 1998). The skeletal remains (though they survived poorly) had great similarities to those from the City discussed by James Rackham in this volume, and seem to reflect the slaughter of aged horses for their hides and disposal of their carcasses.

In connection with my discussion of the evidence for the size of medieval horses (pp 22–32), I am grateful to Mary Littauer for a copy of her note 'How great was the "Great Horse"' (1963), which I had not seen. She concludes that 'you are left with . . . 15 hands 1 inch for the most massive candidate for the role of Great Horse'.

Finds

There seem to have been no extensive groups of medieval horse gear published recently apart from that from York (Ottaway & Rogers 2002, 2956–66); this contains some interesting comparative material, including a very early curry comb that contradicts the typological development we suggested here on pp 162–4.

Some publications on individual types of object are worth recording, however.

Bits: No parallels to the strange curb-bit discussed on pp 51–3 have been noted, but an excellent example of an early medieval curb-bit from Ludgershall Castle (found in a context dated 1280–1300) has now been published (Goodall 2000, 153–5), which itself is a closer parallel for the one in the Metropolitan Museum of Art that we refer to, and may provide a better explanation of the 'triangular' shape of the cheeks of curb bits in such illustrations as our Fig 39. A similar bit is reported from Gordons Lodge, Northamptonshire (pers comm. Jonathan Thomas). A later curb-bit of more 'normal' form, a close parallel to that from Tannenberg Castle (*c.* 1399) illustrated by Ward Perkins (London Museum 1940, 78 fig 18.2), has since been acquired by the Museum of London, a metal-detected find from the Thames foreshore (MoL acc no 95.319; illustrated Kentucky Horse Park 2003, 123 no 21.5b).

Harness pendants: Although confined to armorial pendants, the volume by Steven Ashley (2002) on finds from Norfolk is a valuable addition to the literature on these items.

Spurs: Blanche Ellis, who contributed the section on spurs to the present volume, has now published a Datasheet on prick spurs for the Finds Research Group AD700–1700 (2002). This clarifies the confusion that can occur between early medieval prick spurs and much later forms. One of her publications that was listed in our original Bibliography as 'forthcoming' has now appeared, and is included under Corrections below.

In addition to these recent publications, we should note that the new Portable Antiquities Scheme is ensuring the reporting and recording of large numbers of finds made by members of the public, mostly metal-detectorists, and many such finds are horse related. Although they have no datable archaeological content, the records and images available through the Scheme's website <http://www.finds.org.uk/> provide a valuable resource for anyone studying the development of horse equipment.

In preparing this new introduction I am grateful for the comments received from the contributors to the original text, and also from my colleagues John Schofield and Alan Pipe. Minor corrections are also listed below, and I am grateful to those who drew attention to the errors.

Supplementary Bibliography

ASHLEY, S, 2002 *Medieval Armorial Horse Furniture in Norfolk* (*East Anglian Archaeology* 101), Dereham

COWIE, R, & PIPE, A, with others, 1998 'A late medieval and Tudor horse burial ground: excavations at Elverton Street, Westminster', *Archaeol J* 155, 226–51

ELLIS, B, 2002 *Prick Spurs 700–1700*, Finds Research Group AD700–1700 Datasheet 30

GOODALL, I H, 2000 'Iron objects' in Ellis, P (ed) *Ludgershall Castle Wiltshire: A Report on the Excavations by Peter Addyman, 1964–1972*, Wilts Archaeol Nat Hist Soc Monograph Series 2, Devizes, 143–56

HYLAND, A, 1998 *The Warhorse, 1250–1600*, Stroud

———, 1999 *The Horse in the Middle Ages*, Stroud

KENTUCKY HORSE PARK, 2003 *All the Queen's Horses: The Role of the Horse in British History*, Lexington, KY

LITTAUER, M, 1963 'How great was the "Great Horse" ', *Light Horse* (December) 350–2

OTTAWAY, P, & ROGERS, N, 2002 *Craft, Industry and Everyday Life: Finds from Medieval York* (*The Archaeology of York: The Small Finds 17/15*), York

SCHOFIELD, J, and DYSON, T, in prep *London Waterfront Tenements 1100–1750*, London

Corrections

p 3 Fig 3 This 'unidentified' engraving is Plate XVII in W J Miles *Modern Practical Farriery: A Complete Guide to All that Relates to the Horse . . .*, originally issued in parts by William Mackenzie, London, Glasgow and Edinburgh, 1868–9

p 46 (the date of the London loriners' ordinances) *for* 1269 *read* 1261

p 128 (the date of the death of Bertrand de Goth) *for* 1342 *read* 1324

The following corrections to publications listed as 'forthcoming' should be made both in the Bibliography and where they appear in the text:

p 130 *for* Blair & Crawford forthcoming *read* Blair & Crawford 1997 p 141 (twice) *for* Ellis forthcoming, no 7 *read* Ellis 2000, 138–9 no 7, fig 6.16

p 178 *for* BLAIR, J & CRAWFORD, B, forthcoming in *Oxoniensia read* BLAIR, J & CRAWFORD, B, 1997 'A late Viking burial at Magdalene Bridge, Oxford?' *Oxoniensia* 62, 135–43

p 180 *for* ELLIS, B, forthcoming (etc) *read* ELLIS, B, 2000 'The spurs' in Ellis, P (ed) *Ludgershall Castle Wiltshire: A Report on the Excavations by Peter Addyman, 1964–1972,* Wilts Archaeol Nat Hist Soc Monograph Series 2, Devizes, 137–42

Introduction: horses and horsemen in medieval London

JOHN CLARK

with contributions by Brian Spencer and D James Rackham

Excavations and finds

This volume is one in a series devoted to the rich variety of medieval finds from excavations carried out in the City of London during the 1970s and early 1980s, chiefly by the archaeological service founded as the Department of Urban Archaeology of the Guildhall Museum in 1973, which transferred under the same name to that Museum's successor, the Museum of London, in 1975. Most though not all of the finds (as will be seen in the map of site locations included in the fuller discussion of the site evidence below – Fig 22) were recovered from the deep series of riverside dump deposits south of Thames Street between Blackfriars (Baynard's Castle) and Custom House, an area reclaimed between the 11th and the 15th century by the building of a sequence of new wharves and waterfronts. Only these major waterfront sites produced quantities of horse-related artefacts in double figures; three sites – 'Baynard's Castle', Billingsgate (lorry park site) and Swan Lane – between them account for more than 60% of the finds catalogued in this volume. Inland sites tended to be smaller, and produced few horse-related finds; the distribution of finds does not seem to be significant.

In general the range and quantity of finds from the riverside sites was astonishing, even before the introduction of metal detectors in the capable hands of members of the Society of Thames Mudlarks increased the rate of recovery on some of the later excavations. Soil conditions resulted in a much better preservation of both metalwork and organic materials than is normally seen elsewhere. The close dating of these contexts, by methods described below, has allowed a much more accurate chronology to be established for finds of all types than was previously possible –

for example, its application to the study of medieval pottery was first summarised by Vince (1985), while the new confidence in dating has been central to all volumes in the present series.

The study of these sites and of the finds from them has added immeasurably to our knowledge of the circumstances of life in medieval London, and by inference that in other urban centres. It is limited only by the overall chronology of the city's waterfront development, which began on most of the sites under review in the mid-12th century and was ended by the construction in the mid-15th century of stone riverside walls which halted the forward march of reclamation. Although a companion volume on the Saxo-Norman evidence has already appeared (Vince 1991), a number of relevant items of earlier date have been included here, both from waterfront and inland sites, where they add to or complete a chronological or typological series.

The subject of this volume is the equipment associated with the medieval horse, either as a means of personal transport, in peace or in war, or as a beast of burden or haulage. However, there are noticeable absences from the range of material included and variations in the relative quantities of each sort of object. Since the waterfront deposits consist largely of dumps of rubbish, including street and stable sweepings, it is not surprising that some finds outnumber others. Horseshoes and spurs, both so easily lost among stable litter or street mud, are relatively common; horseshoes, which had in any case a short life and were made for all types of horse, outnumber all other objects. Unfortunately, the established method of dealing with common finds from these very productive sites meant that all nails were treated as bulk finds; it has not proved possible to separate horseshoe nails from the other types of nail present – though they would in theory be easily distinguishable. However, sufficient nails remained *in situ* in horseshoes for their typology and chronology to be recognised.

Another stable loss is the curry comb, which has been recovered in unexpectedly large numbers. On the other hand large pieces of harness and harness-fittings are rare – for example, not one identifiable saddle or saddle fragment was recorded – though it is possible that fragments of leather harness exist unrecognised among the unidentified leatherwork from these sites. Large iron buckles have been included in our catalogue, on the assumption that they are likely to have come from horse harness; on the other hand some buckles and strap fittings already included in the previous volume in this series on *Dress Accessories* (Egan & Pritchard 1991) may be unrecognised horse-equipment. Also omitted are non-specific iron rings and chain-links that might have been used in harness. Identifiable cart fitments have been noticeably absent, though medieval carts clearly carried a wide range of ironwork. A list of the stock of a London cart-builder in 1454 included 'hengys, hokes, chare nayles, boltes, . . . cheynes, styroppes, lachetes, garnetes, lensys, carte clowtes' (hinges, hooks, cart nails, bolts . . . chains, stirrups, latchets, garnets, linchpins, cart clouts) (Clark 1984, 24). The relationship of such miscellaneous ironwork to horse transport could easily have escaped recognition.

For none of the excavated material can we categorically state that it relates to a London-based horse rather than one passing through; indeed there is a suggestion that some material recovered from the so-called Baynard's Castle excavation (BC72) reflects the activities of the nearby Royal Wardrobe (Dyson 1989, 12; Grew & de Neergaard 1988, 29, 90; Egan & Pritchard 1991, 3), and thus the horse-gear from there might relate to the essentially mobile royal stable.

Even where large numbers of particular types of object are present there are limits to the conclusions that can be drawn. For example, as will be seen, we cannot differentiate between the shoes of riding horses and those of draught horses. We cannot recognise the shoes of destriers or coursers, though London farriers

1 Head of shoeing hammer or carpenter's claw hammer, perhaps late medieval, from Thames foreshore at Bankside (MoL acc no 85.467/2)

2 Signet ring, first half of 16th century, showing horseshoe, shoeing hammer, butteris and pincers (British Museum – after Dalton 1912, 88)

charged extra for shoeing them – perhaps reflecting the high value of the horse and the extra care required rather than any difference in the actual shoe (Riley 1868, 256).

Given the important role of the farrier or marshal, discussed further below, it is disappointing that we have failed to recognise farriers' tools among the many finds from the sites included in this project. Appropriate smithing tools – hammer, tongs, sets (handle-held chisels), and pritchel (nail-hole punch) (Hickman & Humphrey 1988, 87–91) – have not been noted, though variations in the form of nail-holes must reflect differences in the cross-section of the pritchel. Nor is there any example of the claw hammer, used for shoeing and shown in early illustrations of farriers (see Figs 12 and 15; also Treue et al. 1965, 132) as well as in the farriers' and marshals' seals in Fig 13. Since a similar tool was used by carpenters, known examples of medieval date cannot be positively identified as farriers' shoeing hammers. Such are those from Winchester (Goodall 1990, 277, no 400, fig 60), Huish, Wiltshire (Thompson 1972, 121, no 27, fig 4) Alsted, Surrey (Ketteringham 1976, 56, no 11, fig 34 – though there is no certainty as to the date of this example) and

Fulmer, Buckinghamshire (Farley 1982, 64, no 12, fig 11), or the less well-dated metal-detector finds from the Thames foreshore (for example Museum of London acc nos 81.543/1 and 85.467/2 – for the latter see Fig 1).

Similarly other tools listed and illustrated by Markham in the 17th century and perhaps reflecting the medieval farrier's toolkit (1662, 589–91), such as pincers, rasp and cutting (paring) knife, would, if excavated, probably not be recognised as specifically horse-related items.

The gouge-like 'butteris which pareth and openeth the hoof' (ibid. no 3), however, is a tool of an unusual form that should be recognisable if it occurred in the archaeological record; indeed, the Roman equivalent is well known (Manning 1985, 61; Webster 1968). The word is recorded quite early in English – as in 1366 when John Wyot was accused of having maliciously wounded a horse at the smithy of John Mareschal in Wood Street with an instrument called a 'botour' (Thomas 1929, 56–7). Apart from Markham's there are other early illustrations of the butteris. A German example of 1467 appears in Treue et al. 1965 (132), others of 1517, 1568 and 1598 in Azzola & Bormuth 1986, pl 1, 25, 43; a butteris is shown together with shoeing hammer, pincers and horseshoe on a signet ring in the British Museum described as 'English 16th century' (Fig 2 after Dalton 1912, 88, no 582) – I am grateful to John Cherry for his comment that it is likely to be of the first half of the 16th century rather than later. Later illustrations, and indeed surviving examples, are not uncommon (Fig 3); however, by the

3 Farrier's tools, including the 'Buttress' (no 5), shown in a 19th-century engraving (the work from which this illustration comes has not been identified)

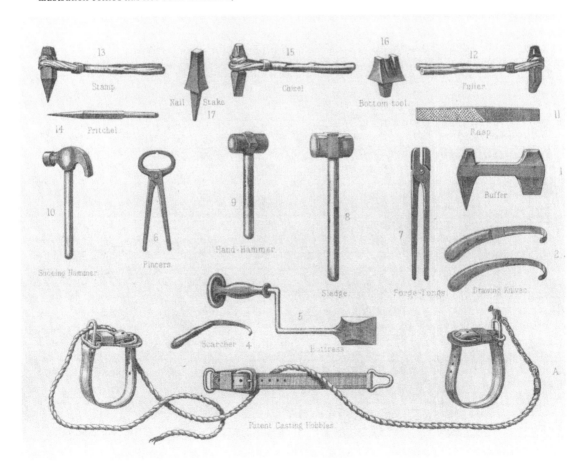

early 19th century the use of the butteris was being actively discouraged: 'The buttress, that most destructive of all instruments, being . . . banished from every respectable forge' (Youatt 1880, 430 – already in the 1831 edition).

The medieval horse and its work

Although the major purpose of this volume is to describe this range of horse equipment from London excavations, the opportunity is taken in this introductory chapter to consider other forms of evidence for the horse itself and for its usage in medieval London. This will serve as a background to the detailed accounts of specific finds that follow.

The horse, from the destrier which carried the knight in battle to the stott or affer which pulled the harrow or took a sack of corn to the mill, fulfilled a vital role in medieval society. Not surprisingly it warrants frequent reference in both contemporary literature and the multiplicity of documents that medieval bureaucracy delighted in. From these sources we can derive lists of names for types or breeds of horse, for their paces and their colours, and evidence for their breeding, their sale and their value at different times. Davis (*The Medieval Warhorse* 1989) and Langdon (*Horses, Oxen and Technological Innovation* 1986) produced detailed studies of particular aspects of the subject, and there are more popular general accounts by Dent & Goodall in their (oddly titled) *The Foals of Epona* (1962) and by Hewitt in *The Horse in Medieval England*

4 'Riding in Cheap'; the coronation procession of Edward VI (1547) (engraving after painting in Society of Antiquaries, London)

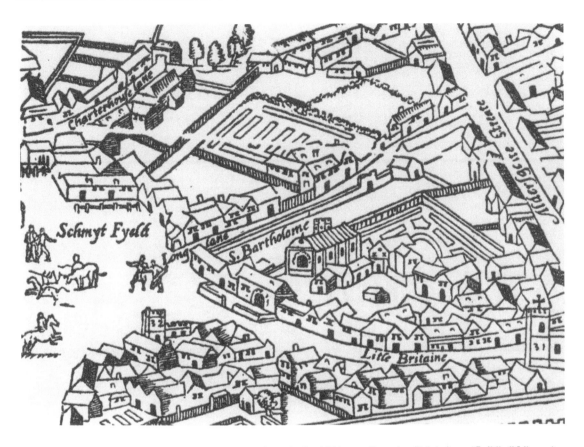

5   Smithfield, shown in the map of London first printed in the 1560s, attributed to Ralph Agas (Guildhall Library)

(1983); for the 16th and 17th centuries there are valuable works by Edwards on *The Horse Trade of Tudor and Stuart England* (1988) and by Dent on *Horses in Shakespeare's England* (1987) – though the latter is sadly lacking in references. Ann Hyland's *The Medieval Warhorse from Byzantium to the Crusades* and Andrew Ayton's *Knights and Warhorses* both appeared while this volume was in press. However, a wealth of evidence remains untapped and the definitive account of the medieval horse has yet to be written.

Professor Davis and Dr Langdon concentrated respectively on the war-horse and its breeding and on the manner in which the horse took over the role of the ox in haulage and farm work; the ordinary riding horse and the urban workhorse, of particular interest to us in the context of archaeological finds from London, have received

scant attention. The archaeological evidence from London, even the study of the skeletal remains of the horses themselves, will in the absence of that definitive study remain somewhat isolated and inconclusive. The following account draws on the published documentary evidence from London, and attempts to highlight the sources that would repay further study as a background to that archaeological work.

Horses of all sorts were a common sight in the streets of medieval London, though a noble or princely cavalcade would still attract onlookers, like Chaucer's ne'er-do-well prentice in the unfinished 'Cook's Tale' who would leave his work and rush to see any 'riding in Cheap' (Robinson 1966, 61, lines 4376–7) – Fig 4. The presence of the royal court at Westminster and of nobles' town houses in the Strand and elsewhere must have ensured such events were not infrequent.

6   Horse-fair at Smithfield *c.* 1820; the scene is reminiscent of that described by William Fitz Stephen 650 years
earlier (etching and aquatint after J L Agasse – Museum of London)

The sight of a whole household or department of state on the move is described by Jusserand (1961, 46–54) and is implicit in surviving royal wardrobe and household accounts with their copious details of expenditure on horses, carts, harness and equipment – for example the published accounts for 1290 (Parsons 1977) and for 1285–6 (Byerly & Byerly 1977). When the king travelled abroad in 1285–6 1000 horses had to be ferried across the Channel to Wissant to provide transport for the royal party (ibid. xxxvii). But the destriers, coursers, palfreys, rounceys, hackneys, cart-, carriage- and pack-horses that made up such a cortège were transient visitors to London, not necessarily representative of the permanent horse population of the city.

The largest concentration of horses regularly seen in London would have been at the horse fair held every Friday at Smithfield, which continued to be held until the 19th century (Figs 5 and 6) and was made famous, at least among historians of London, by the description of it written soon after 1170 by William Fitz Stephen, secretary and biographer of Thomas Becket. It forms part of William's description of London, and a Latin text is contained in Kingsford's edition of John Stow's *Survey of London* (1908, vol 2, 223–4) and an authoritative English version by H E Butler in Stenton 1934, 28–9. Dent & Goodall (1962, 96–9) discuss William's description of the 'smooth field', where 'whether to buy or just to look, everyone in town comes – earls, barons, knights and great numbers of townsfolk', and it is quoted by others, such as Davis (1989, 66–7).

William describes different types of horse exposed for sale, and in spite of the obscurities of his flamboyant Latin they can be identified as follows:

7 Huntsman on horseback, depicted in an early 14th-century English manuscript; the horse's ambling pace is clearly shown (Queen Mary's Psalter – British Library Royal MS 2 B VII f151b)

2 'horses which better suit esquires, moving more roughly but speedily' – Williams's description of their pace is once more obscure, but he is referring to horses which *trot*.

3 young horses, 'colts not yet well used to the bridle'.

4 *summarii*, 'sumpters' or pack-horses 'with stout and agile legs' (a passage omitted in Butler's translation).

5 *dextrarii*, 'destriers' – expensive warhorses, *staturae honestae* 'of noble size', predecessors of the 14th-century 'great horse' discussed by Davis (1989).

6 'mares suitable for ploughs, sledges (*trahis* – perhaps William means harrows) and carts', apparently shown with the cattle. Some are in foal, others have foals at their sides. Unfortunately William has little to say about these workaday draught horses, but his comments are notable at a time when horses were only just beginning to challenge the pre-eminence of oxen for haulage (Langdon 1986, ch 2, summarised p 79).

1 *gradarii*, 'amblers' – riding horses with that easy pace so odd to modern eyes, in which the horse moves both legs on the left forward together, then both legs on the right (Fig 7). On her way to Canterbury, the well-remembered and well-endowed Wife of Bath sat 'upon an amblere esily' (Robinson 1966, 21, line 469 – and see Fig 8), and horses broken to this pace seem to have been the popular choice of the inexperienced rider seeking comfort on a long journey; by all accounts they required little skill in horsemanship. As late as 1678, an author who hid his identity under the initials 'E.R.' (and derived much of his material and his opinions from earlier writers) commented 'Now if you select for Ease, great Persons Seats, or long Travel, then Ambling is required . . . There is not any Motion in a Horse more desired, more useful . . .' (R 1720, 65 and 54). However, and certainly by the time of the 1720 edition of his work, his advice would have been regarded as old-fashioned, as horses trained to the trot became more popular for everyday use – for some discussion of gaits and riding styles see Dent 1987, 61–7.

8 The Wife of Bath, riding on an ambler (from a facsimile of the 15th-century Ellesmere Manuscript of Geoffrey Chaucer's *Canterbury Tales*)

William Fitz Stephen tells us nothing of the organisation or management of the Smithfield horse-fair, and there seems to be surprisingly little reference to it in the published City records. In 1372 the 'coursers' or 'corsours' (horse-dealers) along with the drovers of the larger cattle-market petitioned the mayor and aldermen, and agreed a toll to be levied on every sale of horses or cattle to pay for the cleansing of Smithfield (Riley 1868, 366–7). Coursers are among the many horse-related crafts and trades that appear in the City records, as in 1300 when William Belebuch, *cossur*, brought a case concerning a bay horse he had sold to Simon de Paris in part-exchange for another horse and four marks (Thomas 1924, 85) or in 1366 when Henry Bosele, *corsour*, was summoned to answer a charge that the horse he had sold to an agent of the Bishop of St David's was not of the quality he had warranted (Thomas 1929, 220). As early as 1276 one Nicholas Curteney complained that a horse he bought at the Smithfield fair was blind. The seller, John de Elylaund, claimed it was not blind but just had poor sight (*defectum visus* – perhaps a reference to the intermittent but progressive disease known as 'moon-blindness' (Youatt 1880, 190–4)); the matter is only recorded because a quarrel broke out and Nicholas struck John with his knife (Weinbaum 1976, 99, no 471 and 103–4, no 488).

Certainly by the 16th century Smithfield fair, its dealers and the stock they sold there had a very bad reputation. Dan Jordan Knockem, a drunken 'horse-courser' in Ben Jonson's *Bartholomew Fair* (1614), has a line in patter and a way of patching up a broken-down nag that a modern second-hand car dealer would be proud of (Dent & Goodall 1962, 152–3), while in his study of the 16th- and 17th-century horse trade Peter Edwards (1988, 98–9, 114) supplies solid evidence to support the impression we get from Jonson's play and from Thomas Dekker's 1608 characterisation of the horse-courser – 'in the Citty a Cogging dissembler, and in Smith-field a common forsworne Vilaine'. Edwards puts the situation succinctly: 'The size and anonymity of the market there certainly attracted shady characters from all over the country, intent on selling stolen animals or palming off worn-out jades at inflated prices.'

The receiving and sale of stolen horses was already a problem in the 13th century. Among the

cases heard by the king's justices when they sat at the Tower of London in February and March 1276 were several involving the theft or receiving of horses (Weinbaum 1976, 78–81, nos 276 etc.), and occasional complaints appear later – two cases in the summer of 1301 for example, recorded in the rolls of the Mayor's Court (Thomas 1924, 113–14).

Whatever the quality of the horses sold at Smithfield or the bona fides of the dealers, it is likely that the majority of Londoners were among those who came (as William Fitz Stephen put it) to look, not to buy. The level of horse-ownership among resident Londoners must have been low. In a town that could be crossed on foot in 20 minutes, few had regular need of a horse for personal transport; horses for riding could be hired (at considerable cost) when the need arose to make a longer journey. From an enactment of 1389 which attempted to reduce expenditure on the annual procession that accompanied the new sheriffs to their presentation at Westminster, it is clear that one of the major expenses objected to was the cost to 'the men of divers trades' of hiring horses to ride in the procession (Riley 1868, 515) – such men did not themselves own riding horses.

Hiring was the necessary expedient of those who could not afford the basic initial purchase price of a horse – at £3 to £10 a riding horse such as a hackney or rouncey would cost six months' or a year's wages for a skilled London craftsman (Davis 1989, 67) – and the very real expense of its keep. Horse-bread, baked of 'pure beans and peas without mixture of other grain or bran' (Sharpe 1907, 107; see Dent 1987, 163 and R 1720, 44, 48–9), a horse's staple food, might cost $\frac{1}{2}d.$ a loaf, and hay for one day $2d.$ (Riley 1868, 323–4); oats were being sold in the city in 1382 at the extortionate rate of $5\frac{1}{2}d.$ a bushel (ibid. 460–1). In 1314–15 the cost of housing and feeding a good horse for a day, including half a basket of oats, varied between $6\frac{1}{4}d.$ and $7\frac{1}{2}d.$ (Davis 1989, 44) and in 1359 Edward III paid $6\frac{3}{4}d.$ a day for each horse when 48 newly acquired horses from Lombardy were boarded at the Black Prince's park at Kennington (ibid. 91). These were obviously horses of high quality, and no doubt a more ordinary steed would live in less style; yet if we can trust the well-known London price and wage edict of 1350 (Riley 1868, 253–4) these figures are slightly more than a skilled craftsman such as a mason or carpenter could expect to earn – even for a long summer day's work – to keep himself and his family in some comfort. In addition there would be occasional expenditure on a set of new shoes (6*d.* or 8*d.* in 1350 – ibid. 256) and, between times, 2*d.* for each 'remove' – the shoes taken off, the hooves cut back and the old shoes replaced (ibid.); a four-to-six-week period between removes is recommended today (War Department Veterinary Department 1908, 241; Hickman & Humphrey 1988, 74–5), but was probably not as regular in medieval times.

With these figures we can compare the costs of hiring a 'hakenei' on the busy Dover road. In 1396 the hackneymen (horse-hirers) of Southwark, Dartford, Rochester and other towns on the route agreed to a royal proclamation to levy specified charges (*Calendar of Patent Rolls* 1905, 712–13): 12*d.* for each of the stages Southwark to Rochester and Rochester to Canterbury, and 6*d.* for the slightly shorter stage onward to Dover. The horses on the Dover road were to be branded to discourage theft, no doubt an ever-present risk to those who hired out horses. On the other hand a risk that faced the hirer is illustrated by a case in 1365, when a horse hired by Thomas Bastard of Essex to carry a sick woman to Canterbury got only as far as Singlewell near Gravesend, where it died, leaving the unfortunate Thomas to pay 4*d.* for damage done to a wall by the sick horse plus an apparently extortionate 10*s.* in hire charges for further horses to Canterbury and back to London; the horse's owner (a tiler, not a professional hackneymen) claimed that the horse had been ridden too hard and too fast and demanded 30*s.* recompense for its value (Thomas 1929, 37–8). Horses for the Canterbury and Dover road could readily be hired in Southwark; the Tabard, the 'hostelrye' in the borough where Geoffrey Chaucer met the 'nine and twenty in a company' on their way to Canterbury, was just one of several such establishments that could provide accommodation for both travellers and their horses, and hire out horses as well (Robinson 1966, 17, lines 19–27). In 1598 John Stow commented on the 'many fair inns for the receipt of travellers' to be found in Southwark (Kingsford 1908, vol 2, 62).

As the hire charges show, a journey to Canterbury on horseback was not a cheap one, and not one to be undertaken lightly or frequently by townsfolk. Of more everyday concern to the ordinary Londoner were the horses used to transport foodstuffs and goods to, from and around the city. Regulations in 1356 for the collection of tolls at the City gates for the upkeep of the roads distinguished between carts and pack-horses carrying victuals or wares for sale, which paid toll, and 'the carts and horses of great people and other folks that bring their own victuals or other goods for the use and the consumption of their own hostels, [for which] nothing shall be taken' (Riley 1868, 291–2). Unfortunately there is no way of estimating the relative proportions of toll-paying (commercial) and non-paying (private) traffic. Though pack-horses are mentioned alongside carts in this document, and such horses were in wide use in rural areas (Langdon 1986, 225–7) and seem to have been used in large numbers for the transport of the royal household, other London records suggest that the cart was the dominant form of transport for most heavy goods in and around the town; a 13th-century list of 'customs payable on victuals', for example, though it refers to corn brought by pack-horse, prescribes chiefly charges for carts bringing corn, bread, pottery, charcoal, wood, nuts and cheese among other things (Riley 1861, 203–5).

For the occasional movement of heavy loads the services of porters or carters could be hired, and it seems likely that few citizens would need the full-time use of a cart and horses to pull it. Prices for the hire of carts carrying sand or clay and other materials were laid down in 1350 – 3*d.* to 4*d.* according to the distance travelled (Riley 1868, 256); as will be seen later, carts would be hired by the day for major jobs. A constant complaint was that royal purveyors and other such officials would requisition carts at short notice, though a fixed price was to be paid for each vehicle taken – 10*d.* a day for a cart with two horses, 14*d.* for a cart with three horses (Jusserand 1961, 46–7). In 1350 it was decreed that only carts owned by 'traventers' – men who let carts out on hire – could be requisitioned, sparing privately owned carts ('those of poor folks who bring victuals and other wares to the city') and those already in use by other hirers (Riley 1868, 256).

The horse-drawn cart was clearly a major factor in London's economy, and a major contributor to

9 Heavily laden harvest cart hauled by three horses, *c.*1340 (Luttrell Psalter – British Library Add MS 42130 f173b)

its traffic. Thus in 1479 there was a complaint that carts waiting to pick up loads at Billingsgate blocked Thames Street, making the route from London Bridge to the Tower impassable (Sharpe 1912, 166–7). It was also used for long-distance haulage; carters drove regular routes linking London with provincial towns and providing carrier services. In 1484 William Naynow, then aged 61, claimed to have been driving the London–Exeter route for 35 years (Bennett 1968, 160). The regular carts to Norwich, like the one which left from the Rossamez Inn in St Lawrence's Lane each week, took three or four days for the journey (ibid. 162); it was the regularity and speed of this service which, for example, allowed Sir John Paston to write from London on Sunday 20 November 1474 asking his brother in Norwich to send him a pewter vessel and some books 'by the next carrier, by the latter end of the week' (ibid. 161; Gairdner 1904, vol 5, 216).

The carts used for both local and long-distance carriage were light two-wheel vehicles, shown so often in contemporary illustrations being hauled by two or three horses in tandem – as in the Luttrell Psalter (Fig 9; cf. Millar 1932, f162, f173b). A carter in Geoffrey Chaucer's 'Friar's Tale' drove a hay cart drawn by three horses

(Robinson 1966, 92 line 1554; cf. Dent & Goodall 1962, 113–14). The Coroners' Rolls of the City of London record the death in February 1337 of Agnes de Cicestre, who was run over by a cart as she walked outside Bishopsgate (Sharpe 1913, 181–2); the cart, empty apart from some old sacks and five pounds of candles, was pulled by three horses. The horses ranged in value from the lead horse (a 'favel' – dun or yellow dun) at 10*s.* and the shaft horse (black) at 6*s.* to the trace horse ('albus', and blind in both eyes) at only 4*s.* The cart itself was valued at just 6*s.* 8*d.* Two years later a small boy, John Stolere, died in Cheapside under the wheels of a water cart drawn by two horses (ibid. 219–20). Even for fairly light loads within town teams of two horses seem to have been the norm. Thus 12 carts bought for use by the City rakers in carting away rubbish in 10 of the City's wards had two horses each; the carts and horses were purchased between 1372 and 1382 at a total cost of £48 6*s.* 8*d.* (Sabine 1937, 23–4; Thomas 1929, 147).

Carts used by the London Bridgewardens to transport building materials were usually drawn by two or four horses (see following section), and Salzman (1952, 349–51) gives details from a number of building accounts, ranging from the use of both one-horse and two-horse carts at Vale Royal in 1278 to the transport of a great alabaster reredos from Nottingham to Windsor in 1367 in 10 carts, each one drawn by 8 horses; in view of the length of this journey one suspects that not all 8 horses were in harness at the same time – having fresh horses in reserve would be advisable. Langdon's study (1986, 224–5) suggests that teams of one or two horses (predominantly the former) were normal for use around the farm, larger teams being reserved for road work; thus at East Dereham (Norfolk) in 1251 villagers carried dung and corn on the lord's demesne with a cart and two horses, but used a cart and four horses for the trip to Norwich.

From such evidence it is clear that the medieval *carectarius* was nothing like a modern carthorse in either size or hauling capacity. It was perhaps a sturdy beast, but to the modern eye a small one for its task; its size and abilities are discussed further below.

10 London carter and porter in 1614, sketched in the album of a Dutch visitor; the use of single horses for carts seems more common in illustrations of this period than earlier (cf. Fig 9), perhaps reflecting a real increase in the horse's pulling power. (Edinburgh University Library Laing MS III 283 f494)

The London Bridgewardens and their horses

Brian Spencer

(The transport requirements and activities of one major London institution were fortunately a matter of public record. The Bridgewardens, responsible not merely for the maintenance of London Bridge but for the management of a large group of properties whose rents went towards the costs of the bridge, organised their own transport services within the 'works department' based at their Southwark headquarters at Bridge House. I am most grateful to be able to publish part of an unpublished essay on the subject by Brian Spencer. This is based upon his research into the surviving account rolls of the Bridgewardens covering the period 1381–99 (Corporation of London Records Office) – JC)

Even at slack times London Bridge had 60 men on the payroll, half of them skilled in the building trades. A boatman and a carter also belonged to the permanent establishment and they organised some part of the bridge's transport facilities. Like the rest of the staff they had their headquarters at

the Bridge House, at the foot of the bridge in Southwark. Here, aside from the masons' lodge, carpenters' shop, sawpits and the like, were builders' yards stacked with all kinds of materials from tin-tacks to houseframes ready for use or for sale to other builders. Here, too, the horses were stabled and guard dogs kennelled, while at the wharves the bridge's boats were moored.

The carter, with 22*d.* a week, came low on the bridge's pay scales. He earned about the same as the cook, whose suppers and packed lunches he doubtless enjoyed for nothing. He earned a little less than the boatman and about half the amount earned by skilled men – masons, carpenters, sawyers, plasterers, paviours. Unlike some employees he had no regular mate and was expected to hire casual labour to help with loading and unloading when away from base. He did, however, get specially high quarterly bonuses and a new outfit of clothing at Christmas. It is conceivable that his low basic pay took account of his particular opportunities for making a little money on the side, not least by undertaking private commissions that coincided with official journeys. Be that as it may, the job was evidently sufficiently gratifying for John Dillwish, late carter of the bridge, to leave the bridge some money in 1382 and for his successor, John Pegrom, to remain bridge carter for 25 years and more.

Horses were not so long-lived. Every other year or so, a new horse was brought in, one for as little as 26*s.* 8*d.*, others ranging through 30*s.*, 40*s.*, 50*s.* to £3. The largest sum paid during the last two decades of the 14th century was 60*s.* 3*d.* paid by the carter to Stephen Frith, armourer of Hatfield Broadoak, Essex, for a bay horse for the bridge carts.

Then there is the endless renewal of worn-out equipment, a minimum of 50 full sets of horseshoes a year, mostly from a John and Thomas Kelsey, smiths of Southwark. They charged 2*d.* for foreshoes and 1½*d.* for hind-shoes, and every year supplied rather more hindshoes than foreshoes.

Maintenance of carts was also never-ending, from regular lubrication services to replacement of parts. Every year axle-trees were renewed, usually at around 12*d.* each, and six or eight pairs of wheels were bought. At the same time, old wheels were overhauled, sometimes by bridge carpenters, who in 1396 bought a wheelwright's

bruzz (morticing chisel) specifically for such jobs. But most work of this kind was put out to specialists. In January 1385, for example, 6*s.* 8*d.* was spent on newly rounding two pairs of wheels. New wheels were often bought at Croydon, from where much of the bridge's supply of prepared timber came at this time. Others came from wheelwrights in Chiltern villages. Occasionally we find the chief carpenter buying a batch of wheels at Bartholomew Fair, Smithfield. Smithfield was a centre for many of London's wheelwrights.

Cart-bodies had also to be renewed. On one occasion, John Pegrom, the carter, bought a cart-body of unspecified design from John Elliott, wheeler of Aldgate Street for 17*s.*, as compared to the 2*s.* he paid for the body of a new cart for transporting gravel and chalk. This last transaction is typical of all the bridge purchases of new vehicles, the basic elements of which, together with several pounds of cart-clouts, were paid for as if they were unassembled, even though the whole kit came from one and the same wheelwright. This may simply reflect the bridge's position of having a team of skilled technicians who could put such things together.

Inevitably harness, too, had to be replaced, collars above all. Most of them were of leather, but there were others that were regularly recovered in coarse cloth called wadmel. The carter also bought a stock of hames (the curved wooden frames of collars) from Edward of Stoke Poges. Saddles, more often called cart-saddles, were another frequent and rather costly replacement. Then aside from halters, girth-straps, traces and such like, special equipment was bought for certain jobs – girth-webs, for instance, to enable horses to drag elm piles. Other items were bought for stabling and grooming horses – curry combs, shovels, grease for the horses' feet, wattle baskets, mangers and bins for oats.

Haymaking was part of the yearly round. Some part of the bridge's meadows in Southwark and at Camberwell, New Cross, and across the river at Stratford were set aside to provide hay for the bridge's horses. In July or early August the grass was mown for 10*d.* an acre. About the same amount was spent on turning, shaking-out, raking and ricking the hay, and further labour was hired to help the bridge carter load and cart this to the bridge. Some years stocks ran low and by May the bridge was buying in hay at 6*s*. 8*d*. a cartload. But more often the bridge felt able to sell a little hay to a few clients in the autumn.

As often as not, bridge horses were away from headquarters for days on end, usually hauling timber, and at such times the carter, who got a weekly allowance of 20*d*. (only slightly less than his own wage) for each horse's provender, was able to put in for nearly as much again in extra subsistence when the horses were having to be fed and perhaps stabled away from base.

London Bridge was not simply a vital public utility but also a lively business concern. And so, when opportunities arose, the bridge made a small part of its annual income by undertaking occasional haulage jobs for customers. On the other hand, the bridge's permanent transport section was quite incapable of meeting all of its own haulage requirements, for its lines of communication were widespread, governed mainly by the whereabouts of supplies of suitable stone and timber.

As often as not, transport was hired by the day and not on piece rates. The records make it clear that for apparently routine jobs carts were often pulled by two or more horses. Even for a short level journey carrying stones from the chapel in the middle of the bridge to the Bridge House at the end, two horses were used to draw the cart. Carts hauled by four horses were regularly hired for such varied jobs as carting elms to the river and framed timber, lime or gravel to building sites and even for leading hay. Maybe the horses in such teams were inclined to be small or broken down, for whole outfits were hired for as little as 16*d*. or 24*d*. More usually a carter would charge 5*d*. or 6*d*. for himself, 6*d*. for each draught-horse and a more variable sum for the cart – 2*s*. 6*d*. a day in the case of one carter who transported timber 10 miles from Sanderstead to the Bridge House during several weeks of 1390.

London marshals and other horsemen

Few urban records match in comprehensiveness the Bridge House records, the above-mentioned

royal wardrobe and household accounts or the building accounts which Salzman drew on for a valuable chapter on 'Carriage' in his study of the medieval building industry (1952, 349–54). Further evidence for the use of the horse in London may be sought in the activities of those individuals involved commercially in the provision of transport services and of services to the traveller – the coursers of Smithfield, the hackneymen, traventers, carters, porters and marshals of the City and Southwark. Even the 'bakers of horse-bread' (Sharpe 1912, 185) and the 'hostelers and herbergeours' who provided stabling and fodder for their guests' horses as well as accommodation for travellers cannot be ignored.

Yet such people make only occasional appearances in the City's records, often accidental or inconsequential. Their names occur as witnesses or participants in law-cases; they are involved in crimes or accidents. Thus three 'mareschals' appraise the value of horses, the property of a man accused of murder (Sharpe 1913, 271); a groom (*garcio*) is thrown from the horse he is watering in the Thames and drowns (Chew & Weinbaum 1970, 20 – there are several other such cases); another is riding a horse which kicks a man in the head so that he dies (ibid. 66–7); two carters flee the scene of a fatal road accident outside Bishopsgate (Sharpe 1913, 181–2); another is killed when his cart overturns (Weinbaum 1976, 14); a hackneyman admits a debt of three tuns of wine he owes to a sheriff in respect of three horses (Riley 1868, 63); William Bracy keeps carts for hire, and his neighbours complain of the disturbance caused by carts driving in and out at all hours of day and night (Thomas 1943, 117).

Of these men, the most essential to the maintenance of London's horse stock was the marshal (*mareschal, marescallus*) or farrier. The title of marshal could be one of high dignity, as in the case of the Earl Marshal of England. Even where the term retained something of its original Germanic meaning of 'horse-servant' (Davis 1989, 84–5) it still covered a wide range of duties and of social status. The royal marshalsea, headed by a clerk, was primarily responsible for transporting the royal household on its continual peregrinations. Byerly & Byerly (1977, xxxv–xxxvii) describe its activities as revealed by the accounts of 1285–6:

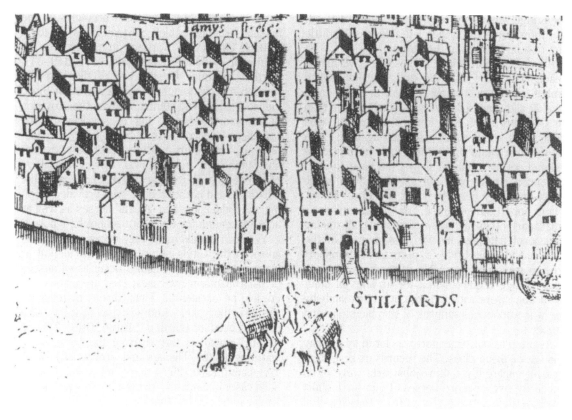

11   Horses in the Thames: a watercarrier filling his casks, shown on a map of London of the 1550s (the so-called 'copper-plate map', Museum of London)

Horses had to be provisioned, equipped, cared for when sick, and replaced when not restored to strength and service. Carts and other conveyances had to be maintained, manned and guarded, and new ones purchased when old ones were worn beyond repair. A small army of grooms, carters, sumpter boys and menials of the stable had to be supervised and provided with the essentials of their offices.

In a smaller household such overall duties would fall to a man with the title of 'marshal', like Master Thomas de Bardeney, marshal to Queen Eleanor of Castile from about 1278 until her death (Parsons 1977, 30–31, 67, n 52).

It does not seem likely that Thomas de Bardeney ever lifted a shoeing-hammer to shoe a horse; this was, however, one of the duties of his namesake Thomas Marchal on the Oxfordshire manor of Cuxham some years later (Harvey

1976, 592) and of the men of London who were known by the same title. Yet it was far from their sole function. We have already seen that London marshals were considered good judges of horse-flesh, able at need to estimate the value of a horse. Clifford Race (1898–1958) – one of the Suffolk informants of the oral historian George Ewart Evans – commented that farmers would always seek the advice of the local blacksmith when intending to buy a horse: 'Few people can judge what shape a particular horse is in better than the smith who shoes him.' (Evans 1960, 197–8) Yet the skill of the medieval marshal went further. In 1285 Thomas de Bardeney was reimbursed the large sum of 11*s*. 3*d*. 'for olive oil, grease and other medicinal items and for poultices bought for six sick horses belonging to the king' (Byerly & Byerly 1977, 13). Like the later far-rier, the medieval marshal was expected to be able to doctor a sick horse. A typical 17th-century work with the all-embracing title *The Experienc'd Farrier* (. . . *bringing pleasure to the gentleman and profit to the countrey-man*), by the pseudonymous 'E.R. gent.', devotes (in its 1720 edition) some 75 pages to breeding, buying and training a horse, 40 to medicine and simple surgery, and just 10 to preparing the hoof and shoeing, before returning to medical matters for a further 50 pages. The second part of over 300 pages contains a list of drugs and herbs, dozens of useful prescriptions and a dictionary of the diseases of horses (R 1720; see Heymering 1990, 39).

Although likely to be the province of one man, the two tasks of doctoring and shoeing were distinct. Among the expenditure on three horses belonging to Alice de Montfort (one of Queen Eleanor's ladies-in-waiting) during the month 6 February to 6 March 1290, when they were stabled in London, was a sum of *2s. 8d.* 'pro mareschalcia unius equorum predictorum et ferrura eorundem' – for the 'marshalsea' of one of the said horses and the shoeing of them all (Parsons 1977, 93). Similar phraseology is used

in, for example, the accounts of Bogo de Clare (younger son of the Earl of Clare) for 1284–6, where the costs of horses stabled in London include a sum 'in mareschaucia et ferrura' (Giusseppi 1920, 49).

In 1356 the London marshals (the mistery of *mareschalcie*) submitted their ordinances to the mayor, Henry Pykard, and the aldermen for approval (Sharpe 1905, 82); they later resubmitted them, with an additional article (ibid. 170; Riley 1868, 291–4). The ordinances define their function as, in Riley's translation, 'horse-shoeing and the farriery of horses' and take pains to distinguish marshals from smiths. Their articles cover: the making of horseshoes and nails; advice to customers on the purchase and cure of horses; undertaking the cure of sick horses; horse-shoeing; and the demarcation of the responsibilities of marshals and blacksmiths.

Of these activities that of making shoes and fitting them is the one that makes most impression on the archaeological record – as will be seen in the catalogue below. It is the only aspect of the marshal's work that is covered directly by the

12 Marshal shoeing a horse, from an English treatise on horse management, first half of 13th century (Bodleian Library MS Douce 88 f51)

a   b   c   d

13   Personal seals of medieval marshals: **a** Thomas Coyners – horseshoe and shoeing hammer (copper-alloy seal
     matrix from Southwell, Suffolk – private collection); **b** Walter le Marshal – horseshoe and nail (after Fleming
     1869, 377); **c** Ralph, the marshal of the Bishop of Durham – horseshoe, hammer and nails (after Fleming 1869,
     379); **d** John the Smith (*Faber*) – shoeing hammer (lead seal matrix from Thames foreshore – private collection)

well-known London price and wage regulations
which followed the Black Death of 1348–9 (Riley
1868, 256). When men who described themselves as 'marshals' came to adopt a device for
their personal seals, they frequently chose a
horseshoe, with or without nails and shoeing
hammer (Fig 13); another London seal matrix,
that of 'Roger Marchal', is in the British Museum,
from Charles Roach Smith's collection (Smith
1855, 146, no 716). Clearly to the man in the
street the horseshoe was an item evocative of the
marshal and his work.

However, the responsibility of the farrier for
the treatment of sick horses was unchallenged
until the rise of veterinary science and the establishment of veterinary schools in the 18th and
19th centuries (Hickman & Humphrey 1988,
7–9). Thereafter, except in an informal way, the
farrier was to be essentially a shoeing smith. The
'Scheme for the Examination and Registration of
Shoeing Smiths' introduced by the Worshipful
Company of Farriers in 1890 and the Farriers
(Registration) Acts of 1975 and 1977 gave statu-
tory backing to this change. Extensive knowledge
of the anatomy and physiology of the horse is still
required of the farrier, but now as an essential aid
to the proper shoeing of the horse (ibid. 15–17;
Prince 1980, 38–9); his expertise is now in equine
chiropody and orthopaedics.

Discussion of the marshals of London is ham-
pered by the development of trade designations
into surnames in the 14th century – we must
dismiss Robert le Mareschal, goldsmith, from our
account (Kerling 1973, 56). On the other hand
Juliana and Maud, both called 'la Mareschale',

accused with others of an assault on a woman
called Galiena in 1243 (Chew & Weinbaum 1970,
67–8), may be an isolated instance of female
involvement in the craft to set beside those
women blacksmiths discussed by Jane Geddes
(1983, 26–9).

In later English the term 'farrier' was to become the norm, and it was as 'the Brotherhood of
Farryers of London' that the London craft in 1674
appealed for and was granted a Royal Charter,
and then in 1692 was recognised by the City
authorities as a Livery Company (Prince 1980,
1–8, 233–5).

'Farrier' and the cognate French *feroun* or
ferrour and Latin *ferrarius* presumably designate
a man responsible for the *ferrura* (shoeing) of
horses – though an ordinance of 1431 which
explicitly defines *ferrones* as *marescallos equorum*
(Sharpe 1911, 121) would imply a responsibility
for the wider aspects of marshalsea and horse
care that we have mentioned. However, the
same or very similar terms are applied to men
described also as 'ferroners', 'ismongers' or 'iron-
mongers'; the ramifications of the trades in which
Latin *ferrum* formed part of the name may have
been as confusing to the ordinary medieval Londoner as it is to us. Presumably the 'ferroners'
who in 1300 complained about the size and quality
of ironwork coming from the Weald were iron-
mongers (Sharpe 1901, 88–9). It is difficult to find
unequivocal evidence that a specific *feroun* or
ferrour was a shoeing-smith rather than an ironmonger or general iron-worker. Even when in
1301 Roger le Ferun complains of the theft of a
bay horse valued at 10 marks we cannot take it

for granted that it was as a marshal that he had possession of the horse (Thomas 1924, 113). However, outside London it seems likely that John le Ferour (keeper of the king's stud at Risborough *c.*1335 – Harvey 1976, 764) and William le Ferrour (a keeper of the king's great horses 1344–54 – Davis 1989, 94) owed their surnames to their responsibilities in positions where the designation 'marshal' might be expected. William de Ferrers, Earl of Derby (died 1254) added a border of horseshoes to his family arms, perhaps in allusion to his name (Fox-Davies 1929, 80–81). He alone of the family seems to have incorporated the horseshoe into his arms – it might have referred also to the family name of his wife Sybilla, daughter of William Marshall, Earl of Pembroke (ibid.); however, there is a suggestion that the horseshoe itself served as a de Ferrers family badge, and as such it was used to decorate pottery made on the Earl of Derby's land at Burley Hill, Derbyshire, in the 13th century (Jewitt 1883, 63 figs 271, 272; McCarthy & Brooks 1988, 128, 276–8; see also Fig 14).

A further complication in terminology is the apparent involvement of general smiths in farriery. The express reason for the 1356 approach by the marshals of London to the mayor and aldermen for confirmation of their ordinances was the damage caused by some 'who kept forges in the said city and intermeddled with works of farriery, which they did not understand how to bring to a good end; by reason of which many horses had been lost' (Riley 1868, 292). One of their articles included an undertaking that no marshal would undertake the work of a smith; nor would a marshal take on a serving-man trained as a smith or allow a smith to employ a qualified marshal. Presumably like the later village blacksmith the London smith was not reluctant to shoe horses. In 1246 Gilbert the Smith (*Faber*) of Bishopsgate Ward was among those accused of having a *travellum* which encroached on the king's highway (Chew & Weinbaum 1970, 147, no 439); as we shall see, a *travellum* is the distinctive feature of the work-place of a shoeing-smith or farrier. Indeed Gilbert the Smith could be the same man as Gilbert the Marshal (*Marescallus*) of Bishopsgate, a tenant of St Bartholomew's Hospital some years later (Kerling 1973, 100, no 996). Similarly a lead seal matrix of 13th-century date, found some while ago on the Thames

14 Pottery jug, 13th-century Burley Hill ware, with horseshoe motif; perhaps the badge of the de Ferrers, Earls of Derby (City of Derby Museums and Art Gallery)

foreshore and now in a private collection, bears the name of 'John the Smith' (*S' IOHIS FABRI*) and as a central device the clawed shoeing hammer of the marshal/farrier (Fig 13d).

Both smiths and marshals had forges. In 1369 there were complaints that Geoffrey Mareschal had obstructed the highway by building a forge in Wood Street (Chew & Kellaway 1974, 138, nos

547–8); both Ralph Mareschall and John Cyl-bryght, *marescallus*, in turn leased a forge from Holy Trinity Priory in the early 13th century (Hodgett 1971, 175, no 900). It is possible that this forge is the one outside Aldgate belonging to the Priory which was noted in a 1246 survey of 'purprestures' (encroachments on the highway) (Chew & Weinbaum 1970, 151, no 470). Other forges standing in the road at this time may well have been intended to take advantage of the needs of travellers for horse-shoeing services (ibid. 137, nos 350–1); this is certainly true of a forge erected by Walter le Brun, marshal, in the Strand in 1235, for which a quit-rent of six horseshoes and their nails was to be paid to the king each year (and is still paid by the Corporation of London in an annual ceremony at the Law Courts (Wilkinson 1825, pl 110 and text; Fleming 1869, 399; Smith 1962, 60–64)).

Also noteworthy among the 1246 purprestures were those where the offending structure was a *travellum* – 11 instances, five of them attributed to marshals and one, as we have seen, to a smith; in the other cases no trade is indicated (Chew & Weinbaum 1970, index sv 'Travails'). Three cases are also recorded in 1276 (Weinbaum 1976, nos 376, 391, 455), the last the property of William le Mareschall; in this later document the clerk adopts the term *trabes*, beams. At both dates the reference is presumably to the structure known in English as a 'travis' or 'trave' (French *travail*). The *Oxford English Dictionary* quotes from 1583 'To set up ane traveis of tymmer for shoeing of horses besyde his smiddy'; forge and travis together defined the shoeing-smith's work-place. The travis was an open wooden frame used to hold the horse during shoeing – and no doubt also during veterinary treatment. It would be particularly useful for a restive horse or one not used to being shod; Alisoun, heroine of Chaucer's 'Miller's Tale', taken unawares in rather indecorous embrace by

15 Horse penned in travis for shoeing *c.*1340 (Romance of Alexander, Bodleian Library MS Bodley 264 f107)

the sprightly clerk Nicholas, 'sproong as a colt dooth in the trave' (Robinson 1966, 49, line 3282).

The travis can be seen in use in a number of early illustrations. The 14th-century Romance of Alexander shows a horse penned in the travis, its rear leg tied to a cross bar while the farrier nails on the shoe (Fig 15; James 1933, f107r). Travises appear in the portraits of three German farriers in the 15th-century housebook of the Mendel brotherhood of Nuremberg (Treue et al. 1965, 89, 265), though another, Hans Pfaffenhoffer 'ein guter hufsmid', is shown shoeing a horse without the aid of a travis (ibid. 132). Dent (1987, 105) reproduces a German woodcut of 1584 showing a horse held in a roofed travis while a farrier pours a drench down its throat – a reminder of the other main purpose of the travis, to hold the horse still during veterinary treatment. Several medieval representations of the proverbial folly of 'shoeing a goose' show the goose held incongruously in a travis: the Romance of Alexander (James 1933, f124v), the manuscripts illustrated by Randall (1966, figs 579–80) and a carved misericord of about 1430 at Whalley Abbey (Lancashire). Jones (1989b, 204 and 213, n 51) and Randall (1986, 200) list other examples of this scene but do not indicate whether in every case the bird is held in a travis.

Diderot's *Encyclopédie* (1763–72, 'Marechal ferrant', pl 1) illustrates a well-made 18th-century *travail* standing inside the forge building, as seems to have been later Continental practice. Certainly the use of the travis has lasted longer on the Continent than in England; Youatt, writing in 1831 when the travis was hardly known in England, commented: 'The *trevis* is a machine indispensable in every Continental forge; even the quietest horses are there put into it to be shod.' (1880, 456) In England the word outlived the thing itself. In talking to Suffolk horsemen and blacksmiths George Ewart Evans came across a word he recorded as 'travus', applied to the partitioned area within a forge where the horse stood for shoeing (1960, 197); later he recognised the derivation of the word from the medieval travis (1970, 163–4).

What is clear from the illustrations is that the basic travis, a free-standing structure of four upright timber posts supporting longitudinal and crossbars, is not one that would leave noticeable archaeological traces. It is unlikely that such a structure would ever be recognised in a London excavation, where the medieval ground surface rarely survives. In more rural areas the association of a group of post-holes with a forge might well repay investigation – though none seem to have been noticed at the forges at Goltho (Lincolnshire), Alsted (Surrey) or Wharram (Yorkshire) (see Beresford 1975, 46; Ketteringham 1976, 25–9; Andrews & Milne 1979, 48–50).

Marshals, like coursers, hackneymen and carters, were directly dependent on the horse for their livelihood; in addition there were many crafts that provided necessary pieces of equipment for the horse – saddlers, spurriers, loriners, wheelwrights etc. In any full study of the horse in London their role would need to be considered. Such trades, like the horse-dealers of Smithfield, served a large clientele, far wider than the immediate population of London; their products certainly occur among archaeological finds. They have variably accessible records; these are often disappointing, and usually more concerned with the election of officials, ceremonial, the protection of trade interests and the training of apprentices than the practicalities of the craft. Official livery company histories are often of little assistance in the study of the history of a craft or technology. Occasionally more detail can be extracted from the available sources: for the cases of two individual craftsmen see Clark 1984 (a wheelwright) and Sutton 1984 (a saddler), while Blanche Ellis discusses some of the documentary evidence for the spurrier's craft below, in the chapter titled 'Spurs and spur fittings'.

Physical remains of medieval horses
D James Rackham

(As is made clear here, there are no large quantities of horse bones recorded among finds from London excavations. The reason is not far to seek. Horse meat was not for human consumption (Langdon 1986, 263–4 and n 43), and though an occasional worn-out horse might be sold as food for hounds (Cummins 1988, 257) – hounds were usually fed on bread and trained to associate meat only with

*their reward after a successful hunt (ibid. 26–7) –
the normal fate of the old or mortally sick horse was
to be buried where it died or to be slaughtered for its
hide. In 1317–24, for example, John de Redmere,
keeper of the king's horses 'South of the Trent', was
selling the hides of royal horses that had died of the
murrain (Davis 1989, 93). Thus the rarity of
single horse bones among archaeological finds and
of remains indicating butchery is not surprising;
after skinning the carcass was simply buried in one
piece or dismembered only for ease of disposal.*

*An ordinance prohibited the skinning and burial
of horse carcasses within the City walls. Thus in
1304 a complaint was made by the Prior of St
Augustine's that one Richard de Houndeslowe had
been slaughtering horses and burying their carcasses within the walls, no doubt close to the priory,
'against the ordinance of the citizens' (Thomas
1924, 161). Richard's plea that men of his trade
(presumably tanning) had always done so was not
accepted, and he was made to take an oath that he
would never again skin horses in the City, nor bury
the carcasses within it, nor cast them in the ditches;
moreover he was to report anyone else he knew of
doing so. Two months later John le Wyttawyere (a
whittawyer, tanning hides with alum to produce
white leather) was brought before the mayor on a
similar charge, that he had 'skinned a black horse'
(Thomas 1924, 164). In 1311 a number of whit-
tawyers were formally sworn not to flay dead horses
within the City or the suburbs, and to report others
guilty of the same offence (Riley 1868, 85–6).*

*It would seem that after about 1300 at least the
disposal of horse carcasses within the City had to be
carried out illicitly. The specific ban on 'casting
them in the ditches' in the case of Richard of
Houndeslowe suggests a particular concern with
instances like the carcasses dumped in the City
Ditch at Ludgate at about this time (below).*

*Tanners were active in the Moorfields and
Smithfield areas; the 'tanners without Newgate'
and the 'tanners without Cripplegate' contributed to
a civic 'gift' to Edward III in 1363 (Riley 1868,
314). It may be in these areas and just beyond the
City boundaries that we should seek London's
horse graveyards. – JC)*

Note: Elements of this report are drawn from
unpublished reports written by Philip Armitage
and Trefor Wilkinson on the horse finds from
Miles Lane (ILA79), Ironmonger Lane (IRO80) –

see Fig 16 – and Ludgate (LUD82). More detailed analysis of the skeletal evidence is contained in the Appendix of this book.

Horse bones rarely represent more than 1% of
the identified bones from archaeological excavations in the City. Two factors appear to be
responsible for this absence. The first is that in
Britain there is little evidence, either historical or
archaeological, for the consumption of horse
meat. On most excavations horse bones are
found relatively intact and often articulated or in
groups from a single animal. Rarely do they bear
any evidence of butchery other than cut marks
probably associated with skinning or dismember-
ment, as in the sample from the City Ditch at
Ludgate (LUD82; see Wilkinson 1983). Although
O'Connor reports (1989) butchered horse bones
from Coppergate, York, where he believes horse
was an occasional element in the diet, there is no
evidence of this in London. In contrast samples of
bone from cattle, sheep and pig – the mainstay of
the medieval meat diet – are always heavily
fragmented and frequently carry evidence of the
chop marks associated with the reduction of the
carcass into 'food' units.

The second factor, implicit in the first, is that if
butchers or slaughterhouses were not taking
horses for commercial exploitation during this
period, other means of disposal would have to be
found. The hides of horses may have been used
(Trow-Smith 1957, 124; see also above) and
there is evidence in many towns of the cannon
(metapodial) bones being used for tool manufacture, but otherwise the horse carcass appears to
have had little value – except on rare occasions
when it may have been purchased to feed dogs
or, during famine, for human consumption (as in
1315–17; Langdon 1986, 263). The burial of a
horse carcass would not have been an activity to
be undertaken lightly in central London, and we
must presume that the carcasses were usually
removed from the City before disposal; the relative rarity of finds possibly supports this pre-
sumption. The high incidence of Roman period
horse burials and bones in the area of the east
London Roman cemeteries (MoLAS report in
preparation) is perhaps a reflection of just this
form of disposal, outside the city walls; other
cultural factors may however be relevant during
this period.

16 Late Saxon horse skeleton, from Ironmonger Lane (IRO80)

Within central London the one type of archaeological feature that has consistently produced numbers of horse burials or bones is the ditch. Excavations of the City Ditch at Ludgate (LUD82) produced evidence of at least six horses, although none were articulated skeletons. Nearby, excavations south of Ludgate Hill in 1986–7 (PIC87) produced two semi-articulated horse skeletons in the fill of a ditch which was possibly that of the Norman fortification known as Montfichet's Tower (Watson 1992, 374–5). Other contexts from which medieval horse bones have been found in London include waterfront dumps, the fill of a dock, and pits. On almost all occasions these finds occur in contexts where a whole or partial carcass could be disposed of without digging a hole, and where general rubbish, probably of an unpleasant or noxious nature, was already being dumped. It seems likely that such 'dumpings' or disposals of whole carcasses were illegal in London (see above). For comparable groups of dumped horse carcasses elsewhere see recent reports from Kingston-upon-Thames (Serjeantson et al. 1992) and Windsor (Bourdillon 1993, 75–9).

The material discussed here and in the Appendix comprises finds from the 8th/9th century to the 16th century. The majority of these come from 13th- and 14th-century deposits, although the results are presented alongside finds of Roman and post-medieval date in London. The quantity of material studied is small and it would be presumptuous to assume that it reflected an accurate cross-section of the capital's horses. The circumstances of many of the finds – animals dumped, possibly illegally – suggest that they represent a socially biased sample and may reflect only the horses used by the poorer sector of London society.

Anatomical clues as to the use of the horses are difficult to interpret. Many of the pathologies typically found in domestic animals but generally absent from members of wild populations may be attributable to either riding or draught. It is common for animals that are ridden to be used occasionally between the shafts of carts or other wheeled vehicles. We perhaps should expect a clear functional division between different horses only in the wealthier sections of society where riding, draught- and war-horses may be specifically bred.

Features of form readily recognised in a live animal become in the skeleton merely differences in scale of both height and robustness. Size *per se*, such as withers height, is unlikely to be a particularly useful variable for establishing the type or function of the horses (see below). Animals from Shetland pony size upwards are all used as riding horses or for pulling vehicles. It may be that the gracility and robustness of an animal is a better indication. For example, it is suggested elsewhere (Rackham 1989), on the grounds of frequency, general size and gracility, that the horses on the medieval manor site at Thrislington, County Durham, were riding animals – possibly from a stud at the manor.

The anatomical evidence discussed below clearly indicates that most of the bones come from adult animals, among which at present only males have been recognised – whether they were gelded or stallions is not possible to ascertain. The size variation of the medieval horses is marked, ranging from small pony-sized horses of barely 10 hands to horses of nearly 16 hands. Nevertheless the majority of finds to date indicate animals of between 12½ and 15 hands. Whether these animals were riding horses, draught-horses or both is uncertain. Some are affected by pathologies indicating stress on the joints and back and have died or been killed relatively early in life. Except through disease or accident a riding pony

is unlikely to die so early unless very badly treated. Some of the bones suggest long-legged, gracile animals, certainly for riding, while one or two others are perhaps as robust as a working Dales pony or Welsh cob. The majority are well-built, slightly stocky animals suitable for both riding and haulage, with perhaps only slight evidence of change from animals of earlier periods.

Whether mules or donkeys are represented in these collections is problematic. Armitage (in Armitage & Chapman 1979) identified a mule from Roman deposits at Billingsgate Buildings (TR74), but no further examples have been recognised. One or two fragments of extremely small equids, for example a portion of a very small metacarpus of Roman date from Chaucer House (CH75), may be donkey, but the remains do not possess the anatomical characteristics necessary to distinguish the species.

The comparison of horse equipment in London with the remains of the actual horse perhaps misses a number of points. Horse equipment, particularly shoes, wears out and is replaced. That found in London, on all types of sites, might be expected to reflect the 'character' of the live horses travelling through London, upon whatever business, needing new harness and shoes. In contrast the horse bones found in London must reflect those animals working and probably permanently stabled in London. Animals ridden into the city might die through accident or illness, but most deaths would be among the working population of draught- and hacking-animals kept in stalls and stables within the city. We cannot assume that our archaeological sample represented a cross-section of all types of medieval horse.

The size of the medieval horse

On the basis of admittedly very limited evidence Rackham has presented a picture of horses in London – and whether they are riding horses or draught- or pack-animals is uncertain – of heights chiefly between 12½ and 15 hands. Modern horses (leaving aside the Shetland and other diminutive breeds) range from such as the Welsh Mountain pony (Section A in the Welsh Stud Book) of a maximum of 12 hands and the larger

Welsh ponies (Sections B and C) reaching 13½ hands, up to the giant Shires of 17 or 18 hands or occasionally more. Riding horses, depending on their use, may be from 14½ hands (such as a small Welsh Cob) to 17 hands or more (an Irish hunter) – with 15 hands or so a good average; police forces sometimes employ particularly tall horses, as in the case of the police horse of 18½ hands referred to by Rackham (see Appendix).

In the 19th century Youatt recommended that the 'Hackney', the everyday riding or road horse, 'should rarely exceed fifteen hands and an inch' (1880, 88). Writing in 1904 Sir Walter Gilbey noted of the Hackney that 'the true type is a horse not exceeding 15 hands 2 inches in height', but also illustrated what he regarded as a gradual improvement over the previous century from a horse of 15 hands or less (Gilbey 1976, 51–2). The Duke of Wellington's famous mount Copenhagen was of no more than 15 hands (Tylden 1965, 18). In 18th-century France a large coach horse might reach only 15 hands 3 inches (Spruytte 1983, 109), while Gilbey referred in 1904 to 'those beautiful match pairs of carriage horses, standing from 15.2 to 16.2' (1976, 1). The Suffolk Punch, an extremely capable heavy draught-horse, rarely exceeds 16½ hands.

Thus even in modern times the very tall horse is a rarity. What is notable, however, in contrast to the medieval situation, is the prevalence today of riding horses of more than 15 hands and of particularly large and heavily built horses employed for haulage; many medieval horses, whether riding or draught, would in modern terms, at less than 14½ hands, be regarded as of pony size.

But what, apart from the skeletal remains discussed by Rackham, is the evidence for the size of the English medieval horse? Central to Professor Davis's magisterial account of the breeding of the medieval war-horse is the concept of the large, specially bred destrier or 'Great Horse', first mentioned in England as *magnus equus* in 1282 (Davis 1989, 88). Davis defines the 14th and 15th centuries as 'the age of the "great horse", perhaps as tall as 17 or 18 hands' (ibid. 69). One recent author describes such horses as 'armour-carrying equine juggernauts' (Dent 1987, 21); another asks, presumably rhetorically, 'Did the average destrier stand sixteen or seventeen hands high?' (Hewitt 1983, 9).

A horse of 18 hands, as envisaged by Davis, would at the withers equal the full height of a six foot man: as tall as the largest modern Shire horse or police horse and exceeding by four to six inches the majority of large thoroughbreds. Not surprisingly some have viewed such horses (on little real evidence) as the ancestors of the modern Shire, and a popular image has emerged of armoured knights galumphing around the field of battle on horses more at home on a brewer's dray! Recently Clutton-Brock (1992, 123–4) has dismissed this concept as legend – with good reason.

The Great Horse certainly existed. It was highly prized; it was imported into England at great expense; its breeding was encouraged and its export banned (Davis 1989, *passim*). It was strong enough to carry not merely an armoured knight but in later years also the weight of its own armour. Yet what is the evidence for its giant stature?

Certainly not, it would seem, the size of surviving medieval horse armour – Mrs Ann Hyland comments (pers comm) that her measurements of examples in the Royal Armouries show that, with allowance for padding, they would sit comfortably on a modern horse of between 15 and 16 hands.

The oft-quoted regulations of Henry VIII, the first laws to define horses in terms of 'handfulls', lend no support to the argument for the existence, even as an ideal, of particularly tall horses; they refer to broodmares of at least 13 hands (1535), to stallions of at least 15 hands (1540) and to the requirement (1541–2) for all men of any status to keep a certain number of saddle-horses (stallions – 'stoned trotting horses for the saddle') of 14 hands or more, to be subject to military requisition if required (Davis 1989, 108–9; Dent & Goodall 1962, 138–42). Indeed there is a suggestion that early measurement by 'hands' followed the contour of the horse's body, rather than being taken vertically (footnote by Mary Littauer in her translation of Spruytte 1983, 109, n 12); if so, the figures in Henry's regulations indicate horses rather smaller than the same figures would represent today. The obvious conclusion would seem to be that it is in the region of 14 to 15 hands (the size of a modern Welsh Cob) that we should expect to find horses bred for military use – not dissimilar to those used by the

17   Sir Geoffrey Luttrell mounted on his war-horse. Luttrell Psalter *c.*1340 (British Library Add MS 42130 f202b)

cavalry of the 17th century, when cuirassiers and harquebusiers rode horses of 15 hands (Tylden 1965, 5).

Nor do contemporary medieval illustrations suggest a particularly large horse. The medieval artist's concept of scale and proportion was not always what a modern technical draughtsman would aim at. It might be claimed that in many scenes the horse is regarded as subsidiary to the rider and therefore drawn at a smaller scale. Yet this certainly could not be argued of the illustration of a group of horses with their grooms, in a manuscript made between 1352 and 1362 for Louis II of Naples, which is reproduced in Davis (1989, 83, fig 36). Here, where the horses are clearly the dominant feature, they are of middling

height; their height at the withers is similar to that of the shoulders of the men with them.

Perhaps the best known of all medieval illustrations of horses by an English artist are those in the Luttrell Psalter of about 1340 (British Library Add MS 42130). At first sight the long-shanked beast on which Sir Geoffrey Luttrell is shown mounted on f202b of the manuscript (Fig 17; Millar 1932, frontispiece) seems to dwarf the ladies standing near it. Draped in the full armorial panoply of the Luttrell family and prepared for a joust, it is clearly Sir Geoffrey's war-horse – perhaps the same 'best horse and its war-trappings' which Sir Geoffrey was to bequeath as a 'mortuary' offering to the parish church at Irnham (Norfolk) where he was buried (ibid. 54).

Yet even here rules of proportion can apply. Sir Geoffrey sits high in his saddle; his wife Agnes stands by the horse's head, handing the knight his helm; behind her their daughter-in-law Beatrice holds his shield. The artist has emphasised the height of the horse and its rider by showing Lady Agnes stretching upwards with the helmet in her hands; but the emphasis is misleading. The knight would, when dismounted, clearly overtop his wife and daughter-in-law by several inches. Skeletal evidence discussed below suggests an average six inches difference in height between medieval men and women, and an average woman's height of 5ft 2in (White 1988, 30–31). If we assume that Agnes Luttrell was of average stature, then her husband's Great Horse, its withers apparently just above her eye level, can have stood no more than 15 hands – an estimate very different from that of Dent & Goodall (1962, 114), who concluded on the basis of the same illustration that Sir Geoffrey's horse 'must have been a good seventeen hands high'.

Sir Geoffrey himself would have stood shoulder-to-shoulder with his horse. Other 14th-century manuscripts show a similar relationship between horse and rider, as, for example, in the early 14th-century English manuscript Queen Mary's Psalter (Warner 1912, 207–8) or the Flemish Romance of Alexander (James 1933, ff92r and 101v, or the groom on f139v and the knights standing by their horses on f161r).

For a later date Trease's study of *The Condottieri* (1970) provides a useful compendium of Italian equestrian portraits, among them the literally monumental painting (that is, it depicts a monument) by Paulo Uccello (died 1475) of the English soldier of fortune Sir John Hawkwood, known in Italy as 'Giovanni Acuto' (Fig 18b – ibid. 154 and fig 107; Davis 1989, 97, fig 40). This shows him in armour on what is surely in this context his war-horse.

At this time (1436) Uccello was experimenting with new techniques of perspective (Kubovy 1986, 116–20), and Sir John and his horse are portrayed virtually in orthographic projection, allowing us to take our measurements with some confidence. If we imagine Sir John dismounted, it is clear that his shoulder would be level with the withers of his horse. Similar proportions are visible in the same artist's well-known battle-scenes such as the *Rout of San Romano* (1454–7)

(Murray & Murray 1963, fig 95).

A survey of some of the existing medieval illustrations, though far from exhaustive, seems to suggest that, at least to the artist, the concept of a horse equalling its rider's shoulder height was a familiar one. Examples are found over a wide chronological and geographical span, from the Bayeux Tapestry to the works of 15th- and 16th-century artists in Italy and Germany; some are collected in the sketches in Fig 18.

To translate these proportions into reality we must know or estimate the height of the human figures shown. The study of human skeletons from medieval cemeteries suggests an average height of 5ft 8in (1.72m) for a man, 5ft 2in (1.58m) for a woman (White 1988, 30–31). Clearly by so much as the well-bred and well-nourished men and women portrayed by our artists exceed this average height – which is derived largely from urban cemeteries and perhaps represents a poorer, unhealthy and underfed population – by so much would their horses exceed any estimate we may make. With that proviso, and allowing 'shoulder-height' for a man at 58 inches, most horses in 15th- and 16th-century illustrations seem to be of something between 14 and 15 hands.

We can test our assumption against some obvious exceptions. One of Dürer's early engravings shows a well-dressed lady riding side-saddle, a man-at-arms at her side (Strauss 1972, no 18). The human figures seem well in proportion; if so the horse is a pony, of about 12 hands. A lady riding alone in a hawking scene in the Duc de Berry's *Très riches heures* (c.1410) is mounted on a horse of perhaps 13 hands – certainly considerably smaller than that in front, on which another lady rides pillion behind a young man (Pognon 1979, 30–31).

The medieval pictorial evidence seems to show consistency. It suggests perhaps that the Great Horse did not differ greatly in height from better quality riding horses; like them it was no more than 15 hands. Its 'greatness' presumably lay not in height but perhaps in nobility – certainly in greater strength and manoeuvrability in combat, as one might reasonably expect.

Working horses – pack-animals, farm- and cart-horses – appear less often in medieval illustrations than do war- and riding horses, yet there is some evidence to allow us to assess their size.

18   Some medieval horses and their riders: **a** *c.* 1225–30 – by Villard de Honnecourt (cf. Bowie 1959, pl 18); **b** 1436: *Sir John Hawkwood* – by Paulo Uccello; **c** *c.* 1452: *Story of the True Cross*, S Francesco, Arezzo – fresco by Piero della Francesca (cf. Murray & de Vecchi 1970, pl XX); **d** 1505: *The Large Horse* – by Albrecht Dürer (cf. Strauss 1972, 97, no 45)

a

b

c

d

19 'Affer' or 'stott' pulling a harrow, *c.* 1340 (Luttrell Psalter – British Library Add MS 42130 f171)

Once again the Luttrell Psalter (British Library Add MS 42130) provides information on the English rural scene, with a horse drawing a harrow (Fig 19 – after f171) and the well-known scene of three horses struggling up hill with a heavily-laden harvest cart (Fig 9 – f173b). Although direct comparison with the human figures is difficult, the small size of the horses is evident. Neither the harrow-horse (presumably an 'affer') nor the cart-horses are particularly large or strongly built.

The distinction between the *affrus* or 'stott', the ordinary peasant workhorse, usually used for ploughing and harrowing and valued at around 2*s.* 6*d.*, and the *equus* or *equus carectarius*, the cart-horse worth three times as much, is clarified by Langdon (1986, 200, 294–6); in the manorial accounts for Cuxham, Oxfordshire, in 1352 the shoeing of affers is listed under expenditure on ploughs, that of *equi* under expenditure on carts (Harvey 1976, 525). For the London area recent research has confirmed the higher value of the cart-horse throughout the period 1250–1400, though suggesting a mean selling price for the affer or stott higher than those quoted by Langdon (66.7 pence – about 5*s.* 7*d.*) and a lower differential, the mean price of the cart-horse being 111.9 pence – about 9*s.* 4*d.* (Centre for Metropolitan History 1991, 12, fig 5 – a preliminary report on a continuing research project described by Galloway & Murphy 1991). In the years 1381 to 1399, for which their accounts survive, the London Bridgewardens consistently paid considerably more than this for horses for their fleet of carts – in one instance as much as 60*s.* 3*d.* (see Brian Spencer's essay, above), a price that would have bought a cheap riding horse (a hackney – see Davis 1989, 67). Similar high prices were paid for cart-horses for the royal household in the late 13th century – from 40*s.* to 106*s.* according to Byerly & Byerly (1977, xxxvi, n 4).

The higher price bought a horse broken to cart harness, presumably better bred, surely sturdier than the ordinary affer. It does not seem to have bought a particularly large horse. French artillery horses of 1697, harnessed in teams of four to two-wheeled carts, were in modern terms small horses or ponies of 13 to 14 hands (Spruytte 1983, 108–9); 100 years later the minimum size of horses requisitioned for the French army was still only 13½ hands (ibid. 111). Medieval illustrations suggest cart-horses of similar size, stocky but by no means heavily built, usually shown in teams of two or three harnessed in tandem to a light cart; documentary evidence discussed above confirms the use of such teams of two or three. The hauling capacity of such a horse, at least over any long distance, could not have been great. There must be some doubt about the veracity of the 14th-century farmer quoted by Langdon (1986, 116 and n 68) who claimed his horse could on its own pull a cart with five quarters of wheat – which, if Langdon's interpretation (2,250lb) is correct, represents a good load for a modern Shire horse.

Spruytte in his study of the efficiency of early harnessing techniques quotes a French 17th-century writer on the use of horses in the artillery (1983, 108–9): four horses of 13 to 14 hands harnessed in file to a two-wheeled cart were expected to haul a load of 675kg (1,400lb) maximum – 350lb per horse. This figure is less for each horse than some of Langdon's authorities assign to a pack-horse (1986, 116), though a more normal recommended load for a pack-animal seems to be between 200lb and 300lb (Leighton 1972, 104; Tylden 1965, 179, 182–3, 191). Perhaps the French figure represents the deliberate underloading of vehicles in military use for speed and endurance. Hauling a four-wheeled wagon, a team of three or four modern Shire horses might well manage a load of three or more tons along difficult roads – a ton (2,240lb; c.1000kg) or so apiece (Brown 1991, 85); Youatt (1880, 98) quotes a figure of 4½ tons as the load regularly hauled by carriers in Normandy with a team of four horses, and one ton as the normal load for a carrier's cart drawn by a single horse on the road between Glasgow and Edinburgh. The haulage ability of the medieval cart-horse must surely lie closer to that quoted by the French military authority, and Langdon's estimate that carrying by cart was twice as effective as the use of pack-horses (1986, 226) may be close to the truth. It would suggest a load of perhaps 500–600lb per horse and a total load of about 15cwt (750kg) for the cart depicted in the Luttrell Psalter; whether such a cart could support that level of loading for long is another matter!

Few of the horse-related artefacts included in our catalogue can give a direct indication of the size of the horse to which they belonged; exceptions are the horseshoes and possibly the bits, though both must be treated with great reservation.

In discussing the use of prehistoric bits as evidence for the size of early horses, Dent & Goodall (1962, 291–2) present with due caution a table of sizes of bit (that is, the width of the mouthpiece measured between the side-pieces) as follows:

3½-inch bit	11 hands
4-inch bit	12 hands
4½-inch bit	13 hands
5-inch bit	14 hands
5½-inch bit	15 hands 'and upwards'

These notional figures differ considerably from some figures for modern pony bits quoted from direct measurement by Ann Hyland in her study of the Roman cavalry horse (1990a, 139–40): 4

inch for a pony of 13 to 13½ hands; 4½ inch for a pony of 13½ to 14½ hands. An average modern snaffle for a horse is around 5½ inches (ibid.). Both sources agree on the great variation in muzzle width found in both horses and ponies, and bit sizes can only be used as an indication of height with hesitation.

Only one bit in our catalogue is complete enough for measurement: the late 14th-century snaffle from Billingsgate (No 3). At about 5½ inches this would represent a horse at the upper end of Dent & Goodall's scale, around 15 hands. It would apparently suit Mrs Hyland's horse Katchina (14 hands 3 inches – see Hyland 1990a, 140), but would also fit many modern horses of much greater stature, particularly where Arabian blood is evident in a finer head. A very similar bit from a contemporary 14th-century context at Lochmaben Castle, Scotland, measures little more than 4½ inches – 13 or 14 hands on Dent & Goodall's scale, around 14 hands according to Hyland (Macdonald & Laing 1974–5, 146, no 1, fig 10).

In the Museum of London collections are many other snaffle bits which, in the absence of an archaeological context, cannot be safely dated – many must be post-medieval if not 'modern'. Three, however, are very similar to the late 14th-century (ceramic phase 11) fragment from Trig Lane (No 5) and may be presumed to be of similar date. Two of these, together with one from Moorfields at that time in Farnham Museum, are illustrated in London Museum 1940 (83, fig 20; see also Fig 33). In the case of the incomplete one (acc no A16814) a mouth size of 4 inches can be estimated; the other two are of 4½ to 5 inches each, while another example in the Museum of London collections (acc no 10207) approaches 5½ inches. Apart from the incomplete example, which suggests a horse of perhaps only 12 hands (Dent & Goodall) or 13 hands (Hyland), the others suit Dent & Goodall's figures for animals of about 14 or 15 hands. Few measurable snaffles of definitely medieval date seem to be recorded from elsewhere; a crude example from Dissolution debris (c.1483–1571) at St Mary's Hospital, Ospringe (Kent) is again of about 5 inches – perhaps 14 or 15 hands (Goodall 1979b, 135, no 111, fig 23).

The complex curb bit from an early 13th-century context at Seal House described in the catalogue below (No 6) has a mouth of about 4½ inches if reconstructed. This would be smaller than the modern English range for curb bits (Hyland 1990a, 139) and, though curbs may be more tightly fitting than snaffles, it might suggest a horse of no more than 14 hands. Though none came from recent excavations, there are a number of decorative curb bits in the Museum of London collections that are similar to those illustrated by Thomas Blundeville in 1565 (Dent 1987, 94–5) – and compare a simple example from 15th- to mid-16th-century levels at Somerby (Lincolnshire) (Mynard 1969, 81, no I.W.28, fig 11) and an early 17th-century one from Basing House (Hampshire) (Moorhouse & Goodall 1971, 47–9, no 89, fig 21). These fine well-made bits were clearly for use on riding horses which were highly valued by their owners. The mouthpieces vary between 4 and 5½ inches, and they suggest perhaps that even in the 16th century the generality of riding horses did not exceed 15 hands.

Horseshoes, applied directly to a part of the horse's anatomy, should theoretically give a reliable indication of size – though only that of the foot, and the size of a horse's foot, like that of its jaw, gives no more than a general indication of its overall dimensions. Measurement of the widths of the front hooves of a group of modern riding horses of between 14 hands 3 inches and 16 hands 2 inches gave figures between 120mm and 140mm (P Armitage pers comm) – the smallest belonging to a horse of 15 hands 3 inches, the largest to one of 16 hands. Thus increase in overall height is clearly not matched *pari passu* by an increase in hoof width. Heavily built draught horses, whatever their height, have larger feet than the lighter riding horses; their hooves might easily be 180mm or more across, and Sparkes (1976, 24) records one 1920s railway horseshoe that was 8½ inches by 8¼ inches (215mm by 210mm).

The fact that in modern practice shoes may be 'close fitting' (slightly narrower than the hoof) or 'wide' or 'full fitting' (extending beyond the hoof all round) is also noted below. With that proviso, but accepting that the shoe size gives some indication of the size of the hoof, it is worth considering the dimensions recorded in the study incorporated in the catalogue of horseshoes, below.

The range of recorded widths remains fairly constant through all four types of shoe discussed in the catalogue; with the exception of a number of very small examples of the early wavy-edged type 2A (less than 88mm wide), all fall between the extremes of 92mm and 120mm, with medians of 101–2mm for types 2A and 2B and of *c.*110mm for the later types 3 and 4. For comparison, measurements of 18 hoof-cores among the medieval skeletal material from London included in Rackham's survey (above), together with two Roman and one post-medieval example, gave figures for the width across the distal phalanx at its widest point of 65mm to 85mm, with a relatively even distribution between these limits. To these must be added a variable allowance for the outer layers of the hoof – a typical cross-section illustrated in Hickman & Humphrey (1988, 54, fig 2.47) suggests that we would not be far wrong if we added a nominal one-third to the width of the bone. Thus the skeletal evidence implies an overall hoof width ranging from just under 90mm to around 115mm, which is certainly not inconsistent with the sizes indicated by the surviving shoes.

Compared with the modern figures quoted above, these measurements are all distinctly small – though not by any means, at the upper end of their range, uncommon among modern horse stock. Fig 20 shows (by courtesy of Ann Hyland) front and hind shoes of Harmony's Legacy, a pure-bred Arabian mare of 15 hands 1 inch and about 950lb weight, alongside shoes of our type 2A (*c.*1050–*c.*1150); the latter, with widths of 119mm and 110mm respectively, are among the largest of the type recorded. On the other hand, Fig 21 shows the largest available shoes (120mm width) of our late medieval type 4 alongside front and hind shoes of Mrs Hyland's stallion Granicus (16 hands 1 inch, *c.*1,200lb); though not at first sight dissimilar, they are a good 10mm narrower than the modern shoes.

If only the largest of medieval horseshoes would fit an average modern horse, it may be safe to conclude that the great majority of medieval horses did not reach the sort of 15 hands height and proportionate bulk that is today expected of an ordinary riding horse – a conclusion similar to our deductions from documentary and pictorial evidence and consistent with the data derived from skeletal remains. Most medieval horses were in modern terms decidedly small.

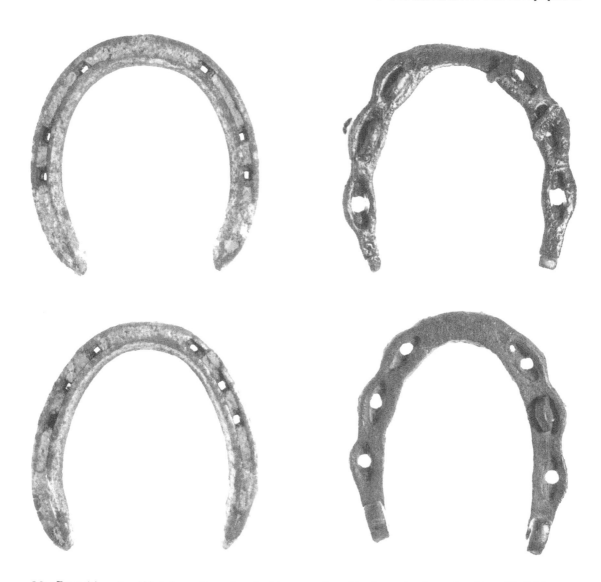

20   Front (above) and hind shoes of a modern Arabian mare alongside shoes of early medieval type 2A (MoL acc nos 59.94/20 and 13105) (modern shoes by courtesy of Harmony's Legacy and of Ann Hyland)

However, if we cannot derive absolute sizes from horseshoes, perhaps we can trace within our period a development in relative terms. Very small shoes, less than 90mm across (3½ inches), are found only among those of the earliest Norman type – common before the mid-12th century – and may perhaps reflect the presence of a few diminutive animals among the horse-stock of the Saxo-Norman period: surely smaller than the 13 to 14 hand horses of this date referred to by

Rackham. There is a noticeable change (see the discussion of the size and shape of horseshoes and Fig 76 below) marked by the introduction during the 13th century of the heavier horseshoe of our type 3. Shoes of this type, which first appear alongside type 2B shoes before 1230 and predominate after 1270, show a variation in size not dissimilar to that of the earlier shoes – indeed the largest are not as wide as the widest type 2 shoes. However, they have a higher median

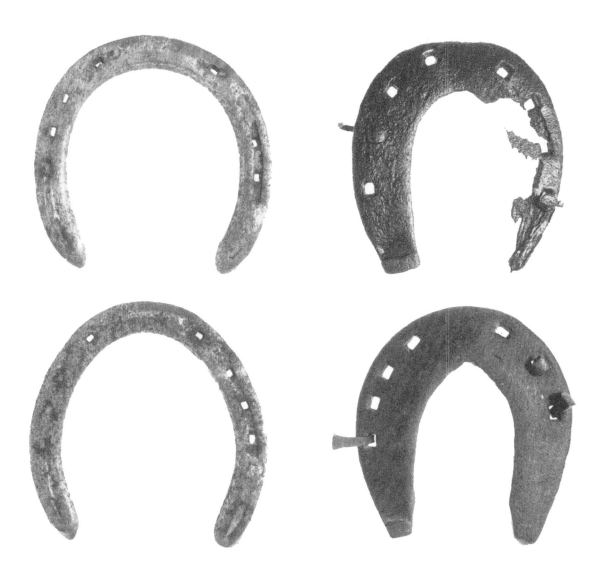

21 Front (above) and hind shoes of a modern 16-hand stallion alongside large examples of shoes of late medieval type 4 (No 230 – BC72 2486 – and MoL acc no 11692) (modern shoes by courtesy of Granicus and of Ann Hyland)

width, of 109mm – and 50% of them lie between 100mm and the maximum 115mm. The succeeding type 4 shoes have a similar median width, but a slightly greater range and less tendency to cluster around the median.

It would be unwise to suggest that the introduction of the type 3 horseshoe directly reflects the breeding or importation of greater numbers of larger (or at least larger-footed) horses. Professor Davis notes, however, that the reigns of John

and of Henry III are the first in which there are glimpses of the administration of the royal horses, and he records increasing evidence during the 13th century of royal attempts to buy good foreign horses (1989, 83–5). When in 1232 three 'horses of Lombardy' appeared on the London market, the king wrote to the mayor and aldermen asking for their assistance in acquiring them for the royal stables. A few years later he sent his marshal to the Champagne fairs, probably to buy more of these desirable north Italian steeds (ibid. 85 and 63–4). Edward I and Edward II both devoted considerable energy and money to the improvement of horse stock for purposes of war; the term *magnus equus* ('Great Horse') first appears in the royal records in 1282 (ibid. 88). If this royal concern reflects the general picture, it may be that the 13th century does in fact see an overall betterment, in quality and size, of the general stock at least of riding and war-horses.

It may be no coincidence that it is in the period 1250–1320 that Langdon records the first instances of farms employing only horses to the exclusion of oxen (1986, 100). The progressive takeover by horses of farm haulage (and in some cases ploughing), which had begun in the Norman period, proceeded rapidly during the 13th century; indeed though the change was to continue in the 14th century the rate of increase seems to have slowed down after the turn of the century (ibid. 254–5, fig 42). The increasing use of horses on farms must surely have depended on, and in turn encouraged, improvements in their stamina and strength; it certainly implies that more good quality animals were becoming available on the market.

But if there was progress in horse breeding during the 13th century, the sample of horse skeletons that has been studied so far is too limited and random to demonstrate it; perhaps the changes we have identified in contemporary horseshoes are the only physical evidence we yet have of an increase in the average size of horses at this time. It should be emphasised that it is this *average* that seems to have risen. As ever horses varied widely in size, but a growing proportion of those in everyday use, at least in London, were no longer of 'pony' but of 'small horse' size.

No single piece of the evidence we have considered can in itself be relied upon to give an exact figure for the size of medieval horses. Even the estimates derived from the skeletal remains are, as has been shown above, no more than that – estimates, based on formulae applied to certain limb bone measurements. However, all our figures are remarkably consistent, and our conclusions about the size of most medieval horses can, I hope, be accepted with some confidence.

Conclusions

In his study of *Horses, Oxen and Technological Innovation* (1986) Langdon was able, thanks to the wealth of evidence available from the Domesday Book onwards, to reach conclusions about the number of horses in use in both demesne and peasant farming and to present the results in statistical tables. Similar statistics are not available for the London horse; the variety of uses to which it was put in an urban situation, the lack of a single central body of related records, the scattered and often anecdotal references surveyed above – all of these severely limit the sorts of conclusion that can be drawn. We cannot estimate the horse population of London, resident or transient.

It is suggested above that among Londoners ownership of riding horses was rare; but horses were clearly kept for hire in large numbers. The importance of the horse-drawn cart is evident from the records – and with two to four horses to each cart a large population of cart-horses may be assumed. No relative, let alone absolute, figures for numbers of riding and draught-horses can be suggested. Rackham was unable to reach a definite conclusion as to whether the medieval skeletons included in his survey were riding or draught-animals (above). One had the slender long legs that might suggest an elegant riding horse; the majority were small, well-built horses that could equally be ridden or used in harness. Some certainly showed signs of hard work and ill use. In any case so small and random a sample can hardly form a sound basis for statistical analysis. Nor have artefact studies been of great assistance; we have not, for example, been able to distinguish riding and draught-horses by the shape or size of their shoes. However, it should not be surprising if some types of archaeological find that relate specifically to the riding horse – such as stirrups and (presumably) curb bits – are relatively rare in London; a large part, if not the majority, of the local horse stock must have consisted of draught-animals.

The excavations

ANGELA WARDLE

This chapter provides a brief background to the main sites mentioned in this book. As in the previous volumes, the most productive were waterfront excavations by the River Thames. Finds were recovered from the dumped fills deposited for land reclamation and from the mixed gravel and silt foreshore deposits that accumulated against the medieval revetments. This reclamation process resulted, over a period of about 300 years (c.1150–c.1450), in the formation of new land to the south of Upper and Lower Thames Street. A larger number of inland sites have been included than in former volumes, reflecting in particular the widespread loss of horseshoes in the City. Preservation of metalwork and organics is generally poor on inland sites, in marked contrast to the waterfront assemblages, and many of the finds, often single examples, are from rubbish pits and wells; an exception is Ludgate Hill (LUD82), which produced material from the City Ditch.

The descriptions of the major waterfront sites given here are largely those of Geoff Egan (Egan & Pritchard 1991, 1–12), adapted to take account of material included in this volume. The dating of the deposits at these sites depends in the first instance on coins, supplemented where possible by dendrochronology. This has permitted key changes in the ceramic sequence to be assigned approximate dates (principally the work of Alan Vince – see Vince 1985, 25–93). The *ceramic phases* thus defined are the linchpin of the dating assigned in this volume to each of the groups of deposits that together constituted a reclamation dump or foreshore etc. Unlike previous volumes, this study includes ceramic phases 1–5 to take account of the earlier development of the horseshoe. (See Table 1.)

In the following accounts general information is given on all sites which produced finds discussed in this book, and more detailed information is given, where available, on the most productive sequences, with a brief summary of the dated

Table 1: Ceramic phasing

Ceramic phase	Date	Pottery fabrics
phase 1	c.900–c.1000	late Saxon shelly ware
phase 2	c.970–c.1050	early medieval sandy and early medieval flinty ware
phase 3	c.1000–c.1050	early medieval sandy and shelly ware
phase 4	c.1050–c.1080/1150	early medieval shelly, early medieval chalk and early Surrey ware
phase 5	c.1080–c.1150	London type ware and coarse London ware
phase 6	c.1150–c.1200	shelly sandy ware
phase 7	c.1200–c.1230	London/Rouen wares
phase 8	c.1230–c.1260	Kingston ware
phase 9	c.1270–c.1350	Mill Green ware
phase 10	c.1330–c.1380	late medieval Hertfordshire glazed ware
phase 11	c.1350–c.1400	Cheam ware
phase 12	c.1400–c.1450	coarse border ware/bifid rims

Note that the pottery fabrics defining phase 4 continue in use throughout phase 5; the latter is distinguished by additional fabrics, which may not always be present in small groups.

sequence proposed for each of the major sites. Post-excavation analysis methods differed from site to site, so that groupings and interpretation may not correspond precisely between the proposed sequences. Simplified site plans of the four major waterfront excavations (BIG82, BWB83, SWA81, TL74), originally published in Egan & Pritchard 1991, can be used to find the location of specific objects in the sequence (see the individual sites), but only contexts which produced horse equipment are listed. Figure 22 shows the location of the sites.

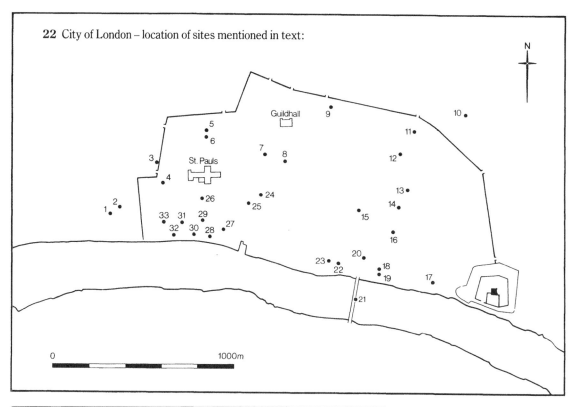

22 City of London – location of sites mentioned in text:

Site	No		Site	No		Site	No
BC72	32		EST83	16		PIC87	4
BIG82	18		GPO75	6		POM79	5
BIS82	11		IME83	14		SH74	22
BOP82	12		IRO80	8		SUN86	27
BOY86	1		LLO78	13		SWA81	23
BWB83	19		LUD82	3		TAV82	26
BYD81	30		MC73	25		THE79	33
CLE81	15		MLK76	7		TL74	28
CUS73	17		OPT81	9		TUD78	2
CUT78	10		PDN81	20		UT74	31
ER1279A	21		PET81	29		WAT78	24

BC72: Baynard House, Queen Victoria Street, 'Baynard's Castle Dock' (site supervisor, P Marsden), Fig 22 (site 32)

The excavations produced two extensive groups of dump deposits attributed to ceramic phase 11, associated with a stone-walled dock known as the 'East Watergate' (Webster & Cherry 1973, 162–3; Vince in Cowgill et al. 1987, 2). One late 14th-century dump (contexts 55, 79, 83, 88, 89, 150) produced a large finds assemblage with material of high quality (Egan & Pritchard 1991, 6; Crowfoot et al. 1992, 3). Among the 24 horseshoes were two with heraldic stamps (Nos 222, 235). The group also contained decorated spur straps (Nos 379–95) and curry comb No 402 together with other miscellaneous items.

BIG82: Billingsgate lorry park, Lower Thames Street, EC3 (site supervisor, S Roskams), Figs 22 (site 18), 23

Excavations revealed an extensive series of revetments, the earliest dating from the 10th or 11th century. To the east lay a row of private tenements (periods 7–12) and behind the riverfront was an undercroft and the Church of St Botolph. The finds considered here came from the sequence of land reclamation dumps and foreshores of ceramic phases 6–8 (12th to 13th centuries), dated by coins, pottery and dendrochronology. In some areas water-lain deposits had accumulated over land reclamation dumps and some deposits defined as foreshores included organic material usually associated with dumps. Consequently it was difficult to identify each context firmly as reclamation dump or foreshore. The structural sequence is complex and further analysis may alter the interpretation (Egan & Pritchard 1991, 4, fig 2).

Two spurs, Nos 357–8, come from contexts dated to ceramic phase 7 (1200–30) – one from a group 10 dump, the other from a group 11 layer – and stirrup No 82 was from a group 9 dump. Dumps dating to ceramic phases 6–8 also produced three horseshoes, Nos 123, 124, 137, and earlier deposits (ceramic phases 4–5) yielded four shoes.

Figure 23 is a schematic plan of the site showing the positions and nature of the main groups of ceramic phase 6 and later. Table 2 gives the contexts used in this volume and the group to which each is assigned.

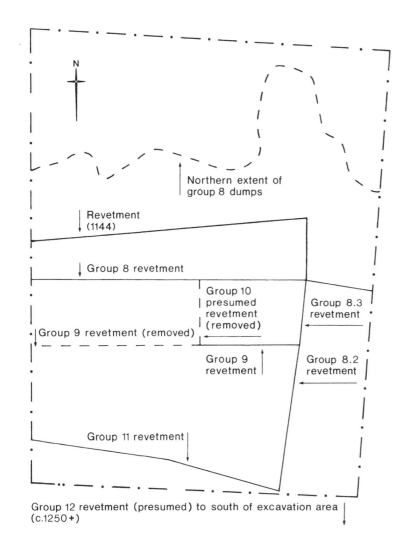

Northern extent of group 8 dumps

Revetment (1144)

Group 8 revetment

Group 10 presumed revetment (removed)

Group 8.3 revetment

Group 9 revetment (removed)

Group 9 revetment

Group 8.2 revetment

Group 11 revetment

Group 12 revetment (presumed) to south of excavation area (c.1250+)

23 Billingsgate lorry park site (BIG82) – schematic plan

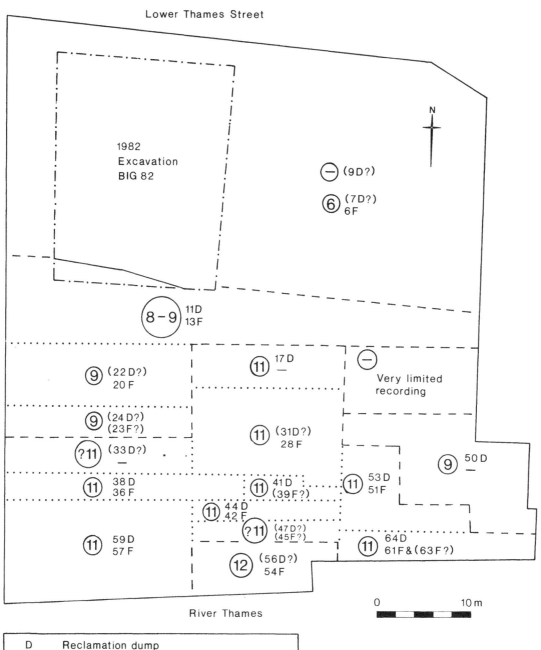

24   Billingsgate lorry park site, watching
brief (BWB83) – schematic plan

Table 2: BIG82 site – context groups and types

Context	Group	Type
2596	12	–
3204	11	–
4100	10.1	dump
4372	10.1	dump
4420	7.7	–
5521	9.2	dump
6980	4.6	–
7073	4.6	–
7336	4.6	–
7462	4.6	–

BIS82: 76–80 Bishopsgate, EC3 (site supervisor, H White), Fig 22 (site 11)

Inland site. Medieval pitting and quarrying overlay Roman levels. A well fill dated to the 13th century produced one horseshoe (No 112).

BOP82: 28–32 Bishopsgate, EC2 (site supervisor, C Evans), Fig 22 (site 12)

Inland site. Late Saxon and medieval pitting produced horseshoe No 99.

BOY86: City of London Boys' School (old site) (site supervisor, C Spence), Fig 22 (site 1)

Late medieval sequence of dumps continuing into the (?) late 15th century: for comparanda. Metal detecting by the Society of Thames Mudlarks.

BWB83: Billingsgate lorry park, watching brief (site supervisor, G Egan), Figs 22 (site 19), 24

The watching brief, which continued after the controlled excavations at Billingsgate (BIG82), produced numerous finds from deposits dating from ceramic phases 6–12. Access to the site was restricted but limited recording of dumps and revetments in three adjacent properties provided a basic sequence in some parts of the site. Most finds, however, came from foreshores and reclamation dumps – some disturbed – after structural features had been removed, and consequently the dating must remain less certain than for other waterfront sites. The sequence is, however, broadly coherent, and a northern limit for deposits attributed to each ceramic phase is given in Fig 24, which also shows the groups to which contexts are assigned (see also Egan & Pritchard 1991, 7). Each group can be located on the plan, which gives its type (dump, foreshore etc.), ceramic phase and position relative to revetments. The very extensive assemblages of finds recovered were the result of metal detecting by the Society of Thames Mudlarks. The horse equipment, mostly horseshoes, came chiefly from contexts dating to ceramic phases 9 and 11, with eight spurs from dumps and foreshores of ceramic phase 11 (1350–1400), in common with the majority of finds from the site.

Table 3 lists contexts used in this book. Bracketed context numbers indicate deposits that were disturbed before retrieval took place; there is the possibility of contamination by earlier, or occasionally later, items among finds recovered from these deposits.

Table 3: BWB83 site – context groups, types and phases

Context	Group(s)	Type	Ceramic phase
4	57/59	m	11
10	20	f	11
15	45/47	m	12
17	unassigned		12
(108)	17	f	10
(110)	28/31/33	m	11
(112)	28/31/33	m	11
(113)	31	d	11
(119)	41	d	11
142	41	d	11
146	59	d	11
(147)	36/38	m	11
(149)	36	f	11
151	36	f	11
157	38	d	11
162	59	d	11
175	unassigned		6–9
(207)	57/59	m	11
216	11	d	9
(222)	9/11	m	9
256	45	f	11
257	39	f	11
(259)	unassigned		?9
(263)	13	f	9
(264)	13	f	9
(265)	45/47/57/59	m	9
(269)	unassigned		?9
274	unassigned		?9
278	unassigned		?12
279	36	f	11
281	unassigned		
282	36	f	11
(285)	23/36	m	9

cont.

Table 3: BWB83 site – cont.

(286)	42/44	m	11
(290)	23/24/36	m	9
291	42	f	11
(292)	57/59	m	11
293	44	d	11
300	unassigned	m	?11
(301)	42/44	m	11
303	36	f	11
(306)	28	f	11
(307)	45/47	m	11
308	38	f	11
(310)	unassigned		?12
318	28	f	11
324	54	f	12
326	54	f	12
329	61	f	11
334	61	f	11
(338)	61/62/64	m	11
343	53	d	11
(354)	57/59	m	11
(359)	51/53	m	11
(367)	48	f	9
369	51	d	11
387	61	f	11

d = dump
f = foreshore
m = mixed dump and foreshore

BYD81: Baynard's Castle, City of London Boys' School (new site), Upper Thames Street, EC4 (site supervisor, J Burke-Easton), Fig 22 (site 30)
The 1981 excavations uncovered the south-east tower and examined the stratigraphy behind the castle (Burke/Easton 1982). Two spurs (Nos 354, 356) came from a large dump in front of the period 2 wall and behind the period 3 wall and tower, dated by the pottery to the late 14th to mid-15th century (Vince 1983, 2). A curry comb (No 408) was from a context also dated to ceramic phase 12.

CLE81: 29–32 Clements Lane, EC3 (site supervisor, C Evans), Fig 22 (site 15)
Inland site. Horseshoe No 313 came from a medieval pit.

CUS73: Custom House, Wool Quay, Lower Thames Street, EC3 (site supervisor, T Tatton-Brown), Fig 22 (site 17)
The excavation of foreshores and dumps took place at the eastern end of the City waterfront (Tatton-Brown 1974, 117–219). Five horseshoes (Nos 150–4) came

from a dump behind a timber revetement dated by pottery and dendrochronological evidence to the early 14th century, ceramic phase 9.

CUT78: Harrow Place, EC1 (site supervisor, S O'Connor Thompson), Fig 22 (site 10)
Inland site. Horseshoes and a spur residual in post-medieval contexts.

EST83: 27–9 Eastcheap, EC3 (site supervisor, S Rivière), Fig 22 (site 16)
Inland site. A series of Saxon and medieval storage pits cut Roman stratigraphy (Rivière 1984), one producing horseshoe (No 95).

GPO75: 76–80 Newgate Street, now British Telecom Headquarters, 81 Newgate St, EC1 (site supervisors, A Thompson, S Roskams), Fig 22 (site 6)
Inland site. Church and cemetery of St Nicholas Shambles. Three horseshoes from contexts containing pottery dating to the 11th/12th centuries and others of medieval date which are residual in later contexts.

IME83: 27–30 Lime Street, EC3 (site supervisor, T Williams), Fig 22 (site 14)
Inland site. Horseshoe No 102 from a well.

IRO80: 24–5 Ironmonger Lane, EC2 (site supervisor, J Norton), Fig 22 (site 8)
Excavations revealed Roman and Saxon structures cut by medieval pits, one of which produced a late Saxon horse skeleton (Armitage 1981a; Norton 1982, 171–6).

LLO78: Lloyds, Leadenhall Place, EC3 (site supervisor, K Flude), Fig 22 (site 13)
Inland site. Roman features and early medieval pits were investigated, one of which produced horseshoe No 314.

LUD82: 1–6 Old Bailey, 42–6 Ludgate Hill, EC4 (site supervisor, P Rowsome), Fig 22 (site 3)
Inland site including the City Ditch. The main ditch fills were dated by a coin of 1302–10 and by documentary evidence of development over the ditch area by 1340, to the middle part of ceramic phase 9 (Vince in Cowgill et al. 1987, 4; Youngs et al. 1983, 194). The early 14th-century fills produced a wealth of finds, among them one horseshoe (No 155) and horse skeletons.

MC73: St Mildred Bread St, 84–94 Queen Victoria St, EC4 (site supervisor, M Guterres), Fig 22 (site 25)

Sequence of Roman buildings, a late Saxon sunken-floored building and the foundations of the medieval and later church (Marsden et al. 1975). Spur No 320 came from a late Saxon/early medieval pit.

MLK76: 1–6 Milk Street, EC2 (site supervisors, S Roskams and J Schofield), Fig 22 (site 7)
Inland site which yielded a series of Saxo-Norman buildings (Horsman et al. 1988, 21–5; Schofield et al. 1986). Horseshoe (No 96) came from a pit associated with the buildings dated by pottery to the 11th to early 12th century.

OPT81: 2–3 Cross Keys Court, Copthall Avenue, EC2 (site supervisor, C Maloney), Fig 22 (site 9)
Inland site. Marshy area reclaimed by the dumping of clay in the 12th century. Horseshoe No 109 came from a dump (ceramic phase 6) and a spur (No 319) from a 12th-century ditch fill (ceramic phase 5).

PDN81: Pudding Lane, 118–27 Lower Thames Street, EC3 (site supervisor, G Milne), Fig 22 (site 20)
Waterfront site. Sequence of Saxo–Norman buildings (Horsman et al. 1988, 16–21). Horseshoe No 89 was found in a deposit dated early to mid-12th century (ceramic phase 5).

PET81: St Peter's Hill/Castle Baynard Street, Upper Thames Street, EC4 (site supervisor, T Williams), Fig 22 (site 29)
Excavations revealed Roman to post-medieval sequence, with Saxon activity prior to the laying-out of Peter's Hill in the 11th/12th century.

POM79: GPO site, Newgate Street, EC4, central area (site supervisors, P Allen et al., Fig 22 (site 5)
Inland site comprising part of the precinct of the Greyfriars (middle area between the two parts of GPO75). Excavations revealed early medieval hearths and fragmentary structures. Horseshoes of type 1 came from various contexts dated to the 12th century, with No 132 (type 2B) and spur No 321 from a late 13th- to 14th-century context.

SH74: Seal House, 106–8 Upper Thames Street (site supervisor, J Schofield), Fig 22 (site 22)
Medieval sequence beginning in the late 11th to early 12th century with a foreshore deposit overlying the Roman quay, ceramic phases 5–8 (Schofield 1975, 53–7; Morgan & Schofield 1978, 223–38). Four successive wharves can be dated after 1133, after 1163–

92 and after 1193 by dendrochronology and to *c.*1250 by pottery. Three horseshoes, Nos 105–7, and spur No 331 were found in the earliest waterfront dumps, all dating to ceramic phase 5, with further shoes and spurs from succeeding dumps.

SUN86: Sunlight Wharf, Upper Thames Street, EC4 (site supervisor, R Bluer), Fig 22 (site 27)
A sequence of reclamation dumps dating from the late 12th to the 15th centuries was recorded. One copper alloy spur of 14th-century date (No 329) is included for comparison.

SWA81: Swan Lane car park, 95–103 Upper Thames Street, EC4 (site supervisor, G Egan), Figs 22 (site 23), 25
A small controlled excavation and subsequent extensive watching brief revealed reclamation dumps and foreshores with as many as 10 successive revetments in three adjacent properties, with a sequence of activity from the late Saxon period to the mid-15th century (ceramic phases 6–12). The helpful contractors (Sir Robert MacAlpine and Sons) permitted prolonged access to the fullest reclamation sequence recorded among the main waterfront sites. Metal detecting by the Society of Thames Mudlarks produced extensive and varied finds assemblages that can be dated closely (Egan 1985/6, 42–50). Figure 25 is a schematic plan of the excavations (see Egan & Pritchard 1991, 10, fig 4), which shows the position and ceramic phase of each group to which contexts are assigned. See also Table 4 overleaf.
The late 12th-century waterfronts yielded three horseshoes, the mid-13th, nine, but the most productive dumps for all categories of material lay in front of the mid-13th-century revetments (ceramic phase 9), with 28 horseshoes, six spurs and two curry combs. Numismatic evidence and pilgrim souvenirs suggests a depositional date after 1270. The early 15th-century waterfront dumps, which produced large quantities of other finds, yielded little horse equipment.

TAV82: 29–31 Knightrider Street, EC4 (site supervisor, J Burke-Easton), Fig 22 (site 26)
Inland site. A small excavation produced evidence of Roman and Saxon occupation. Horseshoe No 121.

THE79: Mermaid Theatre, Puddle Dock, EC4 (site supervisor, P Herbert), Fig 22 (site 33)
Waterfront site; mid–late 13th-century revetment. Horseshoe No 290.

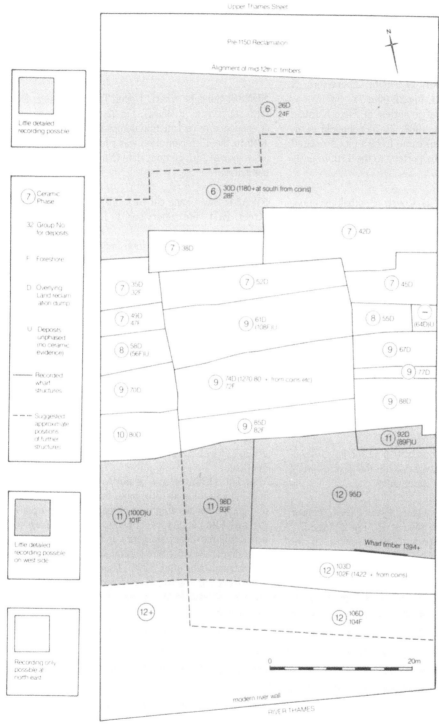

25 Swan Lane site and watching brief
(SWA81) – schematic plan

Table 4: SWA81 site – context groups and phases

Context	Group	Ceramic phase
1040	unassigned	–
1630	unassigned	–
1847	109	6
2000	70	9
2017	74	9
2018	74	9
2038	74	9
2040	74	9
2042	85	9
2046	74	9
2051	74	9
2052	58	8
2055	85	9
2056	85	9
2061	74	9
2066	74	12
2070	74	9
2071	74	9
2075	74	9
2083	103	12
2114	103	12
2124	35	7
2126	77	9
2127	74	9
2130	49	7
2131	85	9
2133	67	9
2134	74	9
2137	74	9
2141	74	9
2144	74	9
2149	74	9
2150	61	9
2157	26	6
2183	26	6
2187	24	6
2188	24	9
2212	61	9
2255	38	7
2257	?38	7
2259	30	6
2266	42	7
2267	45/4	7
2270	61	9
2278	unassigned	–
2279	42	7
2280	42	7
3779	unassigned	–
3848	unassigned	–

TL74: Trig Lane, Upper Thames Street, EC4 (site supervisor, G Milne), Figs 22 (site 28), 26

A sequence of reclamation dumps and foreshores dates from *c.*1250 to *c.*1440 (ceramic phases 8–12) (Milne & Milne 1982). The 17 revetments/repairs and foreshore structures in three adjacent properties were dated by dendrochronology, coins and pottery. Figure 26 is a schematic plan of the excavations showing the main features with the location of the structural groups (see also Egan & Pritchard 1991, 11, fig 5). The field records do not permit specific identification of all contexts as either foreshore or reclamation dump deposits.

Most of the finds, eight spurs, nine horseshoes and a curry comb are from contexts dated to ceramic phases 11–12, chiefly revetment group 11 and group 15, the river wall and associated deposits.

Table 5: TL74 site – context groups, types and phases

Context	Group	Type	Ceramic phase
4	18	–	–
117	17	–	12+
275	15	d	12
291	11	d	11
317	16	–	12
368	15	d	12
378	15	d	12
414	7/11	d	11
415	11	d	11
1595	2	d	9
1596	2	d	9
2442	3	d	9
2532	2	d	9

d = dump

TUD78: 1–3 Tudor Street, EC4 (site supervisor, A Thompson), Fig 22 (site 2)

A watching brief recovered evidence of reclamation and revetting of the west side of the Fleet Valley in the medieval period (Thompson 1979). Horseshoe No 207 came from a deposit dated to ceramic phase 9.

UT74: Upper Thames Street, (Baynard House), EC4 (site supervisor, D Jones), Fig 22 (site 31)

Two parallel walls, thought to be part of Baynard's Castle, were revealed. Horseshoe No 291 was residual in a later sewer trench.

WAT78: Watling Court, 41–53 Cannon Street, EC4
(site supervisor, D Perring), Fig 22 (site 24)
The Saxon and medieval periods were represented by
three late Saxon cellared buildings, overlain by medieval structures with cess pits (indicating separate properties) which fronted on to Watling Street to the north
and Basing Lane to the south.

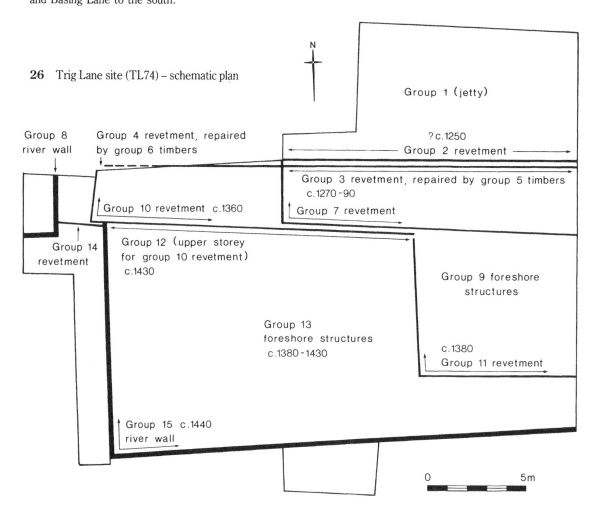

26   Trig Lane site (TL74) – schematic plan

Harness fittings

JOHN CLARK, GEOFF EGAN AND NICK GRIFFITHS

Introduction
John Clark

Whether ridden, carrying a load or hauling a cart, a horse must be harnessed, and the part played by the development of harnessing systems in mankind's use of the horse has long been recognised as fundamental (Lefebvre des Noëttes 1931; White 1962, 1–38, 59–61; Vigneron 1968; Spruytte 1983; and the many references therein to other discussions of saddles, stirrups, bits and methods of attachment to a vehicle).

In the medieval period royal and other accounts show major purchases of the necessary equipment. For example, the index to Byerly and Byerly's edition of Edward I's Wardrobe accounts for the one year 1285–6 (1977, 296–7) contains over 100 references for 'bridles and reins', 'collars and traces', 'girths', 'halters', 'saddle cloths and covers' and 'saddles and stirrups' as well as the ubiquitous 'other harness' (*pro aliis hernesiis*). Expenditure varied between £35 4*s.* for seven saddles decorated with pearls, gold and silver (ibid. 44) to 3*s.* for 'one rein, one halter, two surcingles and four girths' (ibid. 1). Similarly an inventory of harness and saddlery in the royal stables in 1483–4 ranges from saddles covered with cloth of gold to 18 fathom of 'guyding lyne' (Sutton & Hammond 1983, 127–30). The quality and sophistication of harness varied immensely, as can be seen in medieval illustrations – from the rope halter of the pack-horse carrying water-budgets in the Luttrell Psalter (Millar 1932, 154, f201) to the decorated but practical equipment of the horse ridden by Dürer's knight in 1513 (Strauss 1972, 151) or the trappings, as fancy as those of their courtly riders, of the horses in the May Day scene in the Duc de Berry's *Très riches heures* (Pognon 1979, 24–5).

The common feature of much harness is of course that it is made of materials of low survival potential archaeologically. The City of London excavations have produced nothing substantial to set alongside the so-called 'Henry V's saddle' in Westminster Abbey (Laking 1920–2, vol 3, 156–60), and it has not proved possible to identify harness leatherwork among the many leather scraps from the waterfront sites – except the spur straps described below (Nos 379–9), and where leather remains attached to an obvious piece of metal harness. Thus this chapter is devoted to the metal parts of harness, from bits and stirrups to the decorative pendants that seem to have been such a feature of better quality horse trappings.

Catalogue

BITS

John Clark

The few finds of horses' bits from the excavations reviewed here add little to the typology or chronology of bits of medieval date. It remains true, as Ward Perkins wrote in 1940, that 'the surviving specimens are . . . bewilderingly varied in type, and it is hardly possible to do more than indicate the commoner forms and the approximate period of their use' (London Museum 1940, 77).

Ward Perkins, writing at a time when his readers could perhaps be expected to be more familiar with horses and their harness than is true now, did not feel it necessary to define the two functional types of bit to which he referred, the snaffle and the curb bit; some definitions are however necessary today.

The *snaffle* consists of a mouthpiece, either a plain bar or made up of jointed links or 'cannons', fastened (usually with a swivelling joint) to cheek-pieces which are basically of ring form, though

a

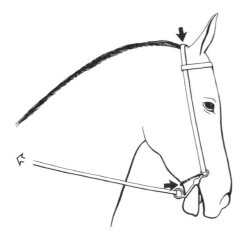

b

27 Snaffle and curb bits: **a** ring snaffle with simple headstall and reins; **b** curb bit with reins pulled back showing pressure from curb chain and on poll

variations on the basic theme in use in Britain today – some of them very specialised (Tuke 1965, 36–49).

In the *curb*, in its simplest form, the cheeks are extended both above and below the point at which they are attached to the mouthpiece; the head strap is fastened to an eye at the upper end of the cheek, the reins at the lower end (Fig 27b). Medieval illustrations suggest that the lower ends of the cheeks of early curb bits were also linked by a rigid bar (as for example in Fig 28; see also the Luttrell Psalter f173b and f202b – Millar 1932, 99 & frontispiece). The mouthpiece may be curved or extended upwards to form a *'port'*, which presses against the roof of the horse's mouth as the bit turns. The port, often quite high – and particularly so in the one curb bit (No 6, from the Seal House site) described below –

28 Medieval curb bit with rigid bar at bottom; St Martin sharing his cloak with a beggar, 13th century (Fitzwilliam Museum, Cambridge, MS 370 f5v)

often extended into wings or bars; to the rings are attached both the straps of the headstall, holding the bit in place in the horse's mouth, and the reins by which the rider controls it (Fig 27a). Within this definition there is great room for variation; Ward Perkins suggested that five different types of cheek-piece and six different types of mouthpiece could be found in medieval usage (London Museum 1940, 80–82 figs 19a, 19b; repeated here Figs 30, 31); Diana Tuke, in a useful 'guide to equine bits', illustrates some 70

seems to have been a regular feature of early curbs; today it is usually gentle or dispensed with entirely – at least in Britain. In modern bits a *curb chain* passes under the horse's chin linking the two upper loops of the cheek-pieces; the chain was clearly present in some if not all curb bits by the 16th century. The attachment of the mouth-piece is usually such that it and both cheek-pieces must rotate together (as in the modern Weymouth bit – Tuke 1965, 34). Depending on the length of these cheeks, greater or lesser leverage can be exerted by the rider pulling on the reins (Fig 27b), controlling the horse by exerting pressure on its mouth and lips directly, on the roof of its mouth through the port, on its jaw through the curb chain and on its sensitive poll (the area of the head between the ears) by the tightening of the head strap (ibid. 26–7). In the accounts of her pioneering experiments on the action of Roman bits found in excavations at the fort at Newstead, Ann Hyland emphasises the importance of this last action of the bit (1990b, 1991).

However, this description does not fully reflect the forms of bit in use today, nor does it explain the occasional appearance in medieval and 16th-century art of bridles with *two* sets of reins: for example, in the early 15th-century *Très riches heures* of the Duc de Berry (Pognon 1979, 25, 31), the *Just Judges* and the *Warriors of Christ* on Hubert and Jan van Eyck's great Ghent altar-piece, completed in 1432 (Dahnens 1980, figs 64–5) and in several of Dürer's engravings and woodcuts of around 1500 (Strauss 1972, nos 34, 71; Kurth 1963, no 109). Where the detail is clear, it can be seen that, as well as the reins attached to the lower ends of the cheeks, another set is attached to the bit at the junction of cheek and mouthpiece (Fig 29). It is noticeable that in several of the early illustrations the rider has left the lower 'curb' rein loose on the horse's neck and is guiding it holding only the upper 'snaffle' rein.

Such a bit resembles the modern 'Pelham' in combining the actions of curb and snaffle in one (Tuke 1965, 34–5). The Liverpool bit – a particular variety of Pelham bit used today almost exclusively for carriage horses – can be seen on occasion fitted with double reins, or with single reins attached either curb-fashion to the lower ends of the cheeks or snaffle-fashion to the

central rings; some late medieval curb bits might have been harnessed similarly with either single or double reins to choice. (This style of bitting should not be confused with the modern double bridle bit, though resembling it at first sight. In the latter the horse is fitted with both a curb bit and a light snaffle, known as a bridoon; each is fastened to a separate head harness strap and each has its own rein (ibid. 33–4).)

In 1940 Ward Perkins noted that, in contrast to their frequent appearance in medieval illustrations, curb bits were much less common among archaeological finds than simple snaffles. This is still true, though curb bits of 16th- and early 17th-century date, usually simpler versions of the complex bits illustrated by Thomas Blundeville in the 1560s (drawn from the works of the Neapolitan Federigo Grisone) (cf. Dent 1987, 94–5) or in the sketch-book of Filippo Ursoni of Mantua (Mann 1938, 270–1, pl XXXI), are found in museum collections and are recorded for example from Basing House, Hampshire, and Sandal Castle, West Yorkshire (Moorhouse & Goodall 1971, 47–9, no 89, fig 21; Goodall 1983b, 250, no 237, fig 10); part of a simpler curb bit, with straight

29 Sixteenth-century curb bit harnessed like modern 'Pelham', with double reins (after Albrecht Dürer, *Knight, Death and Devil* 1513)

cheeks, was also found at Sandal (ibid. no 236).

The prevalence of curb bits in part was due, Ward Perkins felt, 'to their exclusive use for riding in its more elaborate forms, which naturally bulks large in contemporary illustration' (London Museum 1940, 77). Certainly it is rare to find an incontrovertible snaffle in medieval art – though the Flemish artist who illustrated a French translation of Giovanni Boccaccio's *Decameron* (1358) between 1430 and 1440 included a mule, ridden by a high church dignitary, with a snaffle bit alongside a horse with a double-reined curb bit (Pognon 1978, 71), among a series of illustrations showing horses with single- and double-reined curbs; the distinction between the two styles of riding is obviously made deliberately. The late 14th-century equestrian monument to Bernabo Visconti in Milan shows a snaffle with cheek-pieces similar to Ward Perkins's type C, though apparently with double reins (Laking 1920–2, vol 3, 160, fig 964); the famous *Rider of Bamberg* (Egan & Pritchard 1991, 211, fig 132) has a complex snaffle; Dürer illustrates Death riding a broken-down nag with a rope bridle attached to some form of snaffle (Struass 1972, 151, no 71). Otherwise the curb bit reigns supreme in art from the Bayeux Tapestry on.

The riding horses in the Luttrell Psalter of about 1340 (British Library Add MS 42130), whether mounted by knights or civilians, are without exception fitted with curb bits, as are the five postillion-driven horses drawing a royal carriage on ff181b–182 (Millar 1932). Indeed, rather incongruously, the same artist portrays a horse pulling a harrow (ibid. f171; Fig 19) – a job for a hard-working but cheap farm horse (an *equus hercatorius* – Langdon 1986, 113) – being led by reins attached to a curb bit on a rope bridle. He is not however the only medieval artist to picture a similar combination: one of the painters who worked on the Duc de Berry's *Très riches heures* illustrates a tough little harrow-horse fitted with what seems to be quite an elaborate curb bit (the scene for October, Pognon 1979, 34–5). It is of course possible that both these artists, moving as they did in aristocratic circles (though circles of very different status), have unthinkingly placed bits more suitable for their patrons' palfreys in the mouths of farm animals.

The depiction of the harness employed on the two carts in the Luttrell Psalter is unfortunately not clear, but it may be intended to represent simple ring snaffles, combined in one case with a headstall of rope rather than leather (Millar 1932, ff162, 173b; cf. Fig 9).

Snaffles certainly could be, and no doubt were, used on riding horses; the prevalence of the curb bit in art may reflect the taste for illustrations of quality people riding horses of quality. The snaffle from the 'Baynard's Castle' site described below (No 2), with the decorative bosses on its cheeks, seems more likely to be from a riding horse; like many of the finds from the series of late 14th-century contexts on that particular site it is of noticeably good quality, perhaps reflecting, as mentioned in the Introduction, the presence in the area of an especially affluent group of consumers or store of equipment – possibly the King's Great Wardrobe (Dyson 1989, 10–12; Egan & Pritchard 1991, 3).

Yet the great preponderance of archaeological finds of snaffles, from London as elsewhere, is surely consistent with the conclusion that many of such bits are from horses used for haulage rather than riding.

Bits, like stirrups, were made by loriners (or lorimers). The London loriners were among the earliest of the city crafts to become organised, procuring approval of their ordinances from the 'Mayor and Barons' of London in 1269 in return for the annual presentation of an 'honourable and seemly bridle and bit' (Unwin 1908, 85–6). They did not however acquire a charter until 1711 (Hazlitt 1892, 562–3), and apart from renewed approval of their book of ordinances in 1488 (Sharpe 1912, 265–7) there is little record of their activities in the medieval period.

SNAFFLES

The typology suggested by Ward Perkins for the mouthpieces and cheek-pieces of medieval snaffles (London Museum 1940, 80–82) is repeated here (Figs 30, 31) in order to simplify the task of describing the excavated bits in the catalogue below. Ward Perkins's typology is not definitive; indeed it can be questioned whether all the types he illustrated can actually be found on incontrovertible medieval bits, and No 4 below has a pattern of cheek he did not record.

Bit No 5, from a ceramic phase 11 (1350–1400) context, appears to confirm the central medieval

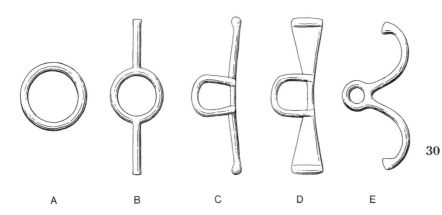

30 Cheek-pieces; typology defined by Ward Perkins (after London Museum 1940, 80, fig 19a)

dating of the bits with cheeks of type D that Ward Perkins published as 'probably a later medieval development' (ibid. 81, fig 20). His reason for proposing this dating is presumably the presence of such a bit among finds from Moorfields, an area rich in material of the later 15th and early 16th centuries. Another bit (No 2) from a late 14th-century context also has the type III mouth, of two cannons with central link carrying a loose

31 Mouthpieces; typology defined by Ward Perkins (after London Museum 1940, 82, fig 19b)

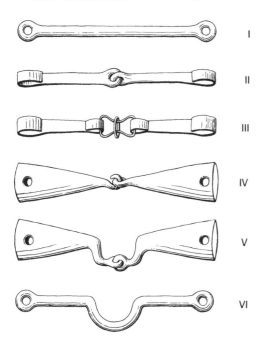

ring, which is common with type D cheeks (cf. ibid. 83, nos 2, 3, fig 20).

Bit No 1, though visible only in X-ray, demonstrates the existence in phase 9 (1270–1350) of mouthpieces consisting of two hollow conical links (type IV) for which Ward Perkins could quote only an example from Tannenberg Castle in Poland (destroyed in 1399) and which is otherwise best known as a post-medieval type, as at Basing House and Sandal Castle (Moorhouse & Goodall 1971, 47–9, no 89 fig 21; Goodall 1983b, 251, nos 244–5, fig 10). Mouthpieces of this form can be seen on a rare medieval illustration of harness that is not in place on a horse – three complete bridles in the background of a portrait of an early 15th-century Nuremberg harness maker (one of which is reproduced here in Fig 32, after Treue et al. 1965, 27).

Though Ward Perkins's typology warrants revision, that cannot be done on the basis of the few finds described in detail here.

The bits are listed below in order of ceramic phase and site. All are of iron, though part of a fine copper alloy bit (with traces of gilding) of type D (very like No 5 below) with a type III mouth exists in the Museum of London collections (acc no A16814 – see Fig 33 and London Museum 1940, 83, no 2, fig 20). The record of a dispute in 1327 between saddlers, loriners and others distinguishes between 'loriners in copper and loriners in iron' (Riley 1868, 156–62). Several of the iron bits show traces of tinning, a practice referred to in the Loriners' ordinances of 1488 – though only with reference to the illicit replating of old bits and stirrups to sell as new (Sharpe 1912, 267) – and a technique also applied to

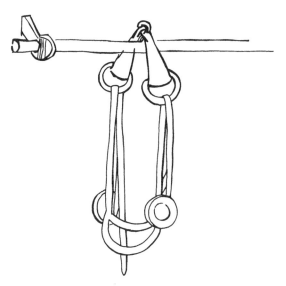

32 Harness hanging up in an early 15th-century German harness maker's workshop, showing conical links of mouthpiece (from the *Hausbuch* of the Mendelschen Zwölfbruderstiftung, Nuremberg, cf. Treue et al. 1965, 27)

spurs, as Ellis discusses elsewhere in this volume.

1 TL74 acc no 1512 (context 2442) ceramic phase 9 Fig 34 (from X-ray)
overall w *c.*240mm, w between cheek-pieces *c.*125mm, external d of rings 60mm
Highly corroded and hidden by concretion, this bit can be seen on X-ray to combine simple rings (Ward Perkins's type A) with a variant of Ward Perkins's type IV mouthpiece, made up of two hollow cones, each with holes through the broad end through which the cheek ring passes – the cones are joined by a central ring-shaped link. The X-ray also reveals traces of plating.

2 BC72 3999 (88) 11 Fig 35
overall w (estimated) *c.*220mm, w between cheek-pieces *c.*110mm, external d of rings 60mm
Incomplete, with a type III mouthpiece with solid forged links pierced with holes at the outer end to take the rings. The central link is missing but the loose ring that encircles the link on this form of mouthpiece (cf. London Museum 1940, 83, nos 2, 3, fig 20) survives.

33 Bits with Ward Perkins's type D cheek-pieces (MoL acc nos 10207 (top), A2439 (bottom right) and A16814 (bottom left)); first two of iron, last of copper alloy (with traces of gilding) with iron centre link and ring (cf. London Museum 1940, fig 20)

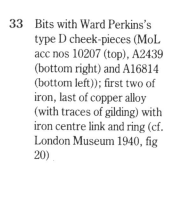

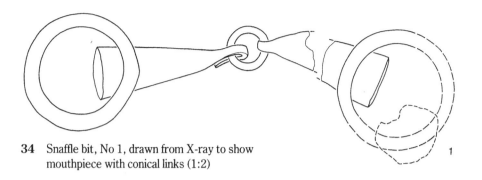

34 Snaffle bit, No 1, drawn from X-ray to show
       mouthpiece with conical links (1:2)

35 Snaffle bits, Nos 2 and 3 (1:2)

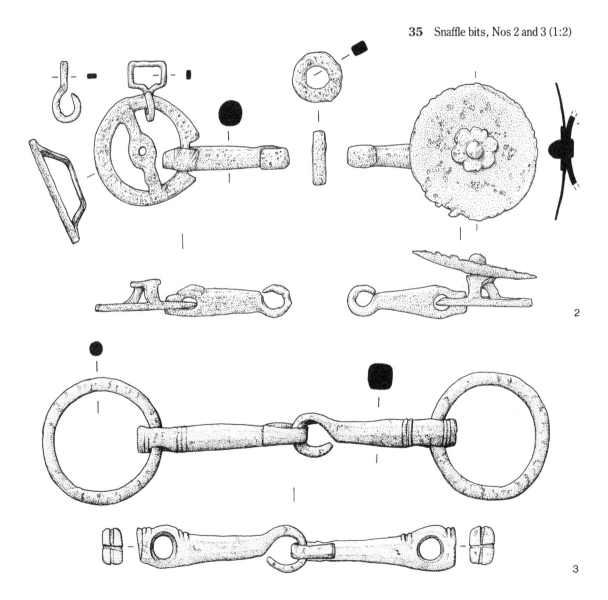

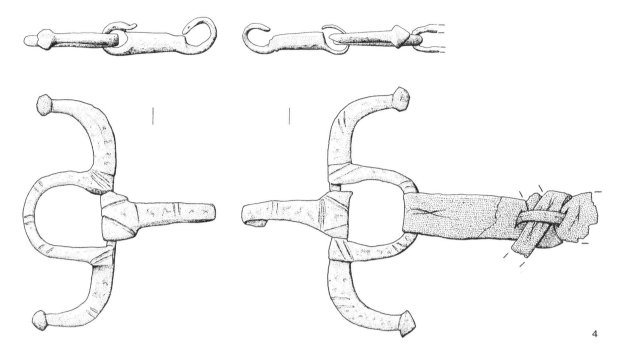

36 Snaffle bits, Nos 4 and 5 (1:2)

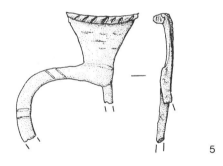

The cheek-pieces are a development of type A, the rings rectangular in section and each with a transverse bar, pierced with a hole to which in one case an ornamental disc or boss – slightly concave and with surviving areas of plating (tin with some traces of lead – AML) – is still fastened by a rivet through a central rosette; traces of similar plating can be seen elsewhere on the rings and mouthpiece. Disc-shaped bridle bosses of this type are discussed further by Egan below; No 12 in particular is very similar. A single strap connector survives attached to the other ring, wide enough to take a 15mm rein or head strap.

A snaffle with a type III mouthpiece and type D cheek-pieces in the Museum of London also has pierced bars across each cheek ring that presumably once carried similar ornamental mounts (acc no 10207, a chance find from Farringdon Street – see Fig 33).

3 BWB83 4 (119) 11 Fig 35
overall w 275mm, w between cheek-pieces 142mm, external d of rings 65mm
Complete ring snaffle with type A cheek-pieces, round in section, and type II mouthpiece. The two mouthpiece links are solid forged and finely made, with holes pierced to take the rings and incised decoration on the front and on the outer ends. A bit of very similar form, with similar incised crosses on the outer ends of the mouthpiece links, is recorded from an apparently contemporary 14th-century context at Lochmaben Castle, Dumfriesshire (Macdonald & Laing 1974–5, 146, no 1, fig 10).

4 BWB83 271 (282) 11 Fig 36
overall w (estimated) c.220mm, w between cheek-pieces c.110mm, width of surviving straps 23mm
Incomplete, with a type III mouthpiece, the central link and ring missing; the cheek-pieces are a developed

form of Ward Perkins's type C, the arms being curved back and ending in knobs. Unlike the mouthpieces of Nos 2 and 3 above, the outer ends of the links are forged flat and bent round to hold the cheek rings, the normal practice in early bits (for example Ottaway 1992, 704–5, nos 3841–3 etc.; Goodall 1976b, 60, nos 57–8, fig 36; Goodall 1983b, 250, no 242, fig 10). There is decoration on the front of both mouthpiece links and cheek-pieces consisting of incised lines; that on the loop of the cheek-pieces in particular is very similar to that on No 5 below. Traces of white metal plating survive in the grooves.

Remains of leather straps are attached to each cheek. In one case the strap is secured by a second short length of leather looped around and held in place by a thong. It seems likely that these straps are fragments of the headstall rather than of reins, and possible that the (apparently incomplete) cross-strap represents a noseband. Nosebands, however, are rarely shown in medieval illustrations of horses; one seems to be depicted on a frontal view of a horse-monster in the Luttrell Psalter (f173b; Millar 1932, 99), while one of the complete bridles in the illustration of a Nuremberg harness maker, referred to above, seems to be so fitted (Treue et al. 1965, 27).

This variant of Ward Perkins's type C cheek-piece is also recorded among finds from the French site of Saint-Vaast-sur-Seulles, a castle attacked and destroyed by the English in 1356 (Halbout et al. 1987, 239, no 997 – the site is discussed ibid. 175). Such a date would agree well with the 1350–1400 dating of our ceramic phase 11, and many of the Saint-Vaast finds might well be relics of the besieging English army rather than of the French defenders.

5 TL74 688 (415) 11 Fig 36
original h (estimated) *c.*105mm
Part of type D cheek-piece with incised decoration on the front of the loop and on the recurved ends of the expanding arms, similar to that on No 4 above and on the type D bit from Moorfields illustrated by Ward Perkins (London Museum 1940, 83, no 3, fig 20).

CURB BIT

(In considering the form and function of the following object I have benefited greatly from discussions with three people – Mrs Ann Hyland, Captain David Horn of the Guards Museum and Mr James White, Past Master of the Loriners' Company – and without their expert advice I would have hesitated to comment on it.)

6 SH74 acc no 320 (context 467) ceramic phase 7 Figs 37, 38
overall l of cheek-piece *c.*240mm (the distortion makes measurement imprecise), original w of mouthpiece *c.*110mm (4½ inches)
One cheek-piece, badly distorted, and part of high-ported mouthpiece of curb bit. The cheek-piece has an angular or stepped profile, with a curved bar linking the top to the lower extension. Two holes are pierced at the bottom end, perpendicular to its profile, presumably to take attachments for the rein and (perhaps) for the sort of spacer bar shown on early medieval depictions of curb bits (as in Fig 28). An eye at the upper end holds remains of a narrow (11mm) leather strap, presumably from the headstall.

The complicated mouthpiece, if correctly reconstructed in Fig 37, had an extremely high but flexible port, the two sides being connected by a chain link at the top and presumably rotating slightly on whatever form of link connected the two holes lower down. The function of the two holes at the top of the port is not clear – though some later curbs have chains linking the top of the port to the cheeks (Dent 1987, 94–5 after Blundeville's illustration of 1565, or the modern 'western spade bit' illustrated by Hyland 1990b, fig 2).

Between the cheek-piece and the port, the mouthpiece carries a rotating cylinder of thin metal. At first sight this would seem in use to have rested on the 'bars' of the horse's mouth (the bare gums between its front and rear teeth), and to have served the same function as the 'rollers' on the mouths of some modern bits (for example Tuke 1965, figs 54, 127). However, it is broken in such a way that it may have been the end of a U-shaped bar similar to those from Grimbosq (Calvados, France) and Ludgershall Castle (Wiltshire) referred to below, pivoting on the mouthpiece.

This item comes from an early context at Seal House – ceramic phase 7, *c.*1200–30. A bit in the Musée de Normandie, Caen, from an 11th-century site at Grimbosq (Halbout et al. 1987, 239, no 998; D'Onofrio 1994, 380, no 10 – strangely reconstructed in the published photograph) and one from a mid-12th-century context at Ludgershall Castle (information from Ian Goodall) are apparently not dissimilar. In these, however, the high port is not flexible but of simple U-shape; a further U-shaped bar of uncertain function, perhaps designed to compress the horse's jaw, seems to have pivoted on the mouthpiece on either side of the port. (For another complex curb bit of early date, from France, see Rippmann et al. 1991, 30, fig 17.)

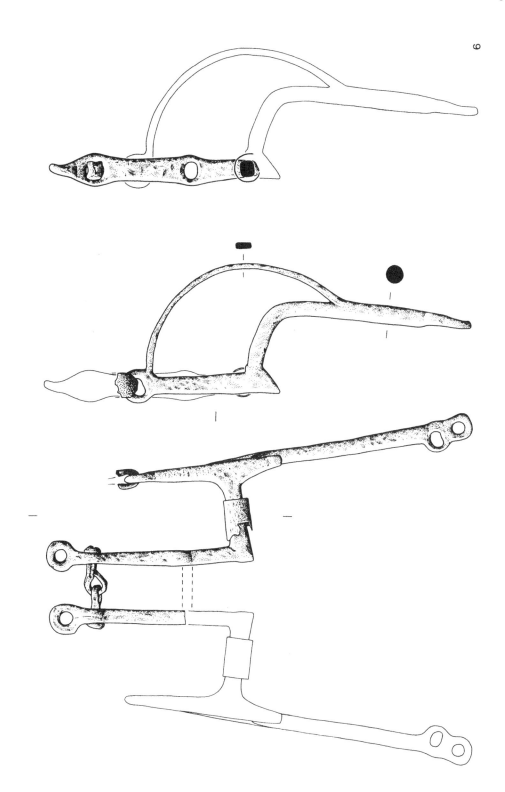

37   Curb bit, No 6, with suggested reconstruction; the distorted shank has been drawn as if straight (1:2)

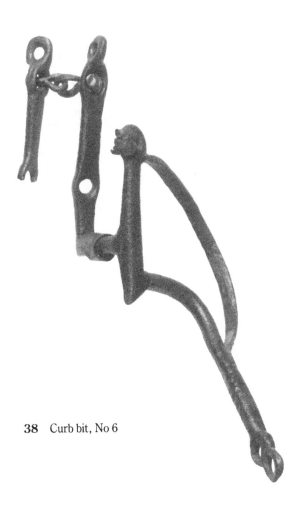

38　Curb bit, No 6

Early medieval illustrations of curb bits are not helpful in interpreting this object. However, the curved reinforcing bars that form part of the cheek-pieces of the Seal House piece *may* be reflected in the triangular shape of the cheeks of some curb bits shown in the Maciejowski Bible of *c.*1250 (Fig 39 – cf. Cockerell nd, 65, f10v). Such curved bars are also a feature of a fine bit in the Metropolitan Museum of Art, New York (illustrated in Laking 1920–2, vol 3, 161, fig 965), though that bit – which has the U-shaped bar of the Grimbosq and Ludgershall examples – would seem to have functioned differently from the London piece.

BRIDLE BOSSES

Geoff Egan

The robust, early 15th-century No 9 is the only certain bridle boss among the items below. The three late 14th-century sheet items (Nos 7, 8, 10) are flimsier than bridle bosses of more recent date; they could be early versions, or other kinds of mounts. Less robust, bossed mounts feature as purely decorative accessories elsewhere on straps in horse equipment, as shown in a misericord carving of a mounted knight at Lincoln (Laird 1986, 28, fig 29; dated to the late 14th century).

A decorated and a plain boss attributed to the late 15th/early 16th century were published by Ward Perkins (London Museum 1940, 85), who dated the introduction of the elaborate curb bits accompanied by paired bosses 'towards the close of the 15th century'. The late 14th-century date assigned to three of the listed items seems to find some support in the equestrian statue of Mastino II della Scala (died 1351) at Verona in Italy (Pope Henessey 1985, 27, fig 50) and a bronze statuette of a knight, apparently from the mid-14th century at the latest (Edge & Paddock 1988, 81, lower photo), on both of which the horse's bridle has a large boss.

Copper alloy

7 BWB83 acc no 1533 (context 256) ceramic phase 11　Fig 40
d 46mm
Sheet roundel; hammered at edges to give convex profile; central gouged hole; crudely engraved with double, six-petalled rose motif in a border of a series of oblique lines.

39　13th-century curb bit with triangular cheeks (after London Museum 1940, fig 18, from the Maciejowski Bible)

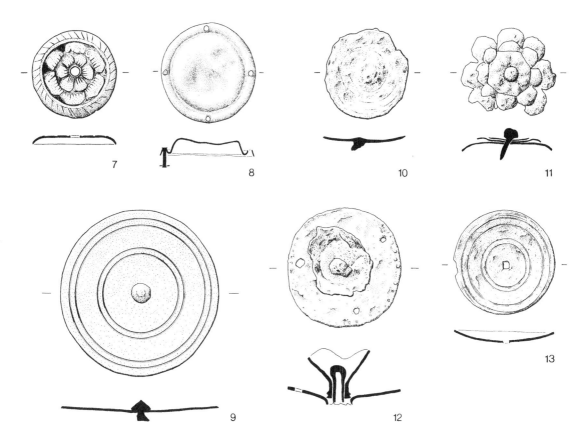

40   Bridle bosses, Nos 7–13 (1:2)

8 TL74 2718 (275) 12 Fig 40
d 52mm

(?) Cast; robust, convex boss with perimeter ridge; turning marks in the groove between boss and ridge; holes for four rivets, of which two survive, with roves; the centre has been distorted (cf. Goodall 1979b, 132, 135, no 114, fig 23).

9 TL74 2683 (368) 12 Fig 40
d 85mm

Relatively robust sheet disc, possible rolling marks on the back; turning marks on the front include deeper, paired grooves near perimeter and half-way towards centre, where a hole has a slightly faceted, conical-headed iron rivet which expands at the back (most appears broken off). The invention of rolling sheet metal has often been attributed to Leonardo da Vinci in the late 15th/early 16th century (cf. Usher 1957, 340–2).

Iron

10 BC72 2735 (79) 11 Fig 40
d 45mm

Incomplete; concave; tin coating on both sides; trace of concentric (?lathe-turning) marks on front. Also published in Egan & Pritchard (1991, 177, 179, no 908, fig 113).

11 BWB83 216 (292) 11 Fig 40
d of largest piece 50mm (the others are slightly damaged)

Three superimposed sheet pieces on a round-headed rivet/pin: one octagon with eight bosses and two octofoils with convex lobes; tin coating on all parts; trace of leather around pin on back.

12 BWB83 5201 (338) 11 Fig 40
d 63mm

Slightly concave disc; stamped beading around perimeter; three crudely pierced and irregularly positioned holes near perimeter, and larger, slightly off-centred one; tin coating; corroded, convex (?petalled) cup having double-ridged collar at the base and iron pin set through this (held by lead solder) and through the disc's largest hole.

13 TL74 2702 (275) 12 Fig 40
d 54mm
Concave disc, with slightly off-centred turning marks on the front, including paired, deeper grooves; rectangular, off-centred hole, crudely pierced; tin coating; small-chord ridge on back.

BUCKLES, HASPS AND STRAP HOOKS

Geoff Egan

The buckles listed below are all of iron. The plain forms have been included in this volume as horse equipment because of their large size; the aperture for the strap is in each case 50mm wide or more. The more robust buckles from the sites are therefore all included here; smaller ones from the same sites have been included in Egan & Pritchard 1991. This rather arbitrary criterion is used because of the difficulty of differentiating horse-equipment buckles from those for a range of other purposes. T-shaped frames (Nos 39–47) apparently indicate pairs of straps of different widths in use together. Stirrup No 82 has a smaller iron buckle (the specific role of which is known only because it remains attached to the original object). Buckles for medieval spurs are smaller still and include examples in copper alloy (see No 372). The T-shaped buckles (Nos 39–47) seem to occur only at the larger end of the scale in medieval London, while oval and D-shaped frames are known in a wide range of sizes.

Many of the more elaborate frame forms published in the *Dress Accesories* volume, including double loops, are not represented among the items in the present catalogue. Decoration on the large iron buckles is almost entirely confined to grooves (sometimes double or triple) on the frames. With the tin coating that is likely to have originally been on all horse buckles, these grooves would have caught the light as they moved. Following Ward Perkins (London Museum 1940, 277, no A2664), identification of excavated harness buckles has in the past tended to be restricted to rectangular iron examples like

No 27, but today buckles of various different metals and with a range of frame shapes are used. No buckle seems yet to have been found in place on an identifiable piece of harness from the medieval period, placing a limit on the usefulness of extended discussion at this stage. Large medieval buckles would also have been appropriate for sword belts and other heavy-duty uses. For further discussion of these points, and for a wider range of buckles that may well include some from horse equipment, see Egan & Pritchard (1991, 50ff).

The function of hasps Nos 48–50 is unknown. The surviving strapping and the fact that they are similar in size to the large buckles seem to associate them with the latter, and for that reason they are included in this present section.

The buckles are listed in order of increasing frame width (second dimension) within each ceramic phase. For the terminology see Fig 41.

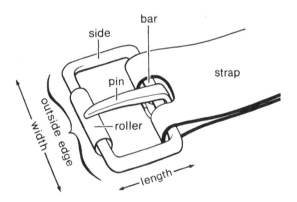

41 Buckle: terminology used in descriptions

BUCKLES

Oval frames

14 SWA81 acc no 1175 (context 2157) ceramic phase 6 Fig 42
47×71mm; frame has lip; tin coating.

15 SH74 270 (536) 6
57×73mm; frame has lip; pin survives.

16 CUS73 799 (XV, 21) 9 Fig 42
44×64mm; frame has lip; pin missing.

17 SWA81 1160 (2188) 9
38×73mm; tin coating.

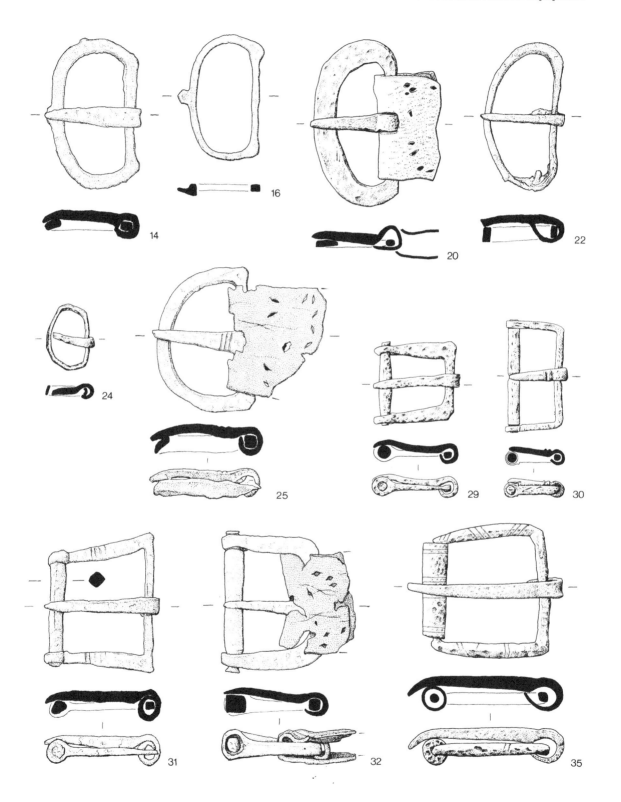

14

16

20

22

24

25

29

30

31

32

35

18 BWB83 5256 (354) 11
44×62mm; corroded; tin coating; pin missing.

19 BC72 1814 (55) 11
35×65mm; pin incomplete.

20 BC72 2419 (79) 11 Fig 42
42×87mm; crude, flat-section frame; pin is bent between loop and shaft; folded leather strap 33×55mm, possibly cut off at both ends.

21 TL74 2694 (368) 12
39×64mm; pin missing; tin coating.

22 BWB83 3114 (278) 12 Fig 42
40×76mm.

23 SWA81 1847 (unstratified)
41×73mm; tin coating; attached to leather strap 40+×71mm.

D-shaped
[Compare London Museum 1940, 277, pl 79, no 4 and Barrère et al. 1990, 262, no 573.]

24 BIG82 acc no 2800 (context 5221) ceramic phase 7 Fig 42
24×34mm; roughly finished; attached to the leather of stirrup No 82. Also published in Egan & Pritchard 1991 (92–3, fig 58).

25 SWA81 720 (2046) 9 Fig 42
53×74mm; pin has three transverse grooves; attached to folded leather strap 50+×60mm, with remains of coarse textile surviving within fold.

25a BC72 4618 (250) 10
58×88mm.

26 BWB83 3826 (146) 11
43×72mm; frame has lip; no trace of tinning; rectangular.

Sides looped for separate solid roller
This distinctive form, requiring particular skill in manufacture, is widely known and has long been associated with horse harness (e.g., London Museum 1940, 277, no A2664; Goodall 1990,

42 Buckles with oval frames, Nos 14, 16, 20 and 22; with D-shaped frames, Nos 24 and 25; rectangular with solid rollers, Nos 29–32; one-piece, No 35 (1:2)

526, 530–1, nos 1302–5, fig 138; Barrère et al. 1990, 261, no 567, dated to the 12th/13th century; see also Egan & Pritchard 1991, 95). Ward Perkins cites parallels from outside London attributed to the 11th and 12th centuries (London Museum 1940, 277). Widths given are exclusive of protruding ends of rollers.

27 SWA81 acc no 2245 (context 2257) ceramic phase 7
52×78mm; both sides and pin have three transverse grooves; fragment of leather strap survives.

28 SWA81 565 (2055) 9
45×43mm; tin coating.

29 BWB83 3142 (269) 9 Fig 42
42×41mm; tin coating. (No 428 in Egan & Pritchard 1991)

30 SWA81 462 (2018) 9 Fig 42
30×63mm; slightly trapezoidal; roller has central constriction; pin has two transverse ridges; tin coating.

31 SWA81 1045 (2131) 9 Fig 42
57×75mm; slightly trapezoidal; two transverse grooves in each side; pin is square in section; tin coating.

32 BC72 2624 (79) 11 Fig 42
52×69mm; on folded leather strap 42+×48mm.

33 BWB83 4309 (329) 11
55×70mm; tin coating.

34 SWA81 2278 (unstratified)
55×74mm; two slightly oblique transverse grooves on pin.

Frames in one piece
35 SWA81 acc no 3508 (context 2141) ceramic phase 9 Fig 42
63×70mm; lozenge-section sides have triple grooves; sheet roller has spiral, tin-filled grooves; robust pin has tip bent over; tin coating (MLC).

36 SWA81 1889 (2137) 9
estimated c.65×c.89mm; fragment of bar and one side; pin survives; tin coating.

37 SWA81 736 (2071) 9
59×72mm; corroded; sheet roller with triple and double, tin-filled grooves; tin coating.

38 BWB83 5249 (334) 11
c.62×c.69mm; incomplete and corroded; flat-section sides, with triple and double transverse tin-filled grooves; tin coating.

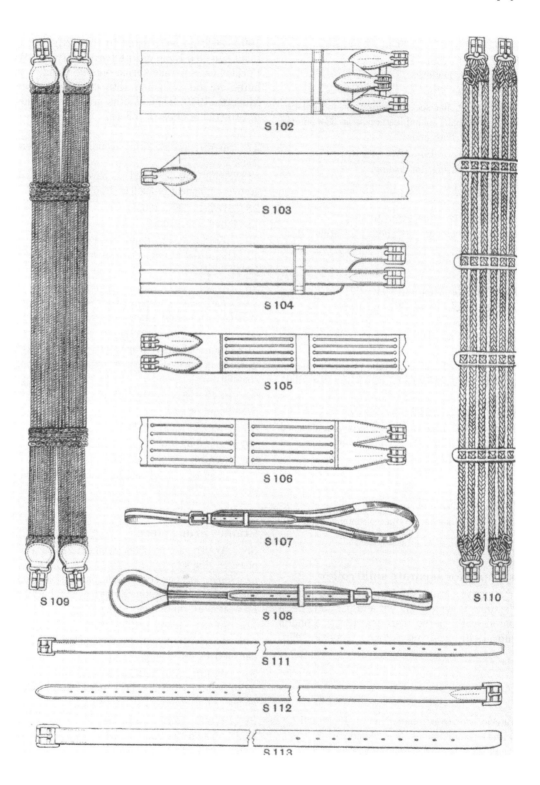

S 102

S 103

S 104

S 105

S 106

S 107

S 109

S 108

S 110

S 111

S 112

S 113

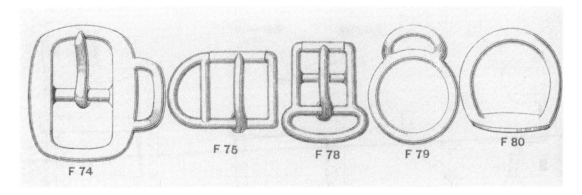

44 Range of harness buckles including T-shaped girth buckle (no F 78) illustrated in Eldrid, Ottaway & Co's catalogue, *c.*1910 (nd, 45)

T-shaped frames

These distinctive buckles, none of which is from a deposit attributed to a period earlier than the late 13th century, are unknown in smaller versions. The form is widespread in the later medieval period (e.g. Goodall 1990, 532–3, no 1315, fig 139; Barrère et al. 1990, 262, no 572 – there called a *harnechement de monture*). The short outside edge implies that they were for attaching a wide strap (fixed to the bar) to a narrower one. Number 45 has the largest strap aperture, at over 90mm, of all the excavated buckles.

Buckles of this form might have been used to link the girth (the broad strap passing under the horse's belly) to girth straps attached to the saddle. This essential fastening is hidden by the saddle flaps in most contemporary illustrations, but a roof boss in Bristol Cathedral depicts two saddles with partly visible buckles at this point, apparently similar to the 'lyre' form (Smith 1979, 16, 21, 26, pl 8, dated between *c.*1470 and *c.*1520; there is a clearer photograph in Cave 1948, pl 32). For the decorative form of these buckles, cf. Fingerlin 1971, 162ff, e.g., nos 273, 278, which are probably for human dress; no buckle of this shape has been found in the medieval deposits at the recent London excavations, so

the form may be of slightly later date than the period considered here. The Henry V saddle of 1422 in Westminster Abbey retains 'two hide strap ends to which double girths were attached', fastened to the saddle tree on one side (Laking 1920–2, vol 3, 156, figs 963a–c). More recent practice has been to use a broad girth of webbing or of plaited leather or cord with two buckles side by side at each end, fastening to a pair of straps on each side of the saddle. In some cases the buckles used on recent girths bear a resemblance to the medieval T-shaped form, as seen in Figs 43 and 44 (from a wholesale catalogue of harness and horse equipment of *c.*1910 – Eldrid et al. nd, 27, 45; cf. Hasluck 1904, 44, fig 12).

The width of each frame at the outside edge is given in brackets – this edge is straight in the buckles, but see hasps Nos 49 and 50.

39 SWA81 acc no 1362 (context 2046) ceramic phase 9 Fig 45
70×*c.*40mm (24mm); broken and distorted; triple and paired transverse grooves on sides; sheet roller; pin missing; tin coating (MLC).

40 BWB83 3916 (120) 9 Fig 45
62×100mm (72mm); sides are looped for the separate, octagonal-section roller.

41 BWB83 1699 (4) 11
53×86mm (61mm); flat-section inside edge; sides looped for robust, solid roller, which expands towards centre, where it has a circumferential groove; pin missing.

43 Page from a wholesale catalogue of harness and horse equipment *c.*1910, showing girths with T-shaped buckles (right and left of illustration) (Eldrid, Ottaway & Co nd, 26)

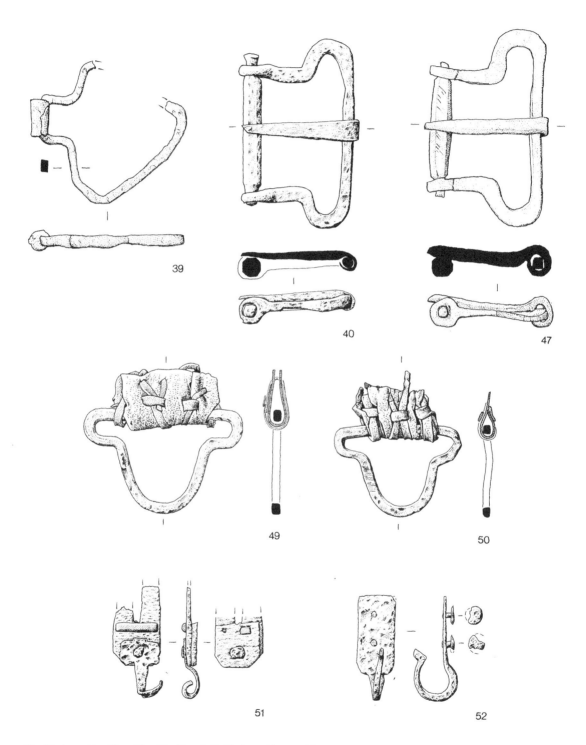

45 T-shaped buckles, Nos 39, 40 and 47; T-shaped hasps, Nos 49 and 50; strap hooks, Nos 51 and 52 (1:2)

42 BWB83 3356 (282) 11
*c.*47×*c.*90mm (*c.*60mm); corroded (described from X-ray); flat-section inside edge.

43 BC72 2871 (83A) 11
62+×91mm (outside edge missing); pin missing.

44 BWB83 2792 (301) 11
77×93mm (37mm); angled sides; sheet roller; pin missing.

45 BWB83 2788 (301) 11
Distorted; *c.*60×*c.*115mm (*c.*70mm); flat-section sides; tin coating (MLC).

46 TL74 2682 (368) 12
45×76mm (39mm); double and triple transverse grooves on sides; tin coating; sheet roller; pin missing.

47 BC72 2078 (unstratified) Fig 45
62×110mm (60mm); solid, square-section roller; tin coating.

T-SHAPED HASPS

These have rounded, narrowed ends; the lack of a hole in the leather in Nos 49 and 50 shows there was no provision for a pin.

48 SWA81 acc no 571 (context 2055) ceramic phase 9
73×50mm.

49 BC72 3509 (250) 10 Fig 45
55×88mm; tin coating; attached to leather strap, w 53mm, l 28mm, with four subsidiary, decorative strips lengthways (the two outer ones w 5mm, the inner ones w 4mm) which are attached by a transverse strip, w 5mm, that is threaded through the main strap and around each strip.

50 BC72 4035 (unstratified) Fig 45
As preceding item, but 50×70mm, and with small notch on the edge (not running the full width); strap, w 45mm, as that on preceding item.

These enigmatic objects presumably had the narrow end looped around a projecting part of the equipment like a robust knop or hook (the tiny notch in No 50 was presumably to cater for this), see Nos 51 and 52. The attached leather is flimsy in comparison with the robust metal of the frames.

These items may have functioned as sliding clasps, the surviving leather being, in effect, a rubber, over which an adjustable length of a main strap (inserted through the wide part of the aperture) could ride.

A decorative strip of leather, perhaps comparable to those associated with the hasps above, survives on the strap (w 36mm) attached to a D-shaped buckle, narrower than the hasps, from a deposit attributed to ceramic phase 12 (no 416 in Egan & Pritchard 1991).

STRAP HOOKS

Iron

51 BWB83 acc no 8 (context 110) ceramic phase 11 Fig 45
32×22mm; outward-curving hook; single rivet; corners cut diagonally at end; tin coating; (no 730 in Egan & Pritchard 1991); on leather strap consisting of two thicknesses of leather with grain side outermost, w 27mm; accompanying bar mount (no 1146 in Egan & Pritchard 1991).

52 BWB83 3970 (307) 11 Fig 45
54×21mm; outward-curving hook; slightly serrated attachment edge; tin coating; two flat-headed rivets with roves (no 731 in Egan & Pritchard 1991).

HARNESS PENDANTS AND ASSOCIATED FITTINGS

Nick Griffiths

Pendants from horse harness and their associated suspension mounts have long been recognised and many individual examples have been published. The London Museum *Medieval Catalogue* (1940, 118) established a basic typology, within the limitations of any catalogue – it included only those types represented in the Museum's collections. Much of the work carried out since has been based on that typology, with additions, but dating has remained vague due to a lack of well-stratified examples. To some extent those with heraldic decoration can be useful, though there is a tendency to place too much reliance on identifications derived from post-medieval reference works. Contemporary, medieval 'rolls-of-arms' are likely to be more reliable but, even so, contradictions and inaccuracies are evident and heraldic identifications should be approached with considerable caution.

Recent work on the pendants suggests that the

date range may be wider than the late 13th to 14th century one often suggested. In part, this is due to the large number of pendants recorded in recent years; sufficient examples are now known for similarities of style and decoration to be recognised. Equally, excavation has produced a number of dated examples, and it is particularly useful to have such close dating for 12 of the objects included here.

A brief survey of the evidence for pendants (Griffiths 1986) was based on the large number now available for study. In summary, horse harnesses appear to have been decorated with pendants of copper alloy from the 12th century onwards; both circular and open-work forms appear in contemporary illustrations and among dated finds. In the 13th century pendants became more numerous, including many rectangular examples bearing a wide variety of decoration, usually engraved and with much gilding; many animal and foliage designs are reminiscent of Romanesque art and may be considered as such. (It has been suggested that artistic styles persist longest in the minor decorative arts, for example on domestic objects – Russell 1939, 135). Perhaps in the second half of the 13th century, both heraldry and enamelling appear on pendants of many shapes, at first on rectangular examples but increasingly on those in the form of small shields, with coats of arms depicted with coloured enamel, silvering and gilding. This display of heraldry on very small items can be paralleled on other horse-related objects and seems to be part of the huge increase in the use of heraldry at this period, perhaps associated with the Welsh and Scottish wars of Edward I (1272–1307).

However, it is noticeable that the pendants are frequently of poor quality and may well have been used by retainers, rather than the knights and nobles who displayed their arms on cloth horse covers (*trappers*) and on their own surcoats, banners, etc. Even their saddles might be painted with their coats of arms.

Some idea of the increase in the number of pendants may be gained from the fact that the shield type, although not represented in the present catalogue, represents some 33% of all known examples. By the end of the 14th century, pendants appear to be in decline; a few large examples, more like Spanish or Italian types, may date to the 15th century, but generally fashions in

horse harness changed to the use of decorative leather or fabric trappings.

In use, the pendants were suspended from the straps by means of small mounts with a hinge, riveted to the leather. There appears to be no direct correlation between the various types of pendant and the mount; in only two instances here are a pendant and mount associated (Nos 69, 71, 76). The *peytrel* or breast-band might carry as many as six on either side; the rear strap may also have been hung with pendants or small bells. Occasionally, a single pendant hung from the brow-band, over the horse's forehead. The representation of a horseman on the Hereford Cathedral *Mappa Mundi*, *c.*1300, provides a good example (Fig 46); here the pendants appear to be alternately shield-shaped and circular, hanging from the peytrel, while bells hang from the rear strap.

Although both pendants and mounts were made of copper alloy, the pin which held the two together was usually of iron; with the movement of the harness, the loop of the pendant frequently wore through, with the consequent loss of the object. It is therefore no surprise that most pendants occur as isolated finds, often from rural

46 Horseman, his horse decorated with a range of harness pendants, *c.*1300 (*Mappa Mundi* – Dean and Chapter, Hereford Cathedral)

areas; few are found on urban, castle or manorial sites. Presumably, if the pendant came away from the harness at home, it could be repaired and returned to use; some examples that have lost their loops have had a hole drilled to take a cord or piece of wire, which would allow the pendant to be reused.

Many questions remain unanswered; for example, where were the pendants made and by whom? Whilst the heraldic pendants, at least, must have been made 'to order', it seems unlikely that there were specialist makers. Possibly the pendants themselves were cast by one of the copper-working tradesmen (for example, the founders, brasiers or girdlers who were accustomed to casting small objects in copper alloy) and then passed to enamellers for finishing. Enamelling as a craft may have derived from France and it is interesting to note the presence of John de Dieppe, enameller, working in London in 1287–8 (Gauthier 1972, 261). However, in 1292 one of five enamellers working in Paris was listed as 'Richardin the enameller, of London', and the craft must have been fairly widespread.

Many of the general shapes found in Britain can be paralleled in France and the Low Countries, whilst Spanish and Italian pendants are usually larger and more elaborate. A few of these have been found in Britain and may have been lost by foreign visitors. The London waterfronts must have seen many such arrivals and departures, and in this context it is interesting to note that the only known parallel (and that virtually identical) to No 69 was acquired by the British Museum in the late 19th century and originated in France or Southern Germany (acc no MLA 94, 2–17, 7).

Although pendants are clearly a feature of horse harness, some of them may have been personal jewellery; two from London with clasps for gemstones are surely personal (Tribbick 1974, 94, no 30, fig 43; Egan & Pritchard, 1991, 321, no 1600). However, their plain equivalents would normally be considered horse-harness pendants. Apart from those decorated with attached gems, those with inscriptions are probably personal, for example a small circular pendant with the inscription IESVICIENLUIDAMI ('I am here in place of a friend', Ashmolean Museum acc no 1921.299).

In the following catalogue, the pendants represent those recovered by excavation, or other means, from the sites covered by the publication; others recorded from London fall outside the scope of this work. Where an item was recovered other than by formal archaeological excavation, it has no identification number and is designated merely by the name of the site. In some cases, objects were recovered from dumps of spoil removed to some distance. Only those objects whose origin is certain, or virtually so, are included. All those without Museum numbers remain in private hands unless otherwise stated.

PENDANTS

53 BIG82 acc no 2496 (context 2596) ceramic phase 8 Fig 47
43×41mm
Rectangular; simple foliate spray of seven leaves, the background filled with punched circles, all within a fine border line. Loop broken and damage to left-hand edge.

54 BIG82 2436 (3135) 7 Figs 47, 48
43×44mm
Rectangular; two plates fastened together by small square rivets at corners, one lost; rear plate roughly cut. Front plate open-work, with a mounted knight within a broad border; border has fine incised line decoration. The knight has short surcoat, mail, shield and sword all picked out with fine lines. In addition, the frame, horse and figure retain traces of gilding; the mailed leg has traces of tinning. Loop lost, but a hole drilled through knight's helmet probably represents an attempt to reuse the pendant.

Although originally identified as a belt-plate, and unparalleled as a pendant, a recent find from Dorset shows that double-plate pendants were not unknown; possibly a coloured material was inserted between the plates.

The style of the knight's costume suggests a 13th-century date, which accords well with the archaeological context.

55 BIG82 2356 (2718) 8 Fig 47
49×41mm
Rectangular with bosses; a variant of the more common rectangular pendant, with a central boss and smaller bosses at the corners, all five hollow on the rear. Central boss has traces of fine punched decoration and is surrounded by a plain band. Between this and the straight edges is a fine engraved zigzag. Near the lower edge is a drilled hole of uncertain purpose. Loop lost. Traces of gilding on front face.

47   Pendants, Nos 53–61 (1:1)

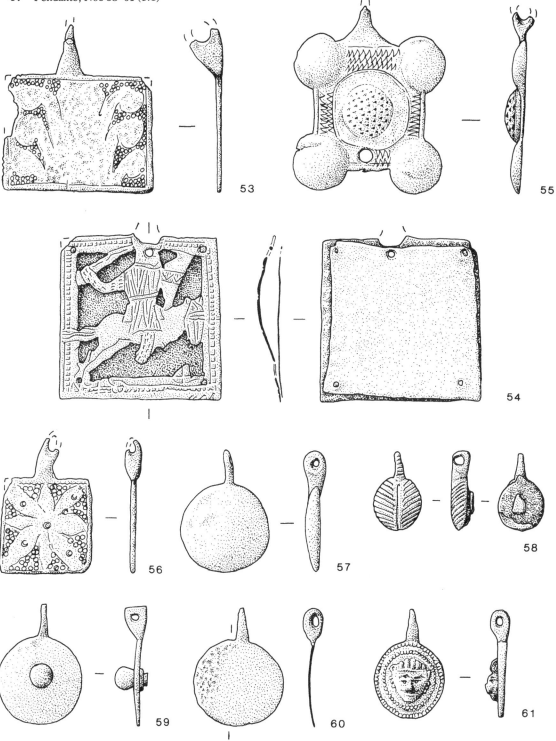

48 Pendant, No 54, showing knight on horseback

56 Billingsgate site   Fig 47
35×25mm
Rectangular; almost square with a fine line border, within which is an octofoil design, defined by a fine line. At the centre is a punched circle, a motif repeated on four of the petals. The background is filled in with punched circles. Loop broken.

57 GPO75 7 (247) – Fig 47
d 24mm
Circular; plain, convex pendant, hollow back. Loop complete and apparently unworn.

58 BWB83 1165 (361) 11 Fig 47
d 13mm
Circular; small, convex pendant of a type that may have been used to decorate reins, etc. Engraved line decoration curving out from central vertical line. Fine notching across front of loop. An irregular rove on the rear retains a piece of decayed leather, which may be the remains of a narrow strap hanging from the pendant. Much gilding survives and the loop is worn but complete.

59 BWB83 3659 (359) 11 Fig 47
d 23mm
Circular; slightly convex, plain pendant with an unusual angular loop. A large spherical stud is fitted at the centre of the pendant and projects 2mm behind. Holes for such studs, and occasionally the studs themselves, are common features of pendants, and as with No 58 above may have held a decorative strap or ribbon.

60 SWA81 3934 (2270) 9 Fig 47
d *c*.24mm
Circular; plain pendant, very thin and slightly convex. Some corrosion on one edge. Loop complete.

61 MoL acc no 88.9/6 (Billingsgate site) Fig 47
d 19mm
Circular; a solid pendant with a lion mask surrounded by a double bead-row. The lion is not well defined; very similar examples, though more realistic, are in the Ashmolean Museum (acc no 1927.6437) and Moyse's Hall Museum, Bury St Edmunds (acc no 1976–253–OS). Interestingly, both come from Suffolk.

62 SWA81 693 (2079) 9 Fig 49
42×29mm
Quatrefoil with angular projections. Although worn, and damaged along the lower margins, the device of a crowned M is clearly visible, probably signifying the Virgin Mary and perhaps an indication of the religious devotion of the owner. Although worn through, the loop appears to have been deliberately closed to make it usable.

63 MoL acc no 84.269 (Billingsgate site) Fig 49
56×42mm
Quatrefoil with angular projections; a large, well-defined pendant. Although there is no surviving enamel, the device of a crowned I is very clear. By analogy with No 62 above, the letter I may indicate a patron saint, although it is worth noting that Spanish pendants, in particular, frequently bear crowned letters, often I or Y; these are usually identified as the initials of noble ladies to whom the pendants were given. On the rear are engraved three heraldic *cross crosslets*; they appear to be unrelated to the pendant itself and suggest that some other item has been reworked.

64 Billingsgate site   Fig 49
34×25mm
Quatrefoil with angular projections. A shield of arms is surrounded by three elongated creatures which serve as space fillers, although the upper one is barely recognisable. The arms are those of England prior to 1340, *gules three lions passant gardant in pale or*; although the red enamel is lost there are traces of gilding, which makes the identification virtually certain. It should be noted, however, that these arms probably continued to be used on small objects after 1340, when the arms of France were added to those of England. The depiction of the lions on this example is not very

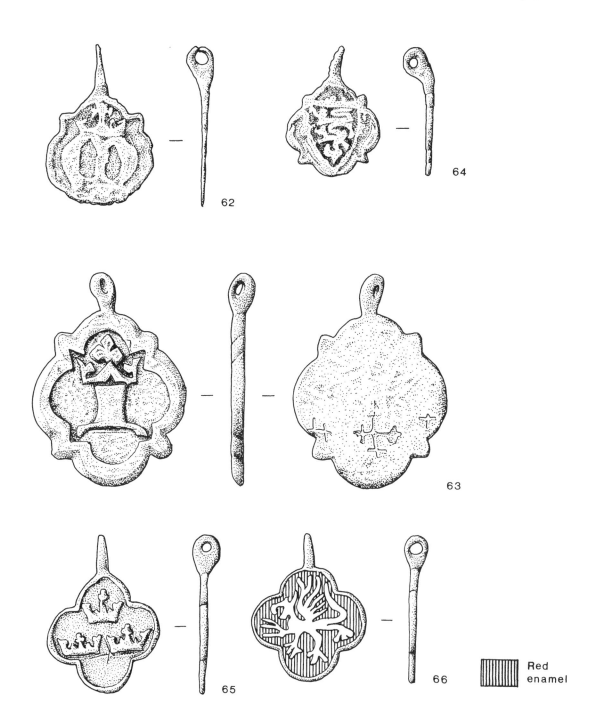

49 Pendants, Nos 62–6 (1:1)

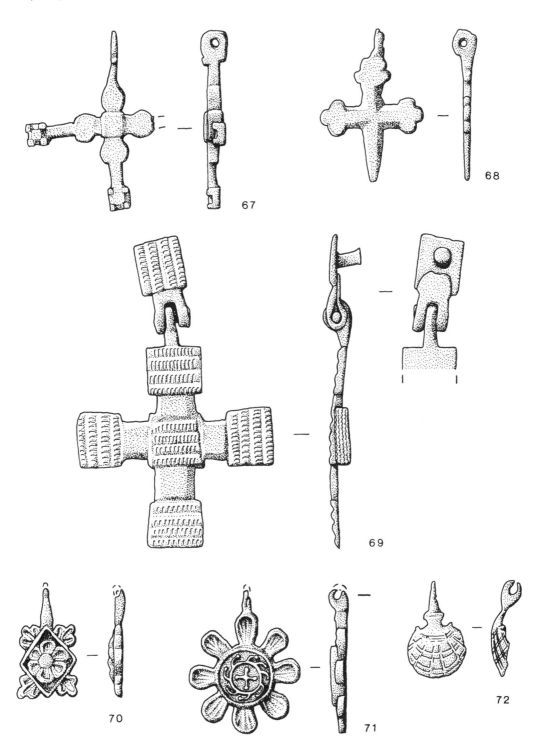

50 Pendants, Nos 67–72 (1:1)

precise, perhaps underlining the lowly status of many, if not all, of these objects. The loop is complete, though it appears to have been bent forwards.

65 Billingsgate site   Fig 49
42×31mm
Quatrefoil; a simpler version of the elaborate quatrefoils, Nos 62–4 above; no enamel survives but the three crowns make it fairly certain that the arms represented are those of East Anglia: *azure three crowns or*. These arms were attributed by heralds in the 13th century to the Saxon Kings of East Anglia, but they appear also to have been used as the arms of St Edmund and therefore of the Abbey and shrine of Bury St Edmunds.

66 Billingsgate site   Fig 49
39×31mm
Quatrefoil; a griffin, silvered, on a red ground. A typical mythical beast, common in medieval art and in this case remarkably accurate in depicting the hindparts of a lion married to the head, breast, claws and wings of an eagle. A very close parallel, perhaps even from the same mould, but with blue enamel, comes from Yorkshire (private collection).

67 BWB83 6025 (298) 11   Fig 50
47×35mm
Cruciform; a cross with four swelling projections from a central square, which in turn extend into narrow arms terminating in faceted rectangles. One arm is lost. Cruciform pendants may be connected with clerics, although they may merely indicate private devotion.

68 Billingsgate site   Fig 50
40×28mm
Cruciform; although, as above, the use of a cross may indicate a religious connection, it is worth noting that the form is that of the heraldic *cross botonny fitchy*. Possibly it represents an element of a coat of arms, used in a decorative fashion.

69 SWA81 441 (2018) 9   Figs 50, 51
63×53mm (pendant), 24×13mm (mount)
Cruciform with mount attached; a very fine cross with rectangular terminals to the arms, which project from a rectangular centre. The centre and terminals are decorated with lines of fine notches; those on the horizontal terminals (and the mount) are arranged in four vertical rows, the remainder in four horizontal rows. The gilding is very well preserved on all front surfaces. Such a pendant might well have decorated the harness of a high-ranking cleric. A very close parallel is in the collections of the British Museum (acc no MLA 94, 2–17, 7).

70 SWA81 585 (2055) 9   Fig 50
28×16mm
Lozenge with fleury projections; a small pendant of purely decorative design; within the lozenge is a sexfoil, originally surrounded by enamel, now lost. The projections from the sides of the lozenge form small trefoils. Loop broken at the top.

71 MoL acc no 86.159/1   (Billingsgate site)   Fig 50
39×32mm
Octofoil; the eight lobes project from a circular centre and are patterned as natural leaves. The central area is divided into two zones, the inner containing a cross, the outer a design probably representing the Crown of Thorns. Very similar pendants are known from Essex, Wiltshire and Kent (respectively British Museum acc no MLA 96, 5–1, 61; Salisbury Museum acc no ii G15; private collection). The Wiltshire find has green and red enamel in the field. The loop is worn through. The

51   Pendant, No 69

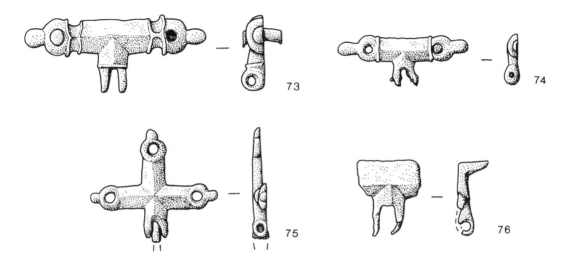

52 Suspension mounts, Nos 73–6 (1:1)

pendant was found in association with, but does not belong to, No 75.

72 Billingsgate site   Fig 50
25×16mm
Scallop-shell; this small shell has the natural form indicated by fine engraved radial and circumferential lines. It may well come from a pair, in which the suspension mount repeated the design but the other way up. The choice of a scallop-shell may have connections with the idea of pilgrimage, deriving from the shell badge of St James, though this must also have been widely used as a simple decorative design. The loop is bent backwards and has worn through.

SUSPENSION MOUNTS

73 BWB83   acc no 1598   (context 292)   ceramic phase 11   Fig 52
49mm
Horizontal mount; a typical, decorative bar mount with the horizontal element separated from the shaped terminals by a double cusp. One complete rivet remains, projecting 4.5mm behind the mount.

74 Billingsgate site   Fig 52
36mm
Horizontal mount; a smaller version of a bar mount (cf. No 73), this differs in not having the double cusps at the end of the horizontal element. Part of one rivet remains, also part of the pin which retained the pendant in place.

75 MoL acc no 86.159/1   (Billingsgate site)   Fig 52
31×35mm
Cruciform mount; a variant of the horizontal bar mount, in which a third arm projects upwards; such suspension mounts were presumably fitted where two straps met at right angles. This example was found with pendant No 71, but the fragment of loop still in place indicates that another, now lost, pendant was once attached.

76 Billingsgate site   Fig 52
17mm
Bar mount; a slightly damaged example of a very common type of suspension mount, with two prongs projecting back from the ends of the bar. The projecting rings through which the pin holding the pendant passed are both broken.

MOUNTS POSSIBLY FOR HORSE HARNESS

In the context of horse harness pendants, one small group of objects deserves attention, since they closely resemble and are often mistakenly described as pendants. These are small shields, or other shapes, of copper alloy, normally enamelled and gilded but lacking any suspension loop. They usually have studs projecting from the rear, or provision for rivets at the angles, and were mounted on to a separate background. A short summary of the more common types, with some suggestions for their uses, has been published (Griffiths 1989) and it is worth discussing

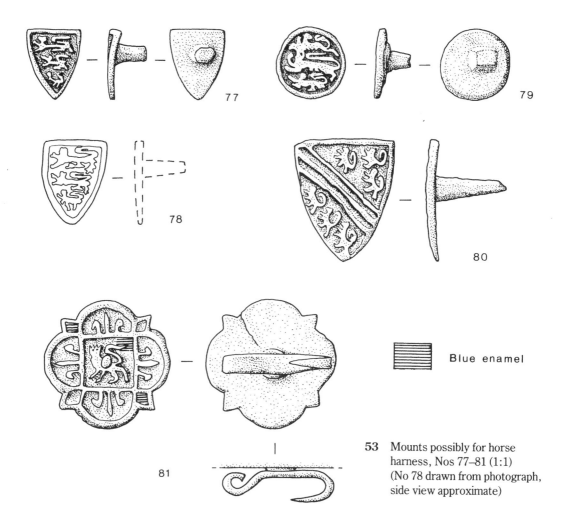

53 Mounts possibly for horse harness, Nos 77–81 (1:1)
(No 78 drawn from photograph, side view approximate)

the examples from London as a group.

The two small shields (Nos 77–8), approximately 20mm in height, can be compared with a shield attached to an iron stirrup from Whapgrove, Oxfordshire. The shield is fastened to the top of the stirrup by a stud, 18mm in length, which passed through the stirrup leather (Griffiths 1989, fig 4a–b). The small, circular and lozenge-shaped mounts (such as No 79) demonstrate the variety of such mounts, the shapes paralleling those of pendants.

Shields such as No 80, of approximately 30–40mm in height, are more difficult to parallel. Uses may include many unrelated to harness, although it seems likely that some at least were used to decorate straps, perhaps in conjunction

with shield-shaped pendants. A fine example of this type of shield, but attached to an iron frame, was recovered from excavations at Baynard's Castle and was published as a type of brooch (Wilmott 1982, 299), an identification since called into question.

The final example in this small group is an interesting example of reuse. A mount of basically similar form to the above, but of an elaborate quatrefoil shape, originally had a rivet or pin on the rear; this has probably broken off but the stump is still visible. It appears to have been filed flat to provide a base for an 'S'-shaped book. This is attached by means of an additional rivet, which projects through the lion on the front face. The purpose appears to have been to convert a broken mount into a hooked fastening, presumably for dress use.

77 Billingsgate site Fig 53
18×14mm
Shield; a stud of roughly hexagonal section, 9mm in length, projects from the rear. No enamel or gilding remains, though the arms are almost certainly those of England before 1340. See No 64 for heraldry.

78 Billingsgate site Fig 53
21×17mm
Shield; a stud projects from the rear. Although badly worn, the arms are those of England, as No 77 above.

79 Billingsgate site Fig 53
d 18mm
Circular mount; a square-sectioned pin, probably broken, projects off-centre from the rear. The crudely rendered arms appear to be those of England, as Nos 77 and 78 above.

80 Billingsgate site Fig 53
32×27mm
Shield; a tapering pin, approximately 20mm long, projects from the rear. No enamel survives but the surviving details must represent the well-known and distinctive coat of arms of the de Bohun family, Earls of Essex and Hereford: *azure a bend argent, cotised and between six lioncels or.* Although the blue ground is lost, traces of gilding remain on the bend. Either slightly damaged, or a faulty casting, the shield has lost the raised border along one side that held the enamel in place.

81 Billingsgate site Fig 53
33×35mm
Quatrefoil with angular projections. As described above, this has apparently been modified into a hooked fastening. The design is not truly heraldic, but allusive, combining the lion from the English royal arms with the fleurs-de-lis of the French in a purely decorative fashion. The inclusion of the fleurs-de-lis suggests a date after 1340, when Edward III incorporated them into the English royal arms. One unusual aspect is the reversal of the background colours, blue for the lion instead of the correct red, and (now lost) presumably red for the fleurs instead of blue. Two of the angles contain blue, the other two may have been marked with red. This unusual treatment is by no means unique and suggests that the design had become purely decorative and of no truly heraldic significance. Some gilding remains.

STIRRUPS

John Clark

For later medieval stirrups from Britain there is as yet nothing to set beside the comprehensive study of Viking Age stirrups by Seaby and Woodfield (1980), which also provides a useful survey of the literature on the origins and early development of the stirrup. Few medieval stirrups have been recorded in well-dated archaeological contexts, and, unusually, Ward Perkins provides little in the way of parallels for the stirrups included here (London Museum 1940, 86–94).

Notable among these stirrups is No 82, which is still attached to its leather. No 84, though incomplete, provides a probable 14th-century dating for a rather distinctive group of stirrups cast in copper alloy (discussed further below); loriners, who made stirrups as well as bits, certainly worked in both iron and copper alloy – in 1327 a distinction is made between 'loriners in copper and loriners in iron' (Riley 1868, 156–62).

In addition to the complete stirrups catalogued here, note should be taken of the two small shield-shaped mounts Nos 77 and 78 described by Griffiths above, which may originally have been attached to stirrups, like an example from Whapgrove, Oxfordshire (Griffiths 1989, fig 4a–b).

82 BIG82 acc no 2800 (context 5221) ceramic phase 7 Fig 54
Stirrup h 157mm, w 130mm; strap w 28mm, extended l 430mm
Iron stirrup of elongated D-shape, the sides of shallow D-section, the footrest curving slightly upwards with central double projection beneath it, a trapezoidal loop at top to take the strap; leather strap, formed of a length of leather folded to a central seam along the back, tapering at one end, where it is edge-stitched and punched with four central holes, and with iron buckle (for which see No 24) at other end; where strap passes through stirrup loop it is reinforced with a thin copper-alloy strip with traces of plating (probably tin), which is fastened by an iron rivet, with lozenge-shaped rove, passing through both thicknesses of leather.

In use, the free end of the strap was presumably passed through an attachment and back to the buckle. Once the buckle was fastened, the total free length of strap would have been around 280–300mm, depending upon which strap-hole was used – not long enough in

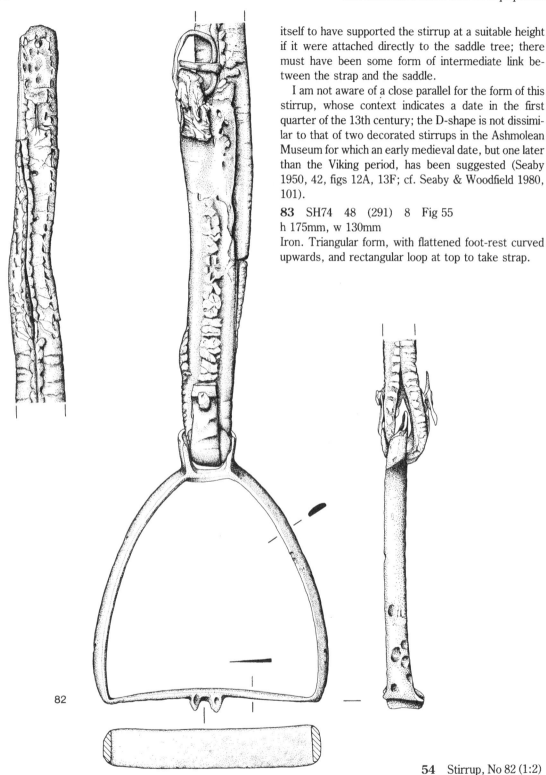

itself to have supported the stirrup at a suitable height if it were attached directly to the saddle tree; there must have been some form of intermediate link between the strap and the saddle.

I am not aware of a close parallel for the form of this stirrup, whose context indicates a date in the first quarter of the 13th century; the D-shape is not dissimilar to that of two decorated stirrups in the Ashmolean Museum for which an early medieval date, but one later than the Viking period, has been suggested (Seaby 1950, 42, figs 12A, 13F; cf. Seaby & Woodfield 1980, 101).

83 SH74 48 (291) 8 Fig 55
h 175mm, w 130mm
Iron. Triangular form, with flattened foot-rest curved upwards, and rectangular loop at top to take strap.

82

54 Stirrup, No 82 (1:2)

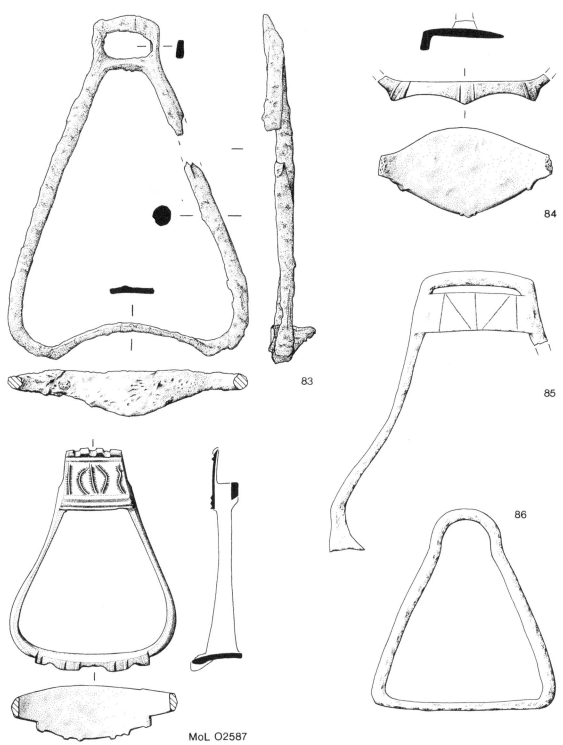

MoL O2587

55 Stirrups, Nos 83–86 and MoL acc no O2587 (1:2)

84 BC72 1772 (55) 11 Fig 55
surviving w 95mm
Foot-rest of stirrup; copper alloy. Cast, with decoration on front edge.

Apparently a fragment of a stirrup of the type represented in the Museum of London collections by acc nos 1816 (from 'London' – Guildhall Museum 1908, 59, no 42) and O2587 (from the Thames at Southwark Bridge – see Fig 55); there are others of similar form in the British Museum (MLA 1836, 9–1, 68; 1909, 3–19, 9; 1910, 4–5, 1; 1913, 12–6, 1 – the second of these being a London find). The type, unusual in being of copper alloy, with in-curving sides and a cover-plate protecting the suspension bar to which the stirrup leather was attached, is referred to by Gaimster (1990, 159) and I am grateful to him for drawing my attention to the British Museum specimens. The BC72 find seems to provide the best dating evidence so far (second half of the 14th century) for the type.

85 BWB83 5428 (293) 11 Fig 55 (from X-ray)
Top and one side of stirrup, h *c.*150mm
Iron. Cover-plate in front of suspension bar, with incised decoration (revealed on X-ray by remains of plating in the grooves).

Probably from a stirrup of what Ward Perkins called 'typically 14th-century asymmetrical form' (London Museum 1940, 89), similar to that illustrated there (ibid. 93, no 2, fig 27, MoL acc no A1398, from Moorfields) and others in the Museum of London collections. A stirrup of similar type from Winchester is published by Goodall (1990, 1042–3, no 3879, fig 332) – and assumed to be residual in its mid 16th- to late 17th-century context.

86 BWB83 4802 (326) 12 Fig 55 (from X-ray)
h 108mm, w 104mm
Iron. Triangular with rounded apex – no loop or slot for suspension.

Though it is included here, the identification of this item as a stirrup is uncertain.

Horseshoes

JOHN CLARK

Introduction

THE FUNCTION OF THE HORSESHOE

Horseshoe: a shoe for a horse, now usually formed of a narrow iron plate bent to the outline of the horse's hoof and nailed to the animal's foot (Oxford English Dictionary)

It is traditional in any publication dealing at length with horse-shoeing to devote space to the origins and history of the practice (see for example Fleming 1869 and Hickman & Humphrey 1988, 1–17). Such accounts, together with the various papers on early horseshoes written in the late 1930s and early 1940s by R W Murray and Dr Gordon Ward (Murray 1937a, 1937b; Ward 1939, 1941a), which are not securely based archaeologically, should be treated with great caution when they refer to shoes of medieval or supposed earlier date.

The introduction of the shoeing of horses was a stage in what Lynn White jr, the American historian of medieval technology, has called 'the discovery of horse-power' (1962, 57), a discovery which had far-reaching consequences for medieval culture and economy – discussed for example by Langdon (1986) and Davis (1989, 11–31) with reference to agriculture and warfare respectively. It is a theme that has concerned historians of technological innovation as well as archaeologists.

There is a huge range of writings related to the origins and history of horse-shoeing, many of them obscure and unhelpful. Heymering's comprehensive bibliography *On the Horse's Foot, Shoes and Shoeing*, originally planned as a 16-page booklet, finally appeared as a hardback book of 366 pages; it lists nearly 1,200 works of which 71 are described as 'primarily historical' (1990, 293–5). The subject is fortunately one in which White has taken a continuing interest; he has provided useful updates and reviews of the evidence in several of his publications (White 1962, 57–9, 156; 1978, 141–2, 287).

That evidence is considered here in so far as it is a necessary background to a study of the horseshoes of medieval date found in London.

It is generally agreed that the function of the nailed-on horseshoe is to protect the horse's hoof, the horny outer covering of its foot, from excessive wear or damage leading to lameness (Hickman & Humphrey 1988, 1). In a paper published in *Antiquity* in 1966, however, Charles Green proposed that this was not its original function (Green 1966). Early shoes have protruding nails and calkins (turned-down extensions to the heels), which would result in the horse, on flat hard ground, standing on a series of stud-like projections rather than on the surface of the shoe. This suggested to Green that it was the nails which were the *raison d'être* of the shoe, serving like hob-nails or football studs to give the horse better grip in soft ground; the strip of iron forming the shoe itself served at first, in his view, simply as a support or spacer for the nails. Discussion followed in later volumes of *Antiquity* (Dent 1967; Littauer 1968). Littauer, pointing out that the grip of the horse's unshod foot was better than that provided by any shoe, concluded that the intention of the early horseshoe was indeed to protect the hoof, and that the protruding nails were an attempt to compensate for the resulting loss of traction and also, in their turn, to protect the shoe itself from rapid wear. Relevant too is the fact that, as discussed below, it is not at all evident that the earliest shoes in medieval Britain (our type 1) were regularly fitted with protruding nails – they certainly did not usually have calkins!

In its natural state and natural habitat the hoof of a wild horse or any of the horse family will, apparently, be worn away by contact with the ground at a rate which is balanced more or less by its rate of new growth (Hickman & Humphrey 1988, 1). In the domesticated horse, heavy labour in haulage or carrying will cause additional wear, while the cold and damp conditions of northern Europe lead to softening of the horn of the hoof, which thus wears rapidly and is prone to damage (White 1962, 57; Dent 1967, 62). On the other hand Chappell (1973, 100–1) quotes documentary evidence from 17th- and 18th-century Virginia and Maryland for the practice of riding horses unshod, a practice the colonists ascribed to the dry climate and the stone-free soil. Even today in Britain shoeing is not regarded as essential in all circumstances. For example, horses turned out to grass in the summer may be left unshod (Hickman & Humphrey 1988, 178–9). The British Horse Society (1988, 167) suggests that working horses unshod 'is quite feasible provided that work on hard, gritty roads or flinty tracks is avoided' and concludes that the unshod hoof develops a harder and firmer horn. Fleming quotes the rather similar opinion of the 14th-century Italian Laurentius Rusius that young horses should be left unshod 'to make the hooves larger and stronger' (1869, 397). One suspects, however, that the modern horse, as an instrument of leisure and ceremonial, has an easier life than its hard-working ancestors and may as a result suffer less wear to its hooves. More generally, in hotter and drier climates, according to Hickman & Humphrey (1988, 179), 'horses are worked on unmetalled roads without hind shoes and mules are not shod'.

There seems to be no readily available evidence from medieval Britain to show how universal the shoeing of horses was, although it certainly seems to have been the norm for horses of all types (White 1962, 59). The 13th-century Calabrian Jordanus Rufus noted the possibility of horses being ridden without shoes even 'per loca montuosa, dura, saxea vel petrosa' (through places mountainous, hard, stony or rocky), but only in order to draw attention to the bruising and damage to the foot that would result (Prévot 1991, 109). If the narrow strip of a contrasting colour at the bottom of the hoof of horses on the Bayeux Tapestry is intended, as seems likely, to represent a shoe, then the great majority of the horses there depicted are shown as shod on all four feet. Almost all are war-horses of course, but a pack-horse in one scene (Stenton 1957, pl 47 and detail) seems to have similar shoes; an exception may be two of the horses being ridden

by English fugitives fleeing after the battle in the final scene, which are apparently shown without shoes – though they are depicted too small for this to be clear (ibid. pl 73). The many horses illustrated in the works of Matthew Paris and his school in the mid-13th century usually exhibit the protruding nails that are the evidence of shoes (for example, James 1920, war-horses *passim*; riding horses and a pack-horse, p 25); it is not clear when they are omitted whether it is deliberate or carelessness. All the horses depicted in the Luttrell Psalter of *c.*1340, whether ridden for war or pleasure (Millar 1932, 157, f202b; 70, f159), hauling carts or harrows (ibid. 76, f162; 94, f1271) or serving as pack-animals (ibid. 68, f158), are clearly well shod, as are those in the well-known Flemish manuscript of the Romance of Alexander of similar date (James 1933 *passim*).

Manorial accounts of the 14th century, such as those from Cuxham (Oxfordshire) contain regular payments for the shoeing of working horses, and indeed for shoeing the plough-oxen: as in 1358–9 when Thomas Marchal (the farrier) was paid a fee of 24s. for the shoeing 'on all feet' of 13 oxen and three cart-horses (*equi carectarii*) for a year from Michaelmas, while a further sum of 2s. 6d. was paid for the shoeing of three 'affers' (*pro ferrura iij affrorum*) for the same period (Harvey 1976, 592). A treatise on estate management and accounting of the mid-14th century comments that 'item affrus laborans cotidie per annum potest ferrari pro vijd per annum' (an affer working every day of the year can be shod for 7d. a year – slightly less than was being paid at Cuxham) (Oschinsky 1971, 473). The distinction between the cheap 'affer', used largely to haul harrows and ploughs, and the more expensive *equus carectarius* is discussed above in the Introduction.

The requirement that Thomas the marshal of Cuxham shoe the animals 'on all four feet' reflects an alternative practice of partial shoeing – the front hooves only. The practice is also indicated by a comment made by Walter of Henley some 70 years earlier about the costs of shoeing a work-horse 'sil deit estre ferre de quatre pez' (if it has to be shod on all four feet) (Oschinsky 1971, 318–9) and by the very specific wording of a Domesday Book reference quoted by Murray (1937a, 29–30), in which a landowner was required to shoe the king's palfrey *upon all four feet* whenever the king visited the manor. Murray also quotes a 14th-century custumal from Minchinhampton (Gloucestershire) which lists among the services required from a particular tenant that 'he keeps shod one horse fore and hind or two horses fore, throughout the year' (ibid. 30). We may also note Hickman & Humphrey's comment (1988, 179) on the working of horses without hind shoes in hot dry climates. None of these references indicate how normal the practice of fore-shoeing only was in medieval times; in any period when it was common we would expect front horseshoes (if they can be distinguished) to outnumber hind horseshoes in any sample – a possibility that is significant for the discussion of shapes and sizes of shoes that follows below.

That Thomas also shod the oxen is not surprising; it remained normal practice as long as the use of oxen for ploughing continued (Jenkins 1962, 51–2; Powell 1991). At West Farleigh (Kent), a manor belonging to the Cathedral Priory of Canterbury, oxen were being shod twice a year in the reigns of Edward II and Edward III, either on front hooves only or both front and rear (information from Nigel Ramsay from notes by J B Bickersteth on the Priory Bedel's Rolls). However, the shoeing of oxen may be a late development. Walter of Henley, writing in about 1286, listed the cost of shoeing a workhorse among the items of additional expenditure that, he believed, made horses less economic than oxen for both ploughing and haulage – for oxen he included no charge for shoeing (Oschinsky 1971, 318–9).

No medieval ox-shoes have been identified from London, though two examples from contexts of the second half of the 16th century were excavated in 1992 at Abbots Lane, Southwark (site ABO92 contexts 184 and 249; Bluer 1993, 145 – I am grateful to my colleague Frances Pritchard for the opportunity to examine these items).

Ox-shoes would not perhaps be expected in an urban context once horses had replaced oxen for road haulage. Medieval and early post-medieval examples are, however, reported from a number of rural sites, such as Waltham Abbey (Essex), Goltho (Lincolnshire), Alsted (Surrey), Hangleton (Sussex) and Wharram (Yorkshire) (Huggins 1972, 122–4, nos 15–21, fig 32 – chiefly 17th century; Goodall 1973, 171, no 38, fig 12; Goodall 1975, 89 (not illustrated); Goodall 1976b, 60, nos 62–4, fig 36; Holden 1963, 173, nos 7–8, fig 38; Goodall 1979a, 123, no 113, fig 65). That from the Roman site at Hod Hill, Dorset (British Museum 1958, 50, fig 23) is surely recent. In other cases it is of course possible that the basic crescent of the ox-shoe (a pair of which fitted each cloven hoof of the ox) might if badly corroded be identified as a fragmentary horseshoe – and vice versa (as, for example, a find from Princes Risborough (Buckinghamshire): Pavry & Knocker 1957–8, 161, no 7, fig 12).

Since other equids (donkeys and mules) may also be shod, we should consider whether any of the medieval shoes discussed here might have served this purpose. Both donkeys and mules were used as pack-animals rather than in draught (Leighton 1972, 63–4). Both could be ridden; a mule was considered an appropriate mount for an ecclesiastic, while to ride a donkey was a sign of asceticism (ibid.). In fact both animals are noticeable for their rarity in medieval documents. Langdon, in discussing the role of horses in medieval farming (1986), included mules and donkeys in his comprehensive statistical survey. Thus, on 406 manors at the time of the Domesday Book, which he considered in detail, there were just 11 donkeys and one mule – 3.9% of the 'working horse' population – while the overall figure for some 4,000 holdings was even lower at only 1.9% (1986, 29). In the 12th century the only reference he found was to 'three Spanish donkeys' at Burton upon Trent (Staffordshire) in about 1114–18 (ibid. 42). In the period 1250–1320, on 625 manors, 14 mules and five donkeys made up just 1% of the working horses in use on the demesne lands (ibid. 86–7); his survey of the peasant holdings in some 335 villages between 1225 and 1332 revealed only five donkeys, all in one Yorkshire village in 1297 (ibid. 187). Unfortunately, the nature of the available evidence did not allow Langdon to provide such detailed statistics for the later 14th and 15th centuries. Yet his figures suggest that neither donkeys nor mules were common as working animals in rural areas. Certainly the study of skeletal material from London excavations discussed by Rackham above, in which no remains could be identified unequivocally as those of either mules or donkeys, seems to confirm the rarity of these beasts.

Nor is shoeing today regarded as essential for either donkey or mule. Hickman & Humphrey

(1988, 79) describe them being 'worked both under load and in draught without shoes'; shoeing is necessary 'in wet weather and when working on modern roads'. A writer of about 1300 comments on the hard-working ass 'withoute nail and scho' (Kurath & Kuhn 1959, 796, sv 'curreien'). The ass ridden by the Virgin and Child in the Luttrell Psalter appears not to be shod, unlike the many horses depicted in the same manuscript (Millar 1932, 30, f88b). In a German engraving of 1474–5 showing a miller driving a pack-ass, the animal seems not to have shoes (Kühnel 1986, fig 79); it is the work of an artist, Martin Schongauer, who delighted in detail and would presumably have depicted the nail-clenches on the sides of the hooves if shoes were present. On the other hand Dürer's 1503/5 woodcut of the *Flight into Egypt* shows a donkey which is clearly shod (Kurth 1963, no 187).

We might then expect to find very few, if any, mule- or donkey-shoes among our sample. Apart from the smaller size of the donkey, both animals have hooves sufficiently different in shape from those of the horse to make the identification of a specially made mule- or donkey-shoe straightforward in principle. In both, the foot is long and narrow, expanding at the heels, and the modern mule-shoe mirrors this shape (Fig 56 after Hickman & Humphrey 1988, 79, fig 4.14; cf. Sparkes 1976, 29–31 and fig). Some five of the medieval shoes from London sites catalogued below are perhaps sufficiently long in relation to their width to approach the form of the modern mule-shoes illustrated (in which the ratio of length to breadth is about 1.24 to 1). These consist of three of our

type 3 from contexts of between 1230 and 1350 (Nos 148, 150, 172) and two of type 4 from 1350–1400 contexts at Baynard's Castle (Nos 222, 225); in all these shoes the length exceeds the breadth by a factor of between 1.2 and 1.27 to 1. None of them is small enough to be a donkey-shoe; none has quite the tendency to everted heels of the modern mule-shoe. However, and particularly in the case of the shoe from Custom House (the longest in relation to its width – by a ratio of 1.27:1 – as well as, in absolute terms, one of the longest shoes among the London finds), we should perhaps conclude that in some instances we are dealing with mule-shoes rather than horseshoes.

HORSESHOES BEFORE THE MEDIEVAL PERIOD

Documents and contemporary illustrations like those described above combine with archaeological sources to provide evidence for the use of the nailed horseshoe in the Middle Ages. However, the early literature of horseshoes is full of shoes apparently dating from the Roman period (or even from the pre-Roman Iron Age (Fleming 1869, chapters III and VI *passim*; Ward 1941a)). Although this is not the place for a full review of the evidence for horseshoes of Roman date in Britain (which is certainly needed), comment is perhaps worthwhile. There is certainly a limited amount of residual material of Roman date in our medieval contexts, and at first sight it would be possible for Roman horseshoes, if they exist, to fall into this category. Thus a horseshoe (No 292) which is apparently of our type 4 ('late medieval') comes from a context at the Billingsgate lorry park site which contained quantities of mid-3rd-century pottery described as 'residual'; contrariwise, from another more recent site (FST85 154) comes a fragment of an obvious type 2A shoe ('Norman'), found in a context with Roman pottery ranging from 2nd to 4th century and with what is described as 'intrusive' medieval pottery. In such cases it is not evident prima facie whether the horseshoe is in context, 'residual' or 'intrusive'!

When in 1962 Lynn White reviewed the evidence for the early use of the nailed horseshoe,

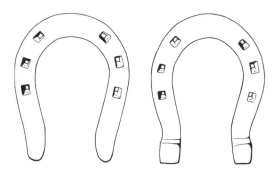

56   Modern mule shoes, front (left) and hind (right)
         (after Hickman & Humphrey 1988, fig 4.14)

he concluded that it was unknown in the classical world but made its first appearance in documentary sources in the late 9th or the 10th century, with almost simultaneous references by Byzantine and Frankish authors (1962, 57–9, 156). The first of his conclusions meets general acceptance, but there has been a tendency, perhaps under the influence of earlier writers, to suggest that while unknown in Rome the nailed horseshoe might have been in occasional use in Celtic Europe during the period of the Roman Empire. However, I am unable to substantiate White's generalisation, made in 1975, that 'British archaeologists still claim to have excavated nailed horseshoes of the third to fourth century after Christ. Continental archaeologists no longer find them before the tenth century, it seems' (White 1978, 287)! A recent survey of the Continental evidence and current views on the problem of Roman horseshoes (Junkelmann 1990–2, vol 3, 92–8) draws attention to the elusive nature of the evidence and the apparent ability of Roman shoes to mimic forms that are definitely found at much later dates (ibid. fig 103). The same seems to be true of finds from Britain.

Manning (1985, 63), whilst omitting horseshoes from his account of the British Museum's collection of Romano–British ironwork on the reasonable grounds that none of those in the collection are stratified finds, comments, 'that horseshoes, both of the lobate and smooth-edged types, were used in Roman Britain is now established beyond doubt'. He refers to the discussion in his own catalogue of Roman ironwork in Newcastle upon Tyne (Manning 1976, 31). In this earlier catalogue he included a number of unstratified horseshoes from Roman sites; some of them (like those illustrated by Junkelmann 1990–2, vol 3, fig 103) look uncomfortably recent (Manning 1976, 32, nos 88–96, figs 19–20).

Other Roman-period horseshoes noted by Manning in 1976 were from Colchester (Camulodunum) and Gloucester (presumably those discussed by Ward (1941a, 10–12) and Ward Perkins (1941, 144), whose context is dubious), Caister-on-Sea (Norfolk), Maiden Castle (Dorset) and Fishbourne (W Sussex). To these we may add finds published as Roman horseshoes from Portchester Castle (Hampshire), Coygan Camp (Dyfed), Chalk (Kent) and Bradley Hill (Somerset). The stratification at Coygan Camp (Wain-

wright 1967, 106, no 3, fig 29), Portchester (Cunliffe 1975, 235, nos 182–3, fig 125) and Fishbourne (Cunliffe 1971, II, 134, no 54, fig 60) is open to debate, as is that at Camulodunum (Hawkes & Hull 1947, 342, nos 2–3, fig 64) where the levels were cut by two modern water main trenches (ibid. fig 13). The items from Bradley Hill (Leech 1981, 214, no 215, fig 17) and Chalk (Johnston 1972, 135, no 2, fig 13) are surely not horseshoes. However, Charles Green's find from Caister seems well stratified and of late Roman date, coming from the surface of a Roman road but sealed by a burial of mid-Saxon date in the soil above (Green 1966, 306), and one hesitates to comment further on it.

Of these 'Roman' shoes most are of our type 2 (below) – more specifically, where identifiable, type 2A (with round nail-holes), to which a date of mid-11th to 12th century is assigned in our own typology. To this type also belong the majority of the 'Iron Age' shoes published by Ward (1941a), for whose date he had no sound evidence. It is not surprising that Ward Perkins concluded in 1941 that 'there is at present no sound criterion by which a shoe of the Romano–British period may be distinguished from one of the twelfth century' (1941, 146–7). Such a conclusion would make horseshoes unique among all but the simplest excavated artefacts; if one excludes basic items like chains, rings and nails there is usually little difficulty in distinguishing medieval small finds from those of the Roman period and defining the differences. The persistence of an object as sophisticated as the type 2 horseshoe without any recognisable development from the 1st century AD until the 12th century – a period of massive cultural change and discontinuity – would surely be unprecedented in the archaeological record. Common sense suggests that if nailed horseshoes of the Roman period exist, the one thing we can be certain of is that they must differ in appearance from the developed shoe of the 'Norman' period!

This last is true of the group of horseshoes and fragments, some 14 in all, recovered by Mortimer Wheeler at Maiden Castle (Dorset) in 1935 (Wheeler 1943, 290–91, pl XXXB) – their form is unclear, but they certainly lack the early medieval wavy edge. They were found in the make-up and on the surface of a late Roman roadway (dated by Wheeler *c*.AD 370) at the east entrance to the hill-fort; Wheeler states categorically that they

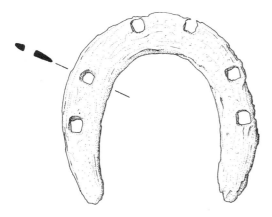

57   Horseshoe from possible Roman context at
Dowgate, City of London (MoL acc no 24607)
(1:2)

were 'sealed beneath later accumulations and
surfaces and are incontestably of late fourth or
early fifth century date'. However, even such an
authoritative statement as Wheeler's can be
questioned. It is clear from elsewhere in his
account that among the 'later accumulations and
surfaces' was the make-up for a farm-track (ibid.
121) and Wheeler recorded the remains of a
16th-century barn just outside the entrance (ibid.
122). The entrance is steep and narrow and
apparently subject to flooding in wet weather;
Wheeler notes that the Roman roadway was
pot-holed by rainwater ponding up on the west
side of the Roman stone gateway (ibid. 121). It is
just the sort of area where farm horses might get
into difficulties in wet weather, churning up the
soil and losing a shoe in deep mud. Given the
difficulty of distinguishing the original make-up of
the Roman roadway from later patchings, and the
obvious dangers of dating a find from a road-
surface by the date of the road rather than by the
levels above it, the context is not necessarily a
securely dated one.

One London find should properly be considered
here, since a Roman period context is claimed for
it, and like those from Maiden Castle it has the
'advantage' of not being immediately identifiable
as an early medieval form; indeed in shape (Fig
57) it is somewhat anomalous. It is formed of a
thin (3–5mm) but broad strip of iron, bent to a
well-shaped regular curve; some slight distortion
to the inner margin at the toe suggests final cold
working to fit it to the hoof. Six square, tapering

nail-holes are spaced fairly regularly around the
perimeter. In this it differs from the more common shoe with three or more nail-holes on each
branch avoiding the toe where (as here) holes are
quickly worn through. The heels are simply
rounded, without calkins. Its nearest parallel
among the well-stratified shoes catalogued below
is one from a mid- to late 14th-century context at
Baynard's Castle (No 215 – see fig 86) which is
itself something of an anomaly, though not entirely without parallel, in that context.

The older find (Museum of London acc no
24607) has been on display in the Museum's
Roman Gallery since 1976, and was illustrated as
Roman (on the present author's recommendation)
by Hickman & Humphrey (1988, fig 1.3, but from
the first edition of 1977). It was found in 1959 by
Peter Marsden on the site of building works for
the Corporation of London's new Public Cleansing
Depot at Dowgate (Upper Thames Street); he
records (pers comm, Marsden Collection no
A893) that it came from river gravels at the
south-east of the site which were being excavated
by contractors prior to the construction of a dock,
and which otherwise produced large quantities of
1st- to 2nd-century Roman pottery. He saw no
obvious sign of intrusion or contamination from
later levels (medieval silts and reclamation dumping), though by the nature of the building site and
in the absence of scientific archaeological excavation such contamination cannot be entirely ruled
out.

In 1941 Gordon Ward established an extremely
long chronology for his 'Iron Age' horseshoe and
its derivatives: 'Our ancestors were making
horseshoes of a characteristic type at the very
beginning of the Roman occupation. . . . Its
various characteristic features were slowly modified during succeeding centuries, but they were
not finally lost until about the twelfth or thirteenth
century A.D.' (1941a, 9) Within that period
Ward's chronology is difficult to interpret. He
would seem to assign his 'normal Iron Age type',
with wavy edge and round nail-holes (our type
2A), in general to the Roman period; the 'Winchester type' (our type 1) to a Saxon date; his
'derived types' (incorporating both our type 2B –
with rectangular nail-holes – and type 3) to late
Saxon or early medieval; and his 'latest derived
types' (also type 3) to an unspecified early
medieval date.

58 Horseshoe –
common modern
terminology

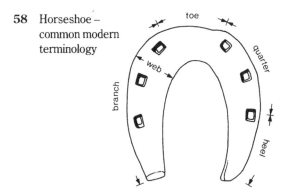

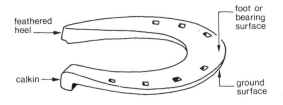

The evidence for this sequence is, to say the least, unconvincing. In a response to Ward's paper Ward Perkins (1941) drew attention to occurrences of shoes of 'Iron Age' type in secure 12th-century contexts, and of 'derived types' in 13th-century contexts (evidence he had discussed earlier in London Museum 1940, 112–17). Accepting the 1st-century date for the Camulodunum shoe, while questioning the evidence for other finds of supposed Roman date, Ward Perkins clearly found it difficult to explain the long life of the basic type and questioned 'whether there was continuity from Roman to medieval times. It is by no means impossible that the medieval horseshoe was an entirely fresh invention.' (1941, 148) In an acerbic reply three months later Ward (1941b) accused Ward Perkins of misrepresentation and called into question his archaeological dating, but he did not present any further evidence for his own hypothesis.

Ward Perkins had commented (1941, 147) that 'judged simply in terms of internal coherence, Dr Ward's classification is often convincing and may yet serve as a valuable basis for some future study'. That is true. If we ignore Ward's uncertain dating and his assignment of the type to the Iron Age, we find in his original paper an excellent survey, with measured drawings of 83 horseshoes out of more than 300 of this class that he had examined in museums and in private collections all over the country. Almost all of these can be readily identified with the type series defined below. We differ in our 'short' chronology and in our sequence of types; but to Ward must go the credit for first identifying the chief distinguishing features of early horseshoes and for providing an unrivalled corpus of comparative material. His work remains valuable, if its basis is unsound.

SHOEING PRACTICE AND TERMINOLOGY

The terminology adopted here for the parts of the shoe (Fig 58) and information on methods of shoeing is derived from modern practice (see in particular Hickman & Humphrey 1988 and War Office Veterinary Department 1908; I am grateful to Mrs Ann Hyland for drawing my attention to the first of these works, to Dr Philip Armitage for the second; Heymering 1990 would provide an abundance of alternative sources). A useful layperson's account of the work of the modern shoeing-smith is in Hogg 1964, 64–103.

Fig 58 shows the familiar curved plate of iron forming the shoe, with the modern terms for its parts. *Calkins* (heels turned down to form projections) of several forms are found on medieval shoes, and all these forms seem to have been in contemporary use. Calkins may be made by *upsetting* (thickening) the heels (Fig 59a), turning them down at right angles (Fig 59b) or folding them (Fig 59c); in rare cases, as on horseshoe No 119 below, the folding is 'double' to produce the 'rolled' effect shown in Fig 59d.

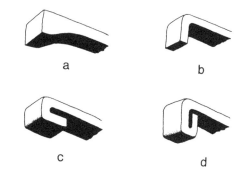

59 Calkins – types found on medieval horseshoes:
a upset or 'thickened' heel; **b** 'right-angle' calkin;
c 'folded' calkin; **d** 'double-folded' calkin

'Calkins provide a good foothold on soft ground and country roads . . . but are of little advantage on modern roads' (Hickman & Humphrey 1988, 62) and they are not in common use today. Where used they are largely restricted to hind shoes (ibid. 63). As early as the 17th century the benefits of calkins were being disputed:

> though they be intended to keep the Horse from sliding, yet they do him more harm than good, in that he cannot tread evenly upon the ground, whereby he many times wrencheth his Foot, or straineth some Sinew, and especially upon stony ways where the Stones will not suffer the Calkins to enter, the Foot slippeth with more Violence: yet some do not think him well shod, unless all his shoes be made with Calkins, either single [ie on one heel] or double [on both heels], yet of the two Evils, double is the less, for he will tread evener with double than with single Calkins. (R 1720, 126 – a work first published in 1678.)

By contrast, particularly where combined with protruding nail heads, calkins are the norm on early medieval horseshoes. Where the presence or absence of calkins was unequivocal, on complete shoes and on heel fragments included in our statistical sample (that is, both the excavated shoes catalogued below and others from more recent City excavations and from Museum of London collections) figures emerge as shown in Table 6. The true figures for calkins may be even higher than shown here, since in some cases a formerly prominent calkin may have been entirely worn down in use.

Table 6: Horseshoes with calkins on one or both heels

Type	Proportion with calkins
2 (Norman/13th century)	72 out of 79 (91%)
3 (13th/mid-14th century)	40 out of 51 (78%)
4 (14th/15th century)	63 out of 118 (56%)

Other features of modern horseshoes, such as *clips*, lugs raised on the edge of the shoe at the toe or quarter to clasp the hoof (Hickman & Humphrey 1988, 61–2), or *fullering*, a groove round the ground surface of the shoe in which the nails sit (ibid. 59), are post-medieval innovations. There is no reason to think that the fullered shoe

published by Ward Perkins (London Museum 1940, 116, no 4, fig 37 – Museum of London acc no A24957), found in the London City Ditch, is medieval; its form suggests an early 17th-century date (cf. Goodall 1983b, 251, no 220, fig 9).

Writing in about 1250 Jordanus Rufus noted that a horse's gait could be corrected by shoes which were higher at the rear than the front (Prévot 1991, 45), but the numerous specially shaped horseshoes of more recent times designed for this purpose or to prevent injury or alleviate lameness (Hickman & Humphrey 1988, 195–222) are notable for their rarity among medieval finds. Of such 'surgical' shoes Ward (1941a, 12 and 16, pl IVa and nos 55–7, fig 5) records three, all of our type 2. All are 'bar shoes', with a bar of iron between the heels, and in two cases a second bar joining the first bar to the toe. The bar transfers some of the weight to other parts of the horse's hoof, and thus bar shoes are 'suitable for treating weak heels and corns' (Hickman & Humphrey 1988, 64, 205). There are no such bar shoes recognised among the medieval London finds.

The modern 'feather-edged shoe', however, in which the inner branch is very narrow, thickened and without nail-holes, and the similar but less exaggerated 'knocked-up shoe' (ibid. 196–7; see our Fig 58) do have their parallels among medieval shoes – for example Nos 185, 186 and 215 below. Such shoes are intended for use in cases of 'brushing', when the horse habitually strikes the inside of one leg with the shoe of the opposite foot.

Other oddly shaped shoes in the archaeological record may represent attempts to deal with particular problems. Ward, for example, published what look like two 'three-quarter shoes' (1941a, nos 58, 59, fig 5; no 59 is our Museum of London acc no A75); Hickman & Humphrey (1988, 195–6, 205–6) note the use of such shoes when treating corns and 'capped elbow'.

In use the horseshoe is fastened by nails of soft iron which pass obliquely through the insensitive wall of the hoof and are *clenched* (bent over) to hold them in place; the manner in which nails were clenched differed from modern practice in the early medieval period and is discussed further below. A modern farrier will often use fewer nails than there are nail-holes in the shoe; 'three nails have been proven to be able to secure a shoe effectively', though six or seven nails are normal (Hickman & Humphrey 1988, 67, 167). Seventeenth-century practice seems to have preferred more nails; Gervase Markham recommends nine (1662, 437–9), the 'experienced farrier' of 1678, eight for a 'perfect hoof' or nine for a 'broad hoof' (R 1720, 121–2). A few medieval shoes have nails *in situ* in all the holes, and it seems likely that all available holes, be it six, seven or eight, were generally used. In the well-known City of London regulations of 1350 setting maximum prices and wages, two figures were given for the fee a farrier could charge for shoeing: 1½*d.* for a horseshoe of six nails, 2*d.* for a horseshoe of eight nails (Riley 1868, 256) – though with higher prices for shoeing a courser or a war-horse, for which no number of nails is quoted.

The shoe must of course be replaced when worn out, and it must be removed periodically, whether worn or not, for the growing hoof to be cut back; if not too badly worn the shoe can then be put back on – a procedure known as a 'remove' (War Office Veterinary Department 1908, 241; British Horse Society 1988, 160–1). In modern practice it is recommended that horses should be reshod every 4–6 weeks, depending on the type of shoe and the use to which the horse is put (War Office Veterinary Department 1908, 241; Hickman & Humphrey 1988, 74–5); according to Clifford Race, a Suffolk blacksmith (born 1898), reported by Evans (1960, 194), 'country horses – horses that worked chiefly on the land – came in once in three months, on the average'. Shoes may be reused several times before they are worn out and may in exceptional cases last a whole season (Hickman & Humphrey 1988, 78).

That the 'remove' was known in the Middle Ages is clear from the Cuxham manorial records, which in 1353–4 note payment 'in dictis ferris equinis remouendis et affirmandis per vices' (for removing and fixing the said horseshoes in turn – Harvey 1976, 533). London's price and wage regulations of 1350 referred to above set a price of one halfpenny (or a penny in the case of coursers and war-horses) for 'taking off' a horseshoe (Riley 1868, 246) – its refixing after paring the hoof is presumably included in the price – in contrast with the cost, ranging from a 1½*d.* to 3*d*, for a new shoe. Fleming (1869, 356) quotes one of the early Italian writers on horse manage-

ment, Petrus de Crescentiis (1307), who refers to both putting on new shoes and fixing old shoes with new nails. (Fleming is presumably misled by a misreading and a resultant mistranslation of his Latin original to write of fastening a new shoe 'with either old or new nails' – an obvious impossibility.) At Cuxham, horseshoe nails were always bought in larger quantities than the number of horseshoes would seem to warrant: 13 shoes and 200 nails 'pro affris ferrandis' and 11 shoes and 100 nails 'pro equis carectariis ferrandis' in 1352 (Harvey 1976, 525), 60 shoes and 700 nails in 1353–4 (ibid. 533), 36 shoes and 400 nails in 1354–5 (ibid. 547); by the manner of their removal horseshoe nails cannot be reused, and the proportions of around 12 nails to each shoe purchased would seem to allow at least one remove for each shoe. A similar proportion is found in Henry III's massive order to 'the good men of Gloucester' in April 1242, to supply 10,000 horseshoes and 100,000 nails and deliver them to Portsmouth by Easter (*Calendar of Liberate Rolls* 1930, 118), while Hewitt (1983, 5) notes a 1356 purchase of 2,000 horseshoes with 20,000 nails, for the Black Prince's campaign in France.

The extreme wear shown in some medieval shoes discussed here – the many cases in which just a single branch survives, due to breakage at the toe which has nearly worn through – illustrates a very poor standard of care. Several of the shoes are so worn at the toe that the hoof itself would have been eroded (see, for example, Fig 60), and the modern practice of frequent removes

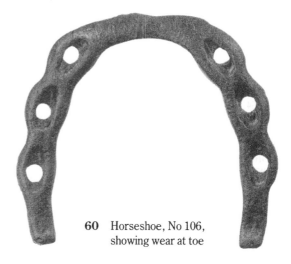

60 Horseshoe, No 106,
        showing wear at toe

and timely replacement of worn shoes was clearly not universal in the Middle Ages.

For a shoe to be removed the *clenches* should be snapped or cut off to allow the nails to be withdrawn; shoes retaining clenched nails are likely to represent accidental losses – though clearly a clumsy farrier might pull a shoe off by main strength with the nails still fastened (a practice not unknown in the 19th century according to Youatt 1880, 429).

MEDIEVAL HORSESHOES FROM THE CITY OF LONDON

The full catalogue of horseshoes below comprises only medieval shoes from sites included within the current publication programme; that is, sites excavated in the City of London on behalf of the Museum of London, and its predecessor the Guildhall Museum, from 1972 to 1983. Nearly 230 horseshoes and fragments (mostly the latter) are listed. These include, for completeness, a number of shoes already published in an earlier volume devoted to 'Saxo-Norman' finds (Pritchard 1991, 253–4).

In the discussion of typology, chronology and size which follow, the opportunity has been taken to draw on a rather larger sample. This includes also the horseshoes from some excavations since 1983 and horseshoes in the Museum of London's core collections. Of post-1983 sites, those listed in Table 7 were included in this survey.

Table 7: Horseshoes from post-1983 sites included in survey

Site	No of horseshoes	Site	No of horseshoes
LEA84	1	CAP86	1
SSL84	1	AMB87	1
TIG84	1	GAG87	3
FST85	2	NEB87	2
GDH85	2	SBG87	1
ABS86	1	PIC87	3
BOY86	9	LSO88	1
MOG86	1	OPS88	1
SUN86	20	ORM88	1
STO86	2		

Of these sites SUN86 (Sunlight Wharf) and BOY86 (City of London Boys' School) were major waterfront sites producing useful bodies of finds. However, for few of these sites is there as yet detailed and definitive dating, and the dates used in our discussion of type sequences are often based on preliminary spot-dating of ceramic groups. Sites producing only shoes of post-medieval date or type are excluded.

In all, finds from over 50 sites excavated in the City of London between 1972 and 1988 have been included in the statistical summary, among which 12 sites produced five or six horseshoes or more – ranging up to 47 from SWA81 (Swan Lane), 48 from BC72 (Baynard's Castle) and 62 from BWB83 (Billingsgate lorry park, watching brief). As with other finds discussed in this publication and in other volumes in the series, the majority of horseshoes are from the large waterfront sites. Interestingly, although the number of metalwork finds made on the 12 most productive sites varies considerably, overall horseshoes seem regularly to make up between 3% and 5% of all accessioned iron objects on both waterfront and inland sites; only on the Billingsgate lorry park site (BIG82) did the figure fall significantly below this – to just 1%. Unfortunately it is not possible to confirm whether the proportion is consistent throughout the historical period under discussion, or varies in a manner allowing us to draw conclusions about the relative abundance of horses or the frequency with which they were shod at different dates. The rule certainly holds true for Swan Lane (largely ceramic phases 7–9 – c.1200–1350), Baynard's Castle (largely phases 10–11 – c.1330–1400) and the Billingsgate watching brief (largely phases 11–12 – c.1350–1450). At first sight it might seem significant that the site with the lowest proportion of horseshoes, BIG82, is generally earlier (phases 4–7 – c.1050–1230); however, preliminary assessment of material recovered from contractors' spoil from the 'Vintry House' site (VRY89), which produced some 30 horseshoes among finds of largely 11th- and 12th-century date, suggests that the 3% to 5% figure holds true on this site even for the earlier date. Given the different finds recovery techniques adopted at each site, both the variation and the similarities in these figures give room for speculation.

In addition to the recently excavated material,

and particularly in the discussion of shapes, sizes and types of horseshoe, some 55 horseshoes of medieval type in the Museum of London core collections (Department of Early London History and Collections – Medieval Collection) have been considered. These are of course not from archaeologically dated contexts, having been acquired over a period of more than 100 years by the former Guildhall and London Museums, largely from workmen's finds made during redevelopments taking place in central London during the late 19th and early 20th centuries (see for example Guildhall Museum 1908, 59 – where they are published as Roman). Find-spots included for example 'Baynard's Wharf' (adjacent to the Museum of London's BC72 excavation site). Several shoes, including some from Moorfields, were acquired by the Guildhall Museum in 1881 in the collection of John Walker Baily (Sheppard 1991, 26–7), having been illustrated by Walker Baily in his own manuscript catalogue, now in the Guildhall Library (MS 17,151/1). They are comparable with the shoes found on the waterfront sites from Baynard's Castle (1972) to Billingsgate (1982) that form the bulk of the excavated items treated here.

In all, some 360 shoes and fragments from the City of London and its environs were taken into consideration in the survey that follows.

TYPOLOGY

The typology here adopted is essentially that which I first published in a 'datasheet' for the Finds Research Group 700–1700 (Clark 1986). At the time, in order to avoid the inflexible succession of types that might be implied by numeric designations, and the foreseeable difficulty of inserting a new type at a later date in an already sequential system, I adopted, with some reservations, a series of generic names, mostly chronological: 'Pre-Conquest', 'Norman', 'Transitional' and 'Later Medieval'. The chronology has been largely borne out by fuller study of the dating evidence – as is discussed below; the evolution from 'Norman' to 'Later Medieval', which is implied by the term 'Transitional', remains questionable. Since the four main types then envisaged seem to have survived reconsideration without the need to insert additional types into the

sequence, they have now been allocated numbers for ease of reference.

Their salient features are summarised here, as a background to the discussions of the dating evidence and of the possible significance of their size and shape. It should of course be recognised that there is a great degree of variability within the types, and an equal degree of subjectivity in the assignment to particular types of individual (often incomplete and corroded) horseshoes. The generally good condition of shoes from the waterfront sites, however, makes the identification of distinguishing features rather easier than would be the case on many inland sites.

61   Type 1 horseshoe

Type 1 (formerly 'Pre-Conquest')

(See Fig 61.) These shoes are generally of crude appearance, rounded and broad (with an overall width about 100mm), wide-webbed but of thin (3–4mm) metal. Nail-holes, usually three to each branch, are round, up to 7mm or 8mm in diameter, with a large rectangular or ovoid countersinking for the nail-head, which may slightly distort the outer edge of the shoe; in the latter case the shoe may well approach our type 2A below. Nails, where found *in situ*, are of T-shape; it is possible that in some, if not all, cases these represent very worn examples of nails of the so-called fiddle-key form familiar in the following type. Nails of this latter form were certainly found at Coppergate (York) in contexts of similar date to those producing horseshoes of the earliest type (Ottaway 1992, 707, fig 308). Nails seem to have been 'double-clenched' as described below. Shallow calkins occur but are rare; the only example from London with a calkin (No 96) occurs in a phase when it would have been contemporary with the regularly calkined type 2 shoes, and is in any case somewhat anomalous. The form is well shown by the complete shoe from the Museum of London collections seen in

Fig 80, and is Ward's so-called 'Winchester Type' in his typology of 'Iron Age' horseshoes (1941a, 16–19).

Type 2 (formerly 'Norman')

(See Fig 62.) The classic type that Ward (1941a) termed 'Iron Age', these shoes are usually well made of narrow (12mm) but thick (more than 5mm) bar iron, averaging (in our sample) just over 100mm in overall width and weighing in the region of 100–130gm. Nail-holes are punched from the front or ground surface; three to each branch are almost universal, though four are occasionally found on one, presumably the outer, branch. In what is here defined as type 2A the nail-holes are round and of similar size to those of type 1 (Fig 63); in type 2B they are neater and rectangular. In both cases they have deep countersunk slots, widening around the hole and with

62 Type 2 horseshoes – type 2A with round nail-holes (left) and type 2B with rectangular nail-holes (right)

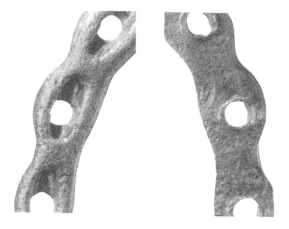

63 Type 2A horseshoe, No 106, showing round nail-holes and indications of punching on reverse

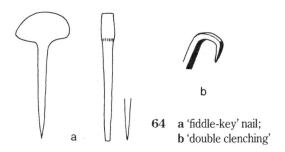

64 **a** 'fiddle-key' nail;
       b 'double clenching'

square or rounded ends. Due to the narrowness and bulk of the metal, the nail-holes – or more truly the countersinking – push the edge of the shoe out to produce the typical 'lobate' wavy edge.

Surviving nails are of so-called fiddle-key form (Fig 64a), with a large head which is semi-circular when seen in profile but of the same thickness as the shank. The shank tapers either to a symmetrical point or to a flat, chisel-like edge. As well as the semi-circular form, nails are known in which the head is of trapezoid form, but still of the same thickness as the shank (for example, Farley 1976, 250, nos 12–13, fig 39 – from an 11th-century midden deposit). The head sits in the long countersinking, protruding by anything up to 5mm, and is often so worn that the nail appears to be T-shaped. To fasten the shoe the nails are 'double-clenched' (Fig 64b), the point being bent over and hammered back into the wall of the hoof.

Calkins are the norm, as indicated above – 91% of shoes of type 2 in our statistical sample have calkins on one or both heels. Calkins of all three types are represented: where the method of manufacture is clear, 9% have thickened or upset heels and 26% have heels bent at right angles, but a considerable majority (64%) have heels 'folded' as in Fig 59c. Of the latter there are one or two examples of the 'double-fold' or 'rolled' type illustrated in Fig 59d. Occasionally the calkins on the two heels are of different types.

Type 3 (formerly 'Transitional')

(See Fig 65.) These are in general heavier shoes, averaging about 220gm, with a broader web (30mm at the widest point is not uncommon) and an overall width around 108mm. They have rectangular nail-holes with narrow rectangular countersunk slots as on type 2B, but have smooth

65 Type 3 horseshoes

rather than wavy profiles; the margin between the nail-holes and the outer edge is sometimes quite broad (Fig 65, right). The number of nail-holes is often increased, four on one branch and three on the other or four/four being not uncommon. Of complete shoes in the sample four have three/three nail-holes, three have four/three and two have four/four; if shoes where half survives and the nail-holes of one complete branch can be counted are included in the reckoning, instances of three nail-holes per branch exceed those of four nail-holes by 20 to 13. There are two examples with five nail-holes on one branch. Modern practice would suggest that where one branch has more holes than the other it is the outer branch that is so treated (Hickman & Humphrey 1988, 67); and compare the 'experienc'd farrier's' comment of 1678 – 'you shall set five Nails on the outside of his Hoof, and four on the inside, because he weareth more without than within' (R 1720, 122).

Fiddle-key nails are found, as in the fine example in the Museum of London collections from the Thames foreshore at Queenhithe illustrated in Fig 83 (acc no 82.411), but so is another type (Fig 66a), which combines a rectangular expanding head with ears which sit in the countersunk slot.

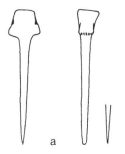

b

66 **a** nail with expanded head and ears; **b** 'spiral' clenching

a

Nails of this type were noted in association with type 3 horseshoes at Winchester (Goodall 1990, 1056); Goodall recognised the type at Waltham Abbey (1973, 174, fig 13, type B) and quotes parallels from generally 13th-century contexts. Fig 66a is based upon a complete and unused nail of this type found in contractors' spoil from the Billingsgate lorry park site (BIG82 and BWB83) and now in a private collection.

Nails are normally double-clenched, but there are examples (Nos 161, 163–4), all from contexts of 1270–1350 (ceramic phase 9) where the tip has been deliberately twisted into a spiral (Fig 66b; see Fig 67). This odd technique, not apparently recorded elsewhere, may have been intended to

67 Fragment of type 3 horseshoe, No 163, showing eared nails with 'spiral' clench

allow the tightening of a nail which has worked loose. With a normal clench, a loose nail must be withdrawn and replaced by a new nail; in theory at least, the tip of a spirally clenched nail can be drawn further through the hoof by grasping it with pincers, then twisted tighter. Whether this technique would successfully serve such a purpose is not clear – it seems to be found only on shoes of this type in phase 9 (1270–1350) and on shoes of type 4 in phases 10–11 (1330–1400) and once in phase 12 (1400–50). It may however be the explanation of the strange portrayal of the hooves of Thomas Becket's horse in Canterbury pilgrim badges of 14th-century date, where a series of small *circles* apparently represent the ends of the nails showing through the wall of the hoof (Fig 68).

Calkins are less common than on type 2 – 78% of the type 3 sample have calkins on one or both heels. 'Folded' calkins are again the most common (just under 50% of instances), the rest being made up of upset and right-angle heels in more or less equal numbers.

69   Type 4 horseshoes

68   Pilgrim badge of St Thomas Becket of
Canterbury, early 14th century, showing the
archbishop on horseback; the close-up of the
horse's hoof (below) shows circles, perhaps
representing the nail clenches (MoL acc no
A24766/1)

These shoes are one of Ward's 'Derived
Types', represented particularly by the group
from the West Orchard site in Coventry (Ward
1941a, 20–3 fig 4), discussed further below.

Type 4 (formerly 'Later Medieval')

(See Fig 69.) Horseshoes of type 4 weigh on
average about 230gm, with a broad web (regularly 30mm at the widest point), sometimes tapering
slightly towards the heels. They are less easy to
characterise than shoes of types 1 to 3, though
the feature which distinguishes them from the

other types is very clear: the form of the nail-
holes and nails. The nail-holes have no separate
countersunk slot for the nail-head, but are square
or rectangular and taper inwards in profile from
the ground-surface of the shoe. Both square and
rectangular holes – the latter normally with sides
in the proportions 3:2 – are found; indeed, one
shoe (No 261) has both! Overall, shoes with
square holes outnumber those with rectangular
holes by 64 to 34. Both forms occur throughout
the period in which shoes of type 4 are found,
from phase 9 (1270–1350) to phase 12 (1400–50).
However, with only one example from a phase 9
context, rectangular holes (the standard in post-
medieval times) seem to have a generally later
distribution than square holes – largely post-
1350.

As in type 3 shoes, nail-holes are usually
arranged three/three, four/three, or four/four –
though some examples with a different arrangement are discussed below. Of complete shoes,
those with the three/three arrangement slightly
outnumber those with four/four; if incomplete
shoes are taken into consideration there are 44
examples where a single branch has three nail-
holes, only 26 with four nail-holes.

Nails have a square or rectangular head which
seems generally to have stood proud of the shoe,
though often worn level – some may have been
intentionally flush with the surface; there are
slight shoulders which taper to match the hole.
The shank of the nail is rectangular in section,
often quite broad (to suit a rectangular hole), and
tapers to a chisel edge (fig 70a). The spiral
clenching previously described is found on a
number of shoes; all are of phase 11 or 10–11
(1330–1400) apart from one of phase 12 (1400–
50), suggesting that the spiral clench is very
much a 14th-century technique – see Nos 212,
214, 222, 229, 238, 239, 250 and 276.

The normal clench is of 'modern' type, the point of each nail being snapped or twisted off before the remaining stub is hammered down flush with the surface of the hoof (Fig 70b, which shows two slightly different forms).

As indicated above, shoes of this type have calkins less frequently than the others, but still on more than 50% of examples; 'folded' calkins are rare (in contrast to types 2 and 3), the norm being either 'right-angle' (42% of recorded calkins) or 'thickened' heels (48%) (see Fig 59a and b).

Within the type it is difficult to define subdivisions. Ward (1939) called it his 'medieval or pack-horse group', but recognised two sub-types within it to which he assigned the names 'Dove' and 'Guildhall' types. The former (Ward 1939, 158) was named from examples found in the River Dove, Staffordshire, in 1831 under circumstances described by Fleming (1869, 410–18) and dated by him to events of 1322. The latter was based on three shoes which Ward was shown at the Guildhall Museum, London (Ward 1939, 161–2, nos 69–71, pl XXV). These three shoes (Museum of London acc nos 10948, 11692, 11693) came from two sites excavated during the construction of the headquarters of the Anglo-Persian Oil Company in Finsbury Circus in the 1920s (see Lambert 1921, 75–110 for the general background – the second two shoes came from a site in West Street not discussed by Lambert). The information that Ward apparently gleaned from the then curator Quintin Waddington, that these shoes came from levels that could definitely be dated between 1415 and 1511, cannot be substantiated from surviving records; however, such a date would not be inconsistent with Lambert's description and the range of other material from the sites (Lambert 1921, 98–104).

Ward's criteria by which he distinguished his Dove and Guildhall types are not clear from his text and illustrations, except that the latter shoes tend to be heavier, with broader webs and usually four nail-holes on one or both branches. Sparkes (1976, 14) and others seem to have assumed that the Guildhall type is characterised by an inner profile approaching that of a pointed arch. This is certainly seen quite dramatically in two of those from Finsbury Circus that Ward illustrates (1939, nos 69–70 – the former is also illustrated in London Museum 1940, 117, no 5, fig 37). However, it is not a feature that Ward himself comments on, and is certainly not common to all those to which he applies the term 'Guildhall'. Among those catalogued below it appears in Nos 222 and 235 and others described in the catalogue as having an 'angular inner profile'.

It is not evident that the distinction between Dove and Guildhall is a tenable one. As the illustrations here show, the width of the web on a type 4 shoe is extremely variable, and Ward's chosen examples do not assist us to define other criteria by which to assign the London shoes to either camp. As for the angular inner profile noted by Sparkes as typifying the Guildhall shoe, it is lacking in the vast majority of shoes considered here (about 90%). There may be some chronological significance in this feature, since the angular type is more common in the ceramic phase 9 to 10–11 (1270–1400) (up to one-third of a small number of type 4 shoes in these contexts) than in phases 11 and 12 (1350–1450); it is notable that examples of this type from Gomeldon, Wiltshire, come from a context dated by the excavators to the end of the 13th century (Musty & Algar 1986, 154, nos 40–41, fig 14). On the other hand the examples from Finsbury Circus suggest the presence of the feature in quite exaggerated form in the 15th century. Where the angle exists it appears as a distinct kink or fold in the web (Fig 71), clearly arising from the method of forming the shoe, and perhaps no more than the result of a final reshaping of a broad shoe to fit a narrow hoof. Such reshaping would obviously distort the broad toe web of a type 4 shoe more than that of the earlier types. In view of the uncertain basis of this Dove/Guildhall distinction the terminology is best avoided.

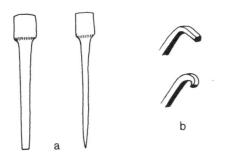

70 **a** tapering nail with rectangular head; **b** standard 'modern'-style clenching

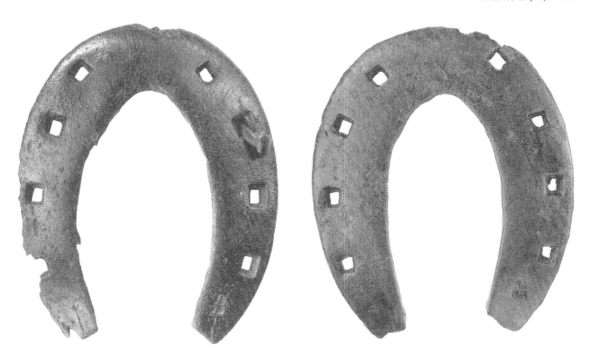

71 Type 4 horseshoes, Nos 222 (left) and 235 (right); well-made shoes with angular inner profile and punched marks on heels

72 Close-ups of marks (shield with cross) on horseshoes Nos 222 (left) and 235 (right)

73 Fragment of type 4 horseshoe, No 238, with punched 'star' or 'sun' mark

However, a small number of shoes do stand out as different – those in which the nail-holes are not grouped along the branches of the shoe, but spaced more or less regularly around the edge, including the toe area (where they are subject to extreme wear). Nos 199, 207, 215, 231, 234, 236 and 274 in the catalogue below are of this type. Similar horseshoes seem to be rare in the archaeological record from other British sites. These shoes have no other distinctive feature in common and cover the complete spectrum of contexts from phase 9 to phase 12; they cannot at present be defined as a separate type or sub-group.

Four of the type 4 horseshoes carry marks, stamped during manufacture into the ground surface of one heel – Nos 212, 222, 235 and 238. All are from the BC72 site from contexts of 1330 to 1400. Nos 222 and 235 are very similar in form and size and have the same mark, a shield bearing a cross (Figs 71, 72, 87, 88). No 212 has a disc within a square, 238 an open sun or star (Figs 73, 86, 88). Maker's marks, though required by the blacksmiths' ordinances of 1372, are not common on medieval ironwork (Riley 1868, 361–2; Clark 1988). A fullered horseshoe with stamps on both heels (Museum of London acc no A24957) is published in London Museum 1940, 116, no 4, fig 37; found in the City Ditch at Aldersgate, it is probably of early 17th-century date (for its form cf. Goodall 1983b, 251, no 220, fig 9). Otherwise, stamped horseshoes seem to be rare or absent from the archaeological record, though there are undated examples in the British and Ashmolean Museums.

Notably all our marked type 4 horseshoes are from one dump group associated with a stone-walled dock known as the 'East Watergate', which has been singled out in earlier research published in this series (Grew & de Neergaard 1988, 29, 90; Egan & Pritchard 1991, 3) for the quality of the material it contained; the suggestion has been made (ibid.; discussed more fully by Dyson 1989, 10–12) that these finds might reflect the presence nearby of the Royal Wardrobe, the king's main purchasing and supply agency in London. These marks – the shield could be read as a cross of St George – could perhaps indicate horseshoes supplied to royal order.

One eccentric item is worthy of comment; the 'miniature' horseshoe No 197 (Fig 86). From a phase 9 (1270–1350) context, this resembles in every respect a type 4 shoe, with nail-holes arranged three/two and with folded calkins, but it is less than half the normal size. It has never been used, and it is hard to imagine any animal to which it could have been fitted. On the other hand it would not function as a shoe cleat, and there is no other obvious practical use for it. Sample, trial-piece or blacksmith's *jeu d'esprit* it might be, or lucky charm – for belief in the luck-bringing and evil-averting powers of the horseshoe has a long history (references in the late 14th century and in 1507 to the luck of finding a horseshoe, and in 1584 to the efficacy of a horseshoe nailed to the threshold in discouraging witches are quoted by Opie & Tatem 1989, 202–4).

CHRONOLOGY

Of the 360 or so horseshoes included in our study group as defined above, about half can be assigned both to a type and to a date provided by their archaeological context (either a ceramic phase or a pottery spot date for the context). From these it is possible to construct a chronological sequence for our typology and to compare it with the published evidence from elsewhere.

The sequence is summarised in Figs 74 and 75. Fig 74 shows the frequency with which each type of shoe appears in a phase or group of phases, expressed as a percentage of the whole sample. The early 'pre-Conquest' phases have been omitted from this diagram since the whole period 900–1050 in London is represented by only three horseshoes – one of them being an apparently precocious example of a type 2A shoe in a context with pottery dating of c.900–1000; no horseshoes are recorded from phases 2 and 3. In the case of phase 10, which overlaps other phases, the figures for each type of shoe have been divided between those adjacent phases.

In interpreting this chart it should be borne in mind that the number of shoes identified within each phase varies considerably, and is generally far too low for reliable statistical use. For example, the figure for phase 8, only four shoes in all, has been combined with the 10 in the slightly more populous phase 7. Similarly, to provide reasonably comparable figures, those for types 2A and 2B have been combined, together with

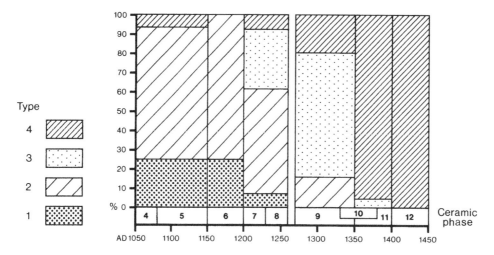

74   Types of horseshoe: relative frequency of each type by date and ceramic phase – phase 4 and later

those for shoes of uncertain type 2. The total number of shoes within each of the blocks shown in the chart was as follows: *phases 4 and 5 – 16; phase 6 – 8; phases 7 and 8 – 14; phase 9 – 51; phase 11 – 65; phase 12 – 8.* Only in phases 9 and 11 is the quantity of finds truly significant, but, if treated with caution, the diagram seems to reflect an actual chronological process.

In Fig 75 the overall chronological span of each type is indicated (including those of the related

types 2A and 2B which are here differentiated) with, emphasised, the period during which the type is predominant (that is, in which it represents 50% or more of all horseshoes present in the sample). The sequence is clear, as is the consecutive but overlapping distribution of types 2A and 2B. This sequence mirrors that demonstrated by published finds from elsewhere. There is clearly a preponderance of type 1 shoes at the beginning, followed in succession by types 2 and

75   Types of horseshoe: overall chronological range of each type and period during which each is predominant and comprises 50% or more of all shoes present

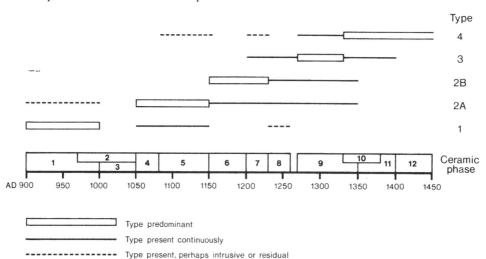

3, and, overwhelmingly, type 4 at the end. In each case there is a considerable overlap; Phase 9 (1270–1350) in particular is noticeable for the range of types of shoe apparently in near contemporaneous use – or at least being dumped at a similar period.

Some of this overlap might reflect residuality. Yet, as has been stated elsewhere, there is little evidence for the presence of large quantities of residual material within the waterfront dumps which provide the bulk of the finds considered in this volume (discussed further in Egan & Pritchard 1991, 1–2); it is clear that much of the refuse deposited there had been discarded only recently, and the obvious assumption must be that those shoes found in a particular context had been in use on horses only very shortly before.

Yet a case might be made for assigning a longer lifespan to some everyday ironwork (usually less intrinsically datable than the smaller more decorative finds discussed by Egan & Pritchard) – a lifespan extended by its survival as (unused) scrap before it was finally discarded. Scrap-iron was presumably used extensively by the medieval smith (though not mentioned by Geddes (1991) nor by Salzman (1952, 286–317)). The Anglo-Scandinavian period iron-working site at Coppergate (York) yielded quantities of broken, clearly scrap, iron as well as 'new' iron in the form of bars and strips (Ottaway 1992, 492–511).

Documentary evidence for use of scrap is scanty. Certainly Richard Crips, a 15th-century London wheelwright and cartbuilder, who owned smithing tools and equipment and seems himself to have manufactured most of the ironwork required for the vehicles he built, possessed no stock of new iron; his stock of raw material apparently consisted only of the '1 cwt 1 qr 8 lb of old iron' listed when an inventory of his property was made in 1454 (Clark 1984, 17). Woodward (1985, 185–6) refers to 16th-century blacksmiths' inventories which occasionally list old as well as new iron (though usually the two are not distinguished) and to the development by the 16th century of large-scale trade in scrap-iron. The scrap-heap of iron waiting for reuse has of course been a prominent feature of blacksmiths' yards in much more recent times, and a practice recorded among, particularly, rural farriers has been the forging of old horseshoes into new (two worn-out shoes would make one new

one – Hogg 1964, 99). Evans (1960, 194) quotes the Suffolk blacksmith Clifford Race: 'New iron wouldn't do for shoes . . . It would be too soft. The more you hammer iron the tougher it gets; so the old shoes welded and hammered together lasted much longer.'

A long-established smith's scrap-heap might well contain at the bottom material that had been there for a generation or more; if such a heap was finally cleared, discarded with more recent rubbish and dumped behind the riverside revetments, only when the forge site was demolished or used for another purpose, its contents could well upset the careful chronologies that we are attempting to establish.

It is thus possible that worn-out horseshoes (and indeed other obvious scrap material) may exceptionally make an appearance in contexts of a much later date, where everything else is a recent discard.

If an argument can be made for the occasional shoe extending the apparent lifespan of a type, the 'precocious' appearance of a type in a context considerably earlier than the bulk of finds is more worrying. For example, the bulk of type 4 shoes are found from phase 9 (after *c.*1270) onwards. There are, however, two apparently earlier examples, one in phase 7 (1200–30) and one (though its classification as a type 4 is perhaps uncertain) in phase 5 (1080–1150); there are none in the adjoining phases 6 and 8. In terms of our typology and the dating of comparable specimens from elsewhere they are intrusive at this early date; perhaps they were also intrusive in the archaeological sense. The undoubted type 2A shoe (No 99) from an apparent 10th-century context, together with another of the same type (No 98) which has also been dated early, present a similar problem; some doubt may be entertained about the dating of the latter – see the catalogue entry below.

Type 1

Though the sparse late Saxon evidence from London does not in itself allow certainty, finds from elsewhere confirm a 'pre-Conquest' date for the beginning of this type. Finds from 10th-century and early/mid-11th century contexts are reported from a number of sites, mostly urban: Cheddar – Goodall 1979c, 267–9, nos 7 (assigned to a date 'pre-930') & 94 (*c.*1000), fig 91; Oxford

– Goodall 1983a, 65, no 10, fig 15, fiche C6 (mid-11th century); Portchester – Cunliffe 1976, 197, no 9, fig 131 ('Late Saxon'); Thetford – Goodall 1984a, 103–5, figs 143–4 (no specific dates quoted); York – MacGregor 1982, 83, no 437, fig 44 (10th century); and Ottaway 1992, 707–9, fig 308 (late 10th and 11th century). The type was recognised by Goodall at Winchester (1990, 1054–5) and in one case (ibid. 1057, no 3939, fig 340) could be assigned to a late 9th-century context; others came from 10th-century contexts (nos 3940–3).

A single complete example from London was found during excavations within the Tower of London (Clark in Chapman 1985, 66, no 31, fig 34), in a deposit related to terracing operations of the mid-11th century which apparently predate the earliest Norman works on the site (Parnell 1985, 23); in that note, written many years before it finally appeared in print, I expressed uncertainty about the dating of the shoe in question. It is now clear that it is a good example of a type 1 shoe in its appropriate chronological context.

In addition to the published examples, two horseshoes of this type in the Ashmolean Museum (acc nos 1954.21, 1954.22) were found during roadworks in Cornmarket Street, Oxford; a late Saxon scramasax from the same site may have been associated with them. Two complete specimens, presumably from London, in the Roach Smith Collection in the British Museum (acc nos MLA 56, 7–1, 2699 & 2700) are totally without context. The Museum of London shoe (acc no 16248 – Fig 80) comes from a site in Barge Yard, Bucklersbury, a Walbrook valley site (now occupied by part of Bucklersbury House) which was developed in 1879 after the building of Queen Victoria Street. The site certainly produced Saxon or early Norman material – spearheads (acc no 7769, possibly 7732) and a small scramasax-form knife (acc no 15262). However, it also produced later medieval objects, including a horseshoe of our type 2B – the type to which a 12th- to 13th-century date is assigned below; the finds from the Barge Yard site no more guarantee the early date of the type 1 horseshoe than does the hoard of 60 coins of Alfred the Great found nearby (Stott 1991, 288 and references therein), though they certainly reflect late Saxon activity in the area.

The largest single group of shoes of this type, however, is that published by Ward in 1941 in his discussion of the 'Iron Age horseshoe' (1941a, 16–19), the 'type specimens' of his 'Winchester Type' shoe. Found during building excavations in Winchester at the city bridge and the east gate, the shoes came from the peat and silt filling of old river channels, and according to Ward 'the associated finds . . . are predominantly Saxon'. Ward Perkins (1941, 144–6) disputed both the association and the date of the associated finds – 'the majority belonged undoubtedly to the Middle Ages and later', a view confirmed by Alison Goodall from her study of the material (information from Ian Goodall). We cannot draw this group into the discussion of the date of the type; however, on the basis of our other evidence we can surely conclude that Ward was in general terms correct!

The two sole examples from London of this type of horseshoe found in definitely 'pre-Conquest' contexts and included in the catalogue below (Nos 87, 95) cannot be dated very closely. The contexts are of ceramic phase 1 (10th century) rather than later – in one case (Ironmonger Lane – No 87) being sealed by phase 2 and 3 deposits (early 11th century) (Horsman, Milne & Milne 1988, 64–5). Thus the London finds need not predate the single late 9th-century example from Winchester referred to above, which is clearly one of the earliest safely dated horseshoes from the post-Roman period. However, Ottaway (1992, 709) refers to a fragmentary horseshoe from a well-stratified 8th- to 9th-century context at Wicken Bonhunt (Essex). I am grateful to Dr Ottaway for information on this item prior to its publication (in Goodall & Ottaway forthcoming, sf437). (From a drawing provided by Ottaway, the one surviving nail-hole on the Wicken Bonhunt shoe appears rectangular and atypical for this early period – in isolation from its secure context the shoe might well have been assigned to a later medieval date.)

An end-date for the type is not easily defined. Finds from 11th-century contexts outside London are listed above. From Winchester, Goodall reports one from a context of late 11th- to early 12th-century date (1990, 1057, no 3945, fig 340). His no 3959, which he suggests is a residual example of this type in a context of mid- to late 13th-century date (ibid. 1055, 1059, fig 341) is

surely one of our type 2A with wavy edge –
though still probably residual. He draws attention
(ibid. 1054, fig 339) to the likelihood that many of
the Winchester horseshoes are residual. The
presence of two dozen horseshoes with countersunk nail-holes (that is, types 1 to 3) in 15th-
century contexts and even later (ibid. 1066) can
have no other explanation, and the Winchester
evidence for the date when this or any other type
went out of use is unsatisfactory.

The type is absent at Castle Acre Castle
(Norfolk), a stone house of the late 11th century
converted to a keep in the 1140s (Coad &
Streeten 1982, 191–2), where finds included
horseshoes of type 2A from conversion period
deposits and of type 2B from the later occupation
(Goodall 1982, 230, nos 126–9 (type 2A), and 130
(type 2B), fig 41). However, a shoe from Woody
Bay (Isle of Wight), published by Ward Perkins
(1940, 115, no 7, fig 36), may from the illustration
be a type 1; if so, its context (in a midden with
12th-century pottery) suggests continuation of
the type.

Our London evidence for the 11th century and
later (Fig 74) comprises two type 1 shoes from
phase 4 (1050–80) contexts, two from phase 5
(1080–1150) and two from phase 6 (1150–1200)
(including a number from contexts for which only
a spot date is available) – something like a quarter
of all the shoes from these contexts. The single
example in a phase 8 (1230–60) context (a fragment whose type is not in fact certain, No 97) is
perhaps best disregarded. This distribution suggests that the type continued in use alongside the
type 2A shoe for a considerable period.

Given the possibility of the presence of residual
material in the form of scrap-iron, discussed
above, this late extension of the type may be
misleading. Yet the most obvious reading of the
London evidence must be that horseshoes of this
earliest type persisted in use into the 12th century.

Types 2A and 2B

Horseshoes of this 'wavy-edged' or 'lobate' form
were familiar in museum collections long before
they could be securely dated. Distinctive enough
to attract the notice of the layperson as well as
the antiquarian if found by chance, they made
their way into 19th- and early 20th-century collections, often labelled 'Romano–British'. In the
1940s Ward Perkins drew attention to shoes of
the type in apparent 12th-century contexts (London Museum 1940, 114–15, nos 2–5, fig 36; Ward
Perkins 1941, 146–7), and the consensus of
evidence from more recent excavations is on that
century as the central date for the type. The
evidence from Castle Acre Castle has already
been referred to above: type 2A associated with
building works of *c*.1140 and type 2B in the
subsequent occupation layers. At Walton (Aylesbury) a fine complete shoe of type 2A almost
identical to our No 119 below came from a
ditch-fill for which the dating evidence included a
coin of 1102–4 in mint condition (Farley 1976,
240–1, no 2, fig 35); the same report includes
another type 2 (2A?) shoe from a 12th-century pit
(ibid. 268, no 14, fig 49). Other sites include
Exeter (Goodall 1984b, 338, no 30, fig 189 – 12th
century – and no 33 – late 13th/early 14th
century); Cheddar (Goodall 1979c, 267, nos 128,
152, fig 91 – early 13th century); and Oxford
(Goodall 1980, 191 and fiche C10, no 59, fig 31 –
late 12th/early 13th century – and no 60 –
mid-13th century), indicating a continuation of the
type through the 13th century.

At Winchester Goodall dates the type from the
late 11th to the 13th century (1990, 1055–6) but
does not distinguish between those with round
and those with rectangular nail-holes. Though he
catalogues two from early/mid-14th century contexts (ibid. 1059, nos 3964–5, fig 341) his earlier
caveat concerning residual finds should be borne
in mind.

Leaving aside Ward's 'Iron Age' examples, the
earliest horseshoe of type 2 from a well-dated
English context known to me is our No 99, dated
to the 10th century by the site evidence. This
single shoe creates something of a problem in
establishing a chronology. Another clearly pre-
Norman example of the type is published by
Ottaway (1992, 709, fiche 2:G12, no 3851) from a
context of early to mid-11th-century date at York;
Ottaway also refers to another shoe with the
wavy edge of our type 2 from Goltho (Lincolnshire) dated to the period 1000–80 (ibid.).

Unfortunately it is often unclear from published
illustrations and descriptions whether a shoe of
this type has round or rectangular nail-holes – the
feature by which we differentiate types 2A and
2B; indeed in the case of a corroded shoe the

distinction may not be evident even on X-ray, while fragmentary heels may often be recognised as of type 2 but broken at the first nail-hole. Among our London finds, where it is possible to recognise the form of nail-hole a chronological difference between the two subgroups is evident (Fig 75). Type 2A is predominant in ceramic phases 4 and 5 (1050–1150); type 2B first appears during phase 6 (1150–1200) and outnumbers type 2A thereafter. However, shoes of both types are still found side by side in phase 9 (1270–1350), though considerably outnumbered by type 3 shoes. In view of what has been said above about the possibility of survival in smiths' scrap-heaps extending the apparent currency of particular types of shoe, we must also allow that type 2 shoes in phase 9 contexts could be residual.

In an English context, then, the designation of these shoes as 'Norman' seems not inappropriate (though using the term purely to define a period and one with an uncommonly extended range). They are hardly known before the Norman Conquest but common thereafter; they predominate throughout the 12th century and are replaced by a heavier, more developed type of shoe (type 3) at some time during the 13th century. The British evidence cannot of course prove that the type is also Norman in the sense of being an introduction from Normandy. The type is certainly known on the Continent at a period contemporary with its use in England (see for example Herrnbrodt 1958, no 79, fig 9 and Halbout et al. 1987, 236–7); much fuller study of the Continental evidence would be needed to ascertain the relative dates of its introduction there and in Britain.

Type 3

Well-dated shoes of this type do not appear to be commonly recorded outside London. Where they are known, a 13th- to 14th-century date seems to be indicated (Goodall 1991, 144, no 546, fig 111 (*c.*1188–1250); Goodall 1984b, 338, nos 31, 32, fig 189 (1250–80), no 34 (1250–1450); Goodall 1976b, 56, no 24, fig 35 (1270–1350); Goodall 1979a, 123, no 107, fig 64 (late 13th to 14th century); Rigold 1967, 109, no Fe6, fig 9 (mid-13th century – a pit-fill possibly of 1247–8 – ibid. 103)). The type appears at Winchester, where Goodall dates its introduction during the 13th

century and notes that it 'continues in use into the fourteenth century, when it was superseded' (1990, 1056). He illustrates only one of the type from Winchester (ibid. 1057, no 3958, fig 341), from a context of the mid- to late 13th century. He also refers to 13th-century examples from the Welsh castles of Rhuddlan and Dyserth (Clwyd) (ibid. 1056) of which Ward Perkins illustrates two from Dyserth, dating them to 1241–63 (London Museum 1940, 117, nos 8, 9, fig 36).

The largest group of shoes of the type previously published is that from Coventry discussed by Ward (1941a, 20–3, fig 4). Found by J B Shelton during works in 1932, they are described by Ward as from 'West Orchard' (a now-vanished street west of the cathedral), coming from the site of an early ford. I am grateful to Ian Soden (Herbert Art Gallery and Museum, Coventry) for the information that Shelton's site in fact lay in Smithford Street (a little to the south of West Orchard) at the crossing of the River Sherbourne. A bridge, Smithford Bridge or later Ram Bridge, seems to have been built during the 13th century to replace the original 'Smythefford' first mentioned in 1161–75 (Stephens 1969, 32). The 22 shoes in Shelton's collection illustrated by Ward (14 of which are now in Coventry Museum – acc nos 49/61/1–14) all seem to be of our type 3; a date for their loss in the last years of the use of the ford in the 13th century, or possibly during the building of the bridge, would seem not inappropriate, though the presence near the site of smiths, implicit in the name of the ford, might be equally significant.

The evidence from London is unequivocal. The type makes its first appearance during ceramic phase 7 (1200–30) alongside type 2 shoes and is predominant during phase 9 (1270–1350) – but must be in the process of replacement towards the end of this phase by type 4 shoes, which already predominate in the overlapping phase 10 (1330–80); only three or four examples occur in phase 11 (1350–1400) and the type is unknown in 15th-century contexts.

Type 4

Horseshoes of this standard 'late medieval' form are frequently reported from 14th- and 15th-century contexts, for example at Southampton (Harvey 1975, 282, no 2048, fig 254 (1300–50));

Oxford (Goodall 1977, 148, nos 59–61, fig 29 (1325–1400)); Exeter (Goodall 1984b, 338, nos 39–40, fig 189 (1450–1500), no 41 (*c.*1500), no 43 (late 15th to 16th century)); Wharram (Goodall 1979a, 123, nos 109–112, figs 64–5 (mid-15th to early 16th century)). Horseshoes with rectangular nail-holes were not common finds on Biddle's Winchester excavations, and many of those published by Goodall (1990, 1066–7) were from post-medieval contexts; the three earliest he illustrates (ibid. 1059, nos 3966–8, fig 342) are dated respectively '13th to 14th century', '14th century' and 'mid-15th century'. What seem to be early occurrences of the form are two from the deserted medieval village of Gomeldon (Wiltshire) illustrated by Musty & Algar (1986, 154, nos 40–41, fig 14); both have the angular inner profile referred to above. They were found with others of similar type in a building which seems to have been in use at the end of the 13th century (ibid. 136). Ward (1939, 156, no 67, pl XXV) illustrates a small example of type 4 from New Winchelsea (Sussex), which he suggests was lost when the new town was laid out in about 1280 – a not impossible date.

The London evidence suggests an introduction of the type during ceramic phase 9 (1270–1350), almost totally replacing type 3 by the end of that phase; in 15th-century contexts it is universal. The sites under review in this volume provide no information on the later continuation of the type; few City of London sites have produced sufficient horseshoes in 16th-century or indeed later contexts to serve as a framework for the study of the post-medieval development of the horseshoe.

SIZE AND SHAPE

The statistics for the size (length, width and weight) of horseshoes in our London sample are summarised in Fig 76, which for each dimension illustrates the overall range, the interquartile range (within which 50% of examples fall) and the median of each type of shoe. The increase in both weight and length associated with types 3 and 4 is noticeable; the two dimensions are of course interrelated – the longer shoe employs more metal – but as the illustrations show the later shoes are also generally thicker and broader webbed. Perhaps more significant are the figures for the overall width, which should reflect closely the size of the horse's hoof.

The relationship is by no means exact; modern practice recognises both 'close fitting', in which the shoe is slightly narrower than the hoof (which may be rasped to fit – bad practice), and 'wide' or 'full fitting', the edge of the shoe extending beyond the hoof by about 1/16th of an inch all round (Hickman & Humphrey 1988, 161–2, 75); early writers recommended 'a straw's breadth' as the width by which the shoe should overlap the foot at the quarters (R 1720, 120, quoting from Thomas Blundeville's work of 1566, see Heymering 1990, 28). It seems likely that type 2 shoes were fitted close – the nail-holes are so close to the outer edge of the shoe; by contrast in some type 3 shoes, such as No 150 (Fig 83), the width of the margin between the nail-holes and the edge suggests that the shoe must have extended some way beyond the hoof.

However, unlike the length, the overall range of recorded widths remains fairly constant through all four types; with the exception of a number of very small (less than 88mm wide) examples of the early type 2A, all fall between the extremes of 92mm and 120mm. Notably, however, both the interquartile range and the median (*c.*110mm) of types 3 and 4 exceed those of the earlier types (with a median of 101–2mm). We might draw one of the following conclusions about the period after the introduction of the new type 3 shoe in the 13th century:

1   that though the overall range of sizes found among horses remained the same, a greater proportion were larger in size; *or*
2   that a similar greater proportion were of breeds with larger feet (since there is no exact correlation between size of hoof and size of horse); *or*
3   simply that the fashion was for full fitting shoes.

The last option, however, would suggest that the horses at the bottom end of the scale in the 13th and 14th centuries were actually smaller or smaller hoofed than those of the preceding period – perhaps unlikely. It might well be that a combination of one or more of these hypotheses is true; their possible significance for the size of the medieval horse is considered in the Introduction to this volume.

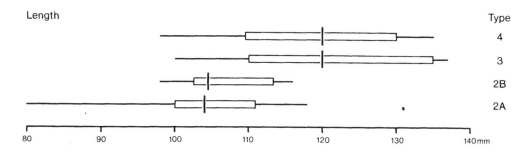

Length

Type
4
3
2B
2A

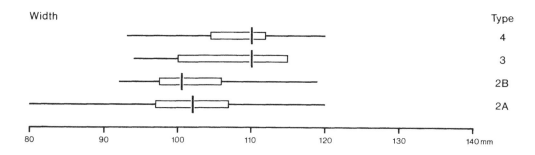

Width

Type
4
3
2B
2A

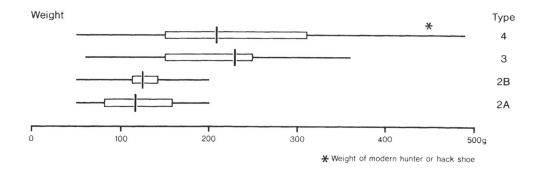

Weight

Type
4
3
2B
2A

✱ Weight of modern hunter or hack shoe

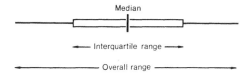

Median

Interquartile range

Overall range

76 Horseshoes, types 2A, 2B, 3 and 4: dimensions and weight of complete shoes

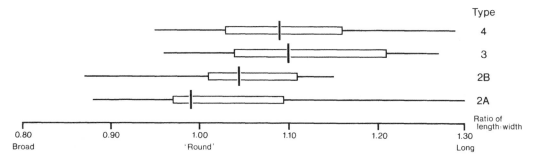

77 Horseshoes, types 2A, 2B, 3 and 4: ratio of length to width of complete shoes

In considering the lengths of surviving shoes it should be borne in mind that wear at the toe can well make a difference of 5mm in the overall recorded length – a factor that hardly affects the width measurement. With that proviso we may note that types 3 and 4 show a much greater difference from type 2 in length than they do in width – a median of *c.*120mm compared to *c.*104mm – and an increased range with a bias towards the higher end of the scale. The length of a shoe need not reflect so closely the form of the hoof as the width should, though it is said to be bad practice to exceed or fall short by very much (Hickman & Humphrey 1988, 162 suggest 3mm as the maximum by which the heels of the shoe may extend beyond the hoof). Heymering (1990, 338), a practising farrier as well as bibliographer, holds to the view that long heels are no bad thing: 'Shoes are more frequently pulled because the heels are not long enough.'

This difference in length is reflected in another set of statistics summarised in Fig 77 – the ratio of length to overall width. Where this ratio is '1' the shoe is as wide as it is long (and might be termed 'round'); 'long and narrow' shoes will have a higher index figure (around 1.10 to 1.20), 'broad' shoes a lower figure (perhaps 0.90). Clearly only complete shoes can be subject to such calculations (83 in the current sample) and both wear at the toe and any distortion of the shape through damage either in use or in the ground may have a major effect on the calculated ratio. In the illustrated graph the line representing the overall range of type 2A shoes in particular is very misleading; its extension to 1.30 at the upper end is due entirely to the presence of one clearly distorted example. Excluding this one the

upper limit is 1.17, much closer to the 1.15 of type 2B. However, although based on a small sample and no doubt statistically unsound the figures are indicative of some broad trends.

There is clearly a distinction between types 3 and 4, with an overall higher range and a median index of around 1.10, and types 2A and B, which – while having a similar overall range to each other – show distinct medians of 0.99 (type 2A) and 1.05 (type 2B). The low median of type 2A shoes is due entirely to the presence of a cluster of shoes which, though varying in overall size (with widths of between 100mm and 120mm), are of very similar proportions. In the sample of 32 complete shoes 10 show a ratio of length to breadth of between 0.96 and 0.98 – slightly wider than they are long. No other obvious factor links these 'broad' type 2A shoes. The majority are from the old Museum of London collections; for only two of the excavated shoes is there external dating – to ceramic phase 4 and ceramic phase 6–9 respectively.

It is noted elsewhere that the extreme length and narrowness of some shoes from 13th- and 14th-century contexts suggests they may be intended for use on mules. However, the front and rear hooves of a horse also differ in both shape and proportion (Fig 78). In the case of a modern horseshoe, fitted closely to the profile of the hoof, there is little difficulty in identifying whether it is a front or hind shoe; the distinction between the 'round' front shoe and the 'oval' hind shoe is usually apparent. The distinction is far from clear in the case of the medieval horseshoes considered here, as the illustrations show. Subjectively, one may conclude that, for example, No 106 is a front shoe, No 119 a hind shoe. An

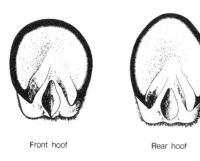

78 Typical shapes of front and rear hooves of modern
horse (after Hickman & Humphrey 1988, fig 2.35)

attempt to define the distinction numerically,
however, is unsuccessful. We might assume that
those shoes in which the ratio of length to width is
high are intended for use on the hind hoof;
unfortunately a histogram of the length/width
ratios of 44 horseshoes of types 3 and 4 (Fig 79)
does not show the bimodal distribution that one
might hope for, with clear peaks representing
'standard' front and hind shoes – though the slight
peak around 0.97 surely comprises front shoes.
When the statistics for type 2 shoes are added to
the diagram, the peak at 0.97 becomes dominant.
This is due to the large number of 'broad' shoes of
type 2A referred to previously. Given the

·documentary evidence for the shoeing of horses
on the front feet only (see the section titled 'The
function of the horseshoe' above) we might conclude that this was a practice more common in the
early period represented by type 2A shoes,
leading to a larger proportion of obvious 'front'
shoes of this type.

Within our type 4 a number of shoes are of the
so-called (by Ward 1939) Guildhall group with an
angular inner profile – showing a slight kink on the
inner margin of the web at the toe. This must
surely be due to cold shaping of the shoe to fit a
narrow, and presumably rear, hoof. Hickman &
Humphrey (1988, 163–7, especially figs 7.61,
7.63) describe the practice and show a farrier
'closing the toe' of a shoe by hammering it on the
side; compare also Hogg (1964, 94–5). There
may have been little real difference at the manu-
facturing stage between front and hind shoes –
though between 1381 and 1399 the London
Bridgewardens were paying less for hind shoes
(1½*d*.) than for front (2*d*.), and consistently
ordering more of them (information from Brian
Spencer, based on a study of the surviving
Bridgewardens' Account Rolls for those years).
The final shaping to suit a front or hind hoof could
be left to the farrier; the degree to which the shoe
accurately fitted the hoof to which it was nailed
was dependent on his level of skill and care.

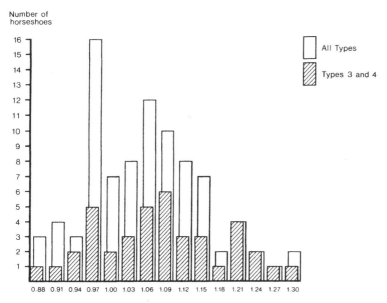

79 Histogram: numbers of
horseshoes with given ratio
of overall length to width

Catalogue

Horseshoes are listed according to the typology established above. Within each type the sequence is basically chronological, according to the *ceramic phase* assigned to each context; within each phase entries are ordered alphabetically by site code. Contexts for which only a *spot date* exists have been inserted in appropriate places in the sequence. Shoes from contexts which were unstratified or for which no date is available have been placed at the end of each type sequence. Shoes whose incompleteness or condition makes assignment to a specific type impossible are listed at the end.

Entries are tabulated under the following headings: *catalogue number*, *site code* and *accession number*, *context number*, *date* (ceramic phase or spot date; '+' indicates an unstratified context), *completeness*, *dimensions*, *presence of nail(s)*, *number of nail-holes* (left/right), *type of calkins* (left/right), *Fig number*, *notes*.

Under 'completeness', the term 'part' implies the survival of about half or more of the original shoe, usually enough to allow its overall form and size to be estimated; a 'fragment' is anything smaller. Where the shoe is complete enough to warrant it, some or all appropriate measurements (overall length, overall width, thickness and weight) have been recorded. Modern farriers' practice is to measure the length of a horseshoe obliquely from the centre of the toe to the end of one or other heel; for simplicity – and because no direct comparison is made with modern shoes so measured – the length quoted for these medieval

shoes is that from the toe perpendicularly to a line drawn between the heels.

Where nail-holes survive they have been indicated in the form 'n/n', where 'n/' represents the number of nail-holes surviving in the left branch (as seen from the ground surface and with the shoe aligned toe-uppermost as in the drawings;, '/n' the number in the right branch; where a single figure occurs without a dividing stroke the nail-holes can be assumed to be regularly spaced, including the toe area, without any clear distinction between left and right. On complete shoes, and on fragments where one or other heel survives, the presence or absence of calkins is recorded in a similar fashion, with a stroke dividing left and right, as follows:

N calkin definitely absent
Y calkin present, but type uncertain
? unclear whether calkin present
T 'thickened' (upset) heel (Fig 59a)
R 'right-angle', turned down calkin (Fig 59b)
F 'folded' calkin (Fig 59c – or where indicated 'rolled' as in Fig 59d)
– heel missing

A Fig number followed by '(X)' indicates that the drawing is derived from an X-ray.

Uncertainties in defining or describing some of the shoes listed here arise from their poor or fragmentary condition. In some cases decisions (and indeed measurements) derive from reference to X-ray plates.

Illustrations will be found in Figs 80–9 on pp.114–23 below.

Table 8: Catalogue of horseshoes

Catalogue no	Site code and acc no		Context	Ceramic phase or spot date	Complete-ness	Dimensions	Presence of nails	Nail-holes (left/right)	Calkins (left/right)	Fig no	Notes & references
Type 1											
87	IRO80	153 (410)		1	fragment		Y	3/–	?/–	Fig 80 (X)	Pritchard 1991, 253
88	GPO75	958 (1201)		5	part	165mm		?/–		Fig 80 (X)	two branches from same shoe?; Pritchard 1991, 254
89	PDN81	260 (609)		5	part			2/3	N/N	Fig 80 (X)	
90	POM79	694 (2595A)		1150–1200?	fragment	175mm		–/3	–/N	Fig 80 (X)	
91	POM79	695 (2595A)		1150–1200?	fragment			–/3	–/N	Fig 80 (X)	
92	POM79	241 (1074)		1150–1350?	part	187mm		3/–	–/?	Fig 80 (X)	
93	GPO75	483 (403)		–	fragment				N/–	Fig 80 (X)	
94	POM79	242 (1134)		–	part	197mm	Y	3/1	N/–	Fig 80 (X)	
Type 1?											
95	EST83	44 (287)		1	fragment	195mm			?/–	Fig 80	Pritchard 1991, 254, no 91, fig 3.22; note 1
96	MLK76	222 (1101)		4	complete	1108mm w 100mm th 4mm wt 119gm		3/3	–/R	Fig 80	
97	BIG82	2565 (2596)		8	fragment			?/–			

Note 1:   A highly developed shoe for this early context; perhaps intrusive? The form of the nail-holes is unclear.

Catalogue no	Site code and acc no		Context	Ceramic phase or spot date	Complete-ness	Dimensions	Presence of nails	Nail-holes (left/right)	Calkins (left/right)	Fig no	Notes & references
Type 2A											
98	PET81	420 (1245)		–	fragment			–/2	–/N		Pritchard 1991, 253; note 2
99	BOP82	83 (313)		900–1000	part	1110mm		3/–	N/–		note 3
100	BIG82	4054 (7462)		4	complete	1101mm w 105mm th 4mm wt 120gm	Y	3/3	R/R	Fig 81	badly distorted; Pritchard 1991, 254
101	BIG82	4997 (7073)		4	fragment	th 6mm			–/R		Pritchard 1991, 254
102	IME83	25 (150)		4	complete	1111mm w 100mm wt 180gm	Y	3/3	?/?		Pritchard 1991, 254
103	GPO75	2300 (1373)		1050–1150	fragment	185mm		–/2	–/?		Pritchard 1991, 254
104	BIG82	3416 (6980)		5	fragment	th 4mm		3/–	?/–	Fig 81	

No											
105	SH74	269	(578)	5	complete	l 100mm w 101mm wt 102gm	3/3		F/F		Pritchard 1991, 254
106	SH74	328	(620)	5	complete	l 101mm w 112mm th 6mm wt 89gm	3/3		R/R	Figs 60, 63, 81	Pritchard 1991, 254, no 88, fig 3.22
107	SH74	454	(620)	5	part	th 7mm wt 60gm	3/3		?/?	Fig 81	Pritchard 1991, 254
108	WAT78	310	(3587)	5	part	l 112mm			?/–		heavily corroded – type uncertain; there is intrusive material in the context
109	OPT81	451	(66)	6	part	l 110mm th 5.5mm	–/3		–/?		
110	SWA81	1537	(2183)	6	fragment				–/F		
111	BWB83	3031	(175)	6–9	complete	l 100mm w 103mm th 5mm	3/3		R/R	Fig 81	
112	BIS82	194	(637)	1230–80	fragment				F/–		
113	SWA81	3503	(2212)	9	fragment				N/–		
114	TL74	1531	(1595)	9	part	l 92mm w 101mm	3/3		?/F		
115	BC72	509	(0)	–	fragment				?/–		
116	GPO75	2158	(1217)	–	part	l 97mm			Y/–		
117	GPO75	2252	(5243)	–	part	l 104mm th 12mm	–/3		–/N		type uncertain, possibly type 1
118	GPO75	406	(585)	–	complete	l 105mm w 108mm wt 82gm	3/3	Y	Y/Y		
119	SH74	661	(863)	–	complete	l 117mm w 107mm th 11mm wt 199gm	3/3		F/F	Fig 81	'rolled' calkins
120	SWA81	1040	(0)	–	fragment	th 4.5mm			–/T		
121	TAV82	108	(61)	–	fragment				?/–		
122	WAT78	731	(0)	–	fragment	l 80mm			?/–		

Note 2:   Published by Pritchard 1991 as '10th century' (ceramic phase 1). However, no pottery is recorded from the context and it is dated stratigraphically, being the last layer of make-up before the laying-out of Peter's Hill, an event assigned to the 11th–12th century; it is a loose deposit only partially sealed beneath the street surface. The shoe might then be rather later than the period previously assigned; otherwise, like No 99, it is a precocious example of the type.

Note 3:   In spite of its apparent early date there is no doubt of the identification of this fragment as of the lobate type 2.

continued

Table 8: *continued*

Catalogue no	Site code and acc no	Context	Ceramic phase or spot date	Complete-ness	Dimensions	Presence of nails	Nail-holes (left/right)	Calkins (left/right)	Fig no	Notes & references
Type 2B										
123	BIG82 2976 (4420)	6	.	complete	l 115mm w 106mm th 5mm wt 129gm	Y	3/3	F/F	Fig 82	
124	BIG82 3677 (5593)	6		part	l 106mm	Y	3/–	F/–		
125	SWA81 1512 (2187)	6		complete	l 98mm w 96mm th 5mm wt 65gm	Y	3/3	–/R	Fig 82	
126	SWA81 2622 (2259)	6		part	l 105mm th 7mm wt 99gm	Y	3/1	F/–	Fig 82	
127	SWA81 2441 (2266)	7		fragment	th 4.5mm			F/–		
128	SWA81 3228 (2280)	7		fragment	th 6mm			R/–		
129	SH74 151 (386)	8		part	l 94mm th 3mm		–/2	–/T		type uncertain
130	BWB83 2569 (259)	9		fragment	th 6mm	Y		–/R		
131	SWA81 3804 (2055)	9		fragment	th 7mm			–/T		
132	POM79 518 (1431)	1250–1350?		part	l 93mm	Y	3/–	F/–		
133	GPO75 60 (221)	–		part	l 101mm		–/3	–/F		
134	SWA81 3848 (0)	–		fragment	th 6mm	Y		R/–		
Type 2: uncertain nail-hole form										
135	BWB83 1518 (222)	9		fragment	th 3.5mm			–/T		
136	BWB83 2552 (216)	9		fragment	th 4.5mm			–/T		
Type 2?										
137	BIG82 5079 (7336)	5		fragment	l 95mm			–/Y		Pritchard 1991, 254
138	SWA81 1123 (2130)	7		fragment	th 6.5mm			?/–		
139	SWA81 2442 (2266)	7		fragment	th 4mm			Y/–		
140	SWA81 3618 (2255)	7		fragment	th 4.5mm			–/F		
141	SWA81 2708 (2075)	9		fragment	th 5mm			–/R		
142	SWA81 3376 (2134)	9		fragment	th 5mm			N/–		
143	SWA81 3630 (2270)	9		fragment	th 6mm			N/–		

Type 3

No.	Site & no.	Context	Period	Completeness	Dimensions	Y	Nails	Calkins	Fig	Notes
144	SWA81 1122	(2130)	7	fragment	th 4.5mm		4/–	F/–	Fig 83 (X)	
145	SWA81 1641	(2124)	7	fragment	119mm; th 6mm			?/–	Fig 83	
146	SWA81 3617	(2255)	7	fragment	th 5mm	Y		–/R		nail-holes regularly spaced
147	WAT78 309	(3953)	7	part	1100mm		3/–	N/–		
148	SWA81 2304	(2052)	8	complete	1137mm; w 113mm; th 8mm; wt 360gm		9	F/F	Fig 83	
149	BWB83 1776	(10)	9	fragment			2/–	N/–		
150	CUS73 26	(III10)	9	complete	1137mm; w 108mm; th 6mm; wt 253gm		4/4	R/R	Fig 83	
151	CUS73 49	(I12)	9	fragment	th 5mm	Y	3/1	–/T	Fig 84	
152	CUS73 50	(I12)	9	part	1108mm; th 6mm; wt 122gm			T/–		
153	CUS73 701	(XV16)	9	part	1105mm; th 6mm		4/–	?/–	Fig 84	
154	CUS73 987	(XII4)	9	part	119mm; th 6mm	Y	–/3	–/F		
155	LUD82 66	(1060)	9	fragment	th 5.5mm			–/R		
156	SWA81 1028	(2126)	9	part	1125mm; th 13mm; wt 154gm		–/4	–/T	Fig 84 (X)	
157	SWA81 1030	(2127)	9	part	1105mm; th 5mm		3/–	N/–		
158	SWA81 1133	(2144)	9	fragment	th 6mm			?/–		
159	SWA81 1186	(2149)	9	fragment	th 5.5mm			–/F		
160	SWA81 1275	(2150)	9	fragment	th 6mm			–/F		
161	SWA81 1357	(2056)	9	part	199mm; w 98mm; th 6mm; wt 100gm	Y	3/3	–/F	Fig 84 (X)	spiral nail
162	SWA81 1495	(2046)	9	part	1118mm; th 8mm; wt 113gm		–/4	–/R	Fig 84	
163	SWA81 1747	(2000)	9	fragment	th 5mm	Y	–/3	–/F	Fig 84	spiral nail

continued

Table 8: *continued*

Type 3 cont.

Catalogue no	Site code and acc no	Context	Ceramic phase or spot date	Complete-ness	Dimensions	Presence of nails	Nail-holes (left/right)	Calkins (left/right)	Fig no	Notes & references
164	SWA81 1757	(2038)	9	complete	1103mm w 98mm th 5mm wt 101gm	Y	3/3	F/F	Fig 84	spiral nail
165	SWA81 1896	(2137)	9	part	1123mm th 5mm wt 142gm		–/4	–/T	Fig 84	
166	SWA81 2479	(2133)	9	complete	1125mm w 110mm th 7mm wt 235gm	Y	8?	T/T	Fig 85	
167	SWA81 2572	(2061)	9	fragment	th 4.5mmh			T/–		
168	SWA81 2608	(2137)	9	part				N/–		
169	SWA81 2981	(2061)	9	fragment	th 4mm			–/R		
170	SWA81 3272	(2141)	9	fragment	th 6mm	Y		–/T		
171	SWA81 3556	(2071)	9	fragment	th 5mm			?/–		
172	SWA81 3763	(2042)	9	complete	1121mm w 100mm th 8mm wt 234gm		3/4	T/F	Fig 85	
173	SWA81 3779	(2031)	9	fragment	th 6mm	Y		–/R		
174	SWA81 3891	(2018)	9	fragment				N/–		
175	SWA81 3908	(2018)	9	part	1119mm th 8mm wt 130gm	Y	–/4	–/T	Fig 85	
176	SWA81 3944	(2040)	9	fragment	th 5mm			N/–		
177	SWA81 466	(2018)	9	part	1100mm th 3mm wt 55gm		4	–/F	Fig 85	nail-holes regularly spaced
178	SWA81 467	(2017)	9	fragment	th 5mm			Y/–		
179	SWA81 566	(2055)	9	fragment	th 5mm			F/–		
180	SWA81 722	(2051)	9	fragment	th 5mm			–/F		
181	TL74 2532	(2532)	9	part	188mm th 5mm		3/–	T/–		
182	BC72 4649	(250)	10	fragment	th 4.5mm			Y/–		
183	BC72 4073	(88)	11	fragment	th 3.5mm			?/–		

No.	Accession	Ceramic phase	Completeness	Dimensions	Measured	Nail-holes	Code	Illus.	Notes
184	BWB83 5241 (334)	11	part			–/3	–/T		feathered heel; heavily corroded
185	BWB83 5601 (300)	11	fragment			2/–	N/–		
186	BWB83 5606 (308)	11	complete	l 135mm; w 115mm	Y	4/3	Y/N		feathered heel; measured from X-ray
187	BC72 3554 (129)	–	part	l 108mm; th 6mm; wt 89gm		–/3	–/N		
188	BWB83 2474 (0)	–	part	l 117mm; th 3mm; wt 54gm	Y	3/–	T/–	Fig 85	
189	TL74 1256 (4)	–	part	l 103mm			N/–		
Type 3?									
190	BWB83 1873 (10)	9	fragment	th 4.5mm			Y/–		type 2 or 3?
191	BWB83 2283 (281)	9	fragment				Y/–		
192	BWB83 5228 (343)	11	complete	l 100mm; w 94mm; th 5.5mm; wt 69gm		3/3		Fig 85	type uncertain – type 1 in late phase?
193	BC72 2077 (0)	–	fragment	th 5.5mm		–/2	–/R		
194	SWA81 1630 (0)	–	fragment	th 6mm			Y/–		
Type 4									
195	BIG82 2941 (4372)	7	fragment	th 4mm		3/–	N/–		type uncertain
196	SH74 785 (326)	1250–1350	fragment			3/2	F/F	Fig 86	miniature horseshoe? – discussed above
197	BWB83 151 (290)	9	complete	l 52mm; w 48mm; th 3mm; wt 13gm					
198	BWB83 3088 (285)	9	part	l 117mm; th 4mm; wt 92gm		4	N/–	Fig 86	angular inner profile; square nail-holes, regularly spaced
199	BWB83 3089 (285)	9	part	th 4mm		3	?/–		square nail-holes, regularly spaced?
200	BWB83 3096 (274)	9	fragment	th 3mm			N/–		
201	BWB83 3103 (285)	9	fragment	th 5mm			N/–		
202	BWB83 3191 (290)	9	part	th 4.5mm		2/–	N/–		square nail-holes
203	BWB83 3294 (367)	9	fragment	th 4.5mm			?/–		square nail-holes
204	BWB83 3296 (367)	9	fragment	th 5mm			N/–		
205	BWB83 3350 (269)	9	fragment	th 7mm		3/–	R/–		rectangular nail-holes

continued

Table 8: *continued*

Type 4 cont.

Catalogue no	Site code and acc no	Context	Ceramic phase or spot date	Complete-ness	Dimensions	Presence of nails	Nail-holes (left/right)	Calkins (left/right)	Fig no	Notes & references
206	TL74 2238	(1596)	9	part	1107mm		3/3	N/N		square nail-holes, regularly spaced
207	TUD78 3	(125)	9	complete	1118mm w 110mm th 5mm wt 189gm	Y	8	N/N	Fig 86	square nail-holes
208	BWB83 4344	(108)	10	part	1108mm th 8mm wt 110gm		3/–	N/–		angular inner profile; square nail-holes
209	BWB83 4676	(108)	10	fragment	th 5.5mm			N/–		square nail-holes
210	BWB83 4824	(108)	10	fragment	th 2.5mm		–/3			
211	POM79 864	(2004)	10	fragment				N/–		
212	BC72 2074	(81)	10–11	part	1117mm th 8mm wt 143gm	Y	4	–/F	Fig 86	angular inner profile; square nail-holes, regularly spaced; mark on heel, disk in square, visible on X-ray; spiral nail
213	BC72 2075	(81)	10–11	part	1100mm th 4.5mm wt 73gm		–/4	–/T	Fig 86	square nail-holes
214	BC72 2133	(81)	10–11	part	199mm th 5mm wt 77gm	Y	4	–/T	Fig 86	angular inner profile; square nail-holes, regularly spaced; spiral nail
215	BC72 3132	(81)	10–11	complete	1114mm w 116mm th 3mm wt 105gm		7	–/T	Fig 86	regular nail-holes; right heel feathered; formerly listed as 2132
216	BC72 3837	(119)	10–11	fragment	th 3mm		2/–	N/–		rectangular nail-holes
217	BC72 3838	(119)	10–11	fragment	th 4mm			?/–		
218	BC72 4202	(118)	10–11	part	1160mm			?/–		
219	BC72 4552	(123)	10–11	fragment						
220	BC72 1744	(55)	11	fragment	th 7.5mm		1/–	T/–		square nail-holes
221	BC72 1798	(55)	11	part	196mm			?/–		square nail-holes

No.	Site	Context		Condition	Dimensions		Nail-holes	Stamp	Figure	Description
222	BC72	1902	(55)	11	complete	l 132mm w 110mm th 7mm wt 232gm	Y	4/4	N/N	Figs 71, 87	square nail-holes; spiral nail; mark stamped on right heel, shield with cross – see Fig 72
223	BC72	2388	(83)	11	fragment	th 7mm		3/4	N/–		square nail-holes
224	BC72	2424	(79)	11	part	l 123mm w 115mm th 6mm wt 132gm			?/T	Fig 87	square nail-holes
225	BC72	2436	(79)	11	complete	l 135mm w 110mm wt 387gm	Y	4/3	R/T		square nail-holes
226	BC72	2443	(79)	11	fragment	th 6mm			T/–		rectangular nail-holes
227	BC72	2483	(79)	11	part	l 119mm th 7mm wt 125gm		–/3	–/N		square nail-holes
228	BC72	2484	(79)	11	fragment		Y	2/–	N/–		square nail-holes
229	BC72	2485	(79)	11	part	l 108mm th 4mm wt 106gm		3/–	T/–		rectangular nail-holes; spiral nail
230	BC72	2486	(79)	11	complete	l 130mm w 120mm th 4.75mm wt 218gm	Y	4/4	R/T	Fig 87	rectangular nail-holes
231	BC72	4163	(88)	11	part	l 112mm th 5.5mm wt 82gm		–/3	–/T	Fig 87	angular inner profile; square nail-holes, regularly spaced (?)
232	BC72	4164	(88)	11	fragment	th 6mm		2/–	R/–		square nail-holes?
233	BC72	4165	(88)	11	fragment				?/–		
234	BC72	4166	(88)	11	complete	l 123mm w 107mm th 4mm wt 171gm		4/4	T/R	Fig 88	angular inner profile; square nail-holes, regularly spaced
235	BC72	4167	(88)	11	complete	l 126mm w 109mm th 6mm wt 254gm	Y	4/4	N/N	Figs 71, 88	angular inner profile; square nail-holes; mark stamped on right heel, shield with cross – see Fig 72
236	BC72	4224	(150)	11	part	w 112mm th 6mm	Y	7	–/?	Fig 88	square nail-holes, regularly spaced
237	BC72	4229	(150)	11	fragment	th 5mm	Y		–/R		square nail-holes?

continued

Table 8: *continued*

Catalogue no	Site code and acc no	Context	Ceramic phase or spot date	Completeness	Dimensions	Presence of nails	Nail-holes (left/right)	Calkins (left/right)	Fig no	Notes & references
Type 4 cont.										
238	BC72 4230 (150)	11	fragment	th 5mm	Y	1/-	T/-	Fig 88	spiral nail; mark stamped on heel, open star or sun – see Fig 73
239	BC72 4307 (150)	11	part	1118mm th 4mm wt 85gm	Y	3/-	T/-	Fig 88	spiral nail
240	BC72 4308 (150)	11	part	1100mm		3/-	?/-		rectangular nail-holes
241	BC72 4763 (255)	11	fragment				?/-		
242	BWB83 632 (157)	11	part	1126mm th 4mm wt 100gm		5	-/R	Fig 89	angular inner profile; square nail-holes, regularly spaced
243	BWB83 2542 (207)	11	fragment	th 4mm			N/-		square nail-holes
244	BWB83 2795 (301)	11	fragment	th 6mm		3/-	?/-		rectangular nail-holes
245	BWB83 2797 (301)	11	fragment	th 4.5mm			T/-		square nail-holes
246	BWB83 2808 (147)	11	fragment	th 4mm		-/2	-/R		square nail-holes
247	BWB83 2903 (306)	11	fragment	th 2.5mm		-/1	-/N		square nail-holes
248	BWB83 2912 (286)	11	fragment	th 4mm			T/-		
249	BWB83 2913 (286)	11	fragment	th 3.5mm			N/-		
250	BWB83 2976 (257)	11	part	1103mm th 4mm wt 95gm	Y	-/3	-/N	Fig 89	angular inner profile; square nail-holes; spiral nail
251	BWB83 2989 (151)	11	part	th 5mm		3/3	?/-		square nail-holes
252	BWB83 3057 (162)	11	fragment	th 5.5mm			N/-		
253	BWB83 3075 (369)	11	fragment	th 4mm		-/2	-/N		square nail-holes
254	BWB83 3158 (279)	11	fragment	th 6mm		-/2	-/N		square nail-holes
255	BWB83 3163 (279)	11	part	192mm		-/3	-/T		square nail-holes
256	BWB83 3164 (279)	11	part	1104mm th 5mm wt 80gm		3/-	N/-		square nail-holes
257	BWB83 3309 (387)	11	fragment	th 5mm		-/3	-/R		square nail-holes
258	BWB83 3322 (279)	11	fragment	th 5mm			?/-		square nail-holes
259	BWB83 3368 (282)	11	fragment	th 4mm			N/-		square nail-holes
260	BWB83 3381 (303)	11	part	185mm th 4.5mm wt 47gm		-/3	-/N		square nail-holes

No.	Ref	Period	Form	Dimensions		Nails	Code	Fig	Description
261	BWB83 3471 (293)	11	part	195mm / th 5mm / wt 53gm		–/3	–/N		two square nail-holes, one rectangular!
262	BWB83 4239 (307)	11	fragment	188mm / th 4.4mm	Y	2/–	R/–		square nail-holes
263	BWB83 4268 (256)	11	part			–/4	–/?		rectangular nail-holes
264	BWB83 5616 (291)	11	part	th 5mm		3/–	?/–		square nail-holes
265	BWB83 638 (157)	11	fragment	th 4mm			N/–		square nail-holes
266	TL74 178 (291)	11	part	l116mm / th 8mm / wt 115gm		4/–	?/–		square nail-holes?
267	TL74 180 (291)	11	fragment	th 5mm		2/–	T/–		square nail-holes
268	TL74 532 (415)	11	part	195mm / th 3mm / wt 38gm	Y	–/2	–/N		square nail-holes
269	TL74 537 (291)	11	part	th 5.5mm		3/1	–/R	Fig 89	rectangular nail-holes
270	TL74 689 (415)	11	part	l102mm / th 4mm / wt 70gm			T/–		square nail-holes
271	TL74 743 (414)	11	fragment	188mm / th 3mm	Y		N/–		square nail-holes
272	BWB83 1721 (17)	12	part			–/3	–/N		square nail-holes
273	BWB83 2922 (265)	12	part			–/3	–/N		square nail-holes; worn through at toe
274	BWB83 3931 (310)	12	complete	l102mm / w 99mm / th 5mm / wt 148gm		6	N/N	Fig 89	square nail-holes, regularly spaced
275	BWB83 4830 (324)	12	fragment	th 4.5mm	Y	?/–			square nail-holes; spiral nail
276	BWB83 547 (310)	12	part	l108mm / th 5.5mm / wt 100gm		4/–	N/–	Fig 89	
277	TL74 1115 (378)	12	part	l105mm / th 7mm / wt 110gm	Y	3/–	N/–		angular inner profile; square nail-holes
278	TL74 1172 (275)	12	part	l114mm / w 116mm	Y	4/4	N/N		square nail-holes
279	TL74 1214 (317)	12	part	l90mm		?/–			rectangular nail-holes
280	TL74 64 (117)	12+	part	195mm		?/–			narrow rectangular
281	BC72 105 (10)	15	part	195mm		–/3	–/N		nail-holes
282	BC72 1457 (23)	15	fragment				T/–		

continued

Table 8: *continued*

Catalogue no	Site code and acc no	Context	Ceramic phase or spot date	Complete-ness	Dimensions	Presence of nails	Nail-holes (left/right)	Calkins (left/right)	Fig no	Notes & references
Type 4 cont.										
283	BC72 50	(10)	15	part	198mm th 3.5mm		1/–	T/–		
284	BC72 488	(0)	+	fragment				F/–		square nail-holes
285	BC72 647	(0)	+	fragment	1102mm			?/–		
286	BC72 3708	(127)	–	part	1129mm th 5.5mm wt 126gm		4/–	F/–		rectangular nail-holes
287	BC72 4289	(259)	–	part	1108mm		3/–	N/–		square nail-holes
288	BC72 4298	(259)	–	part	174mm			?/–		
289	PET81 411	(49)	–	fragment				–/N		rectangular nail-holes
290	THE79 2	(70)	–	part	1109mm th 5.5mm wt 81gm		4/–	N/–		square nail-holes
291	UT74 10	(35)	–	part	1106mm		3/–	?/–		angular inner profile; rectangular nail-holes
Type 4?										
292	BIG82 5190	(7350)	240–50?	fragment				?/–		context containing residual Roman material? intrusive? – looks modern
293	OPT81 230	(20)	5	fragment	th 6mm		2/–	R/–		
294	BWB83 1775	(10)	9	fragment				?/–		
295	BWB83 407	(359)	11	fragment	th 5.5mm			T/–		rectangular nail-holes; type uncertain
296	BWB83 2925	(286)	11	fragment	th 5mm			?/–		
297	SWA81 4651	(2114)	12	fragment				?/–		rectangular nail-holes
Uncertain type										
298	WAT78 397	(3512)	5	fragment				N/–		
299	POM79 417	(1015)	1150–1350	fragment						
300	SWA81 2539	(2267)	7	fragment	th 5mm			–/F		
301	WAT78 160	(3953)	7	fragment	1102mm		3/–	?/–		
302	BC72 4648	(250)	10	fragment	th 3.5mm					
303	BC72 2612	(79)	11	fragment	th 3.5mm		N/–			
304	BC72 4386	(89)	11	fragment	th 6mm			–/R		
305	BWB83 4364	(112)	11	fragment						probably not horseshoe

306	BWB83 4646	(110)	11	fragment	th 7.5mm	N/–	
307	BWB83 4785	(318)	11	fragment	th 3.5mm		
308	BWB83 5337	(110)	11	fragment	th 3mm	?/–	
309	BWB83 3778	(149)	11?	fragment		–/F	
310	BWB83 1771	(15)	12	fragment			not located
311	BC72 295	(0)	+	fragment		?/–	
312	BC72 868	(5037)	–	fragment	th 4.5mm	N/–	
313	CLE81 52	(12)	–	fragment			
314	LLO78 82	(367)	–	fragment			not located
315	MFS76 337	(013?)	?	fragment			not located

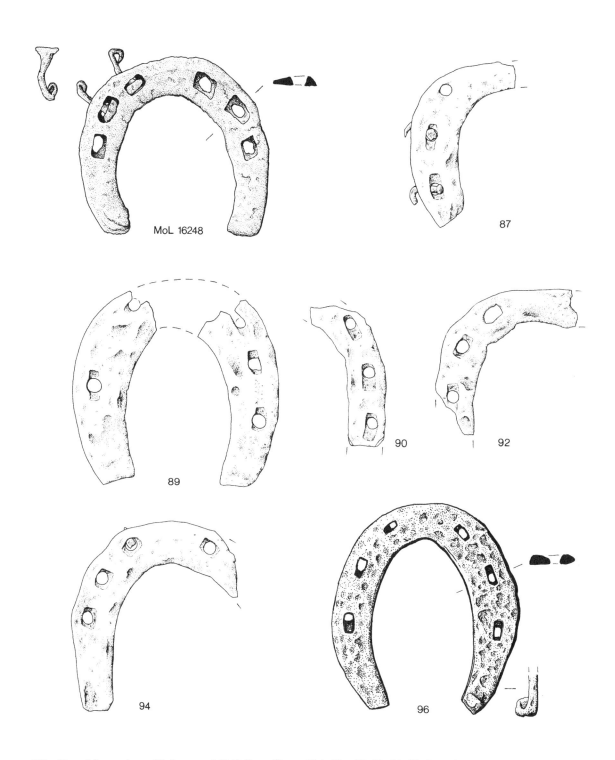

80   Type 1 horseshoes, MoL acc no 16248 (from Cheapside), Nos 87, 89, 90, 92, 94 and 96 (1:2)

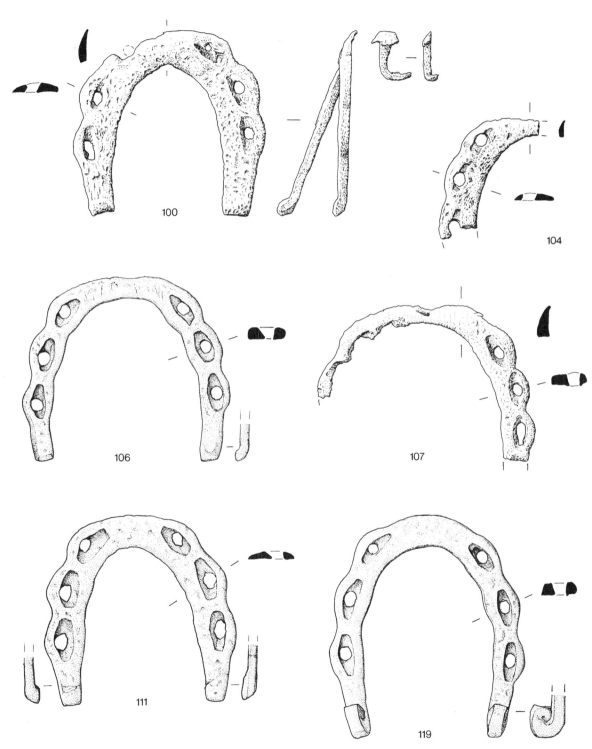

81　Type 2 horseshoes, Nos 100, 104, 106, 107, 111 and 119 (1:2)

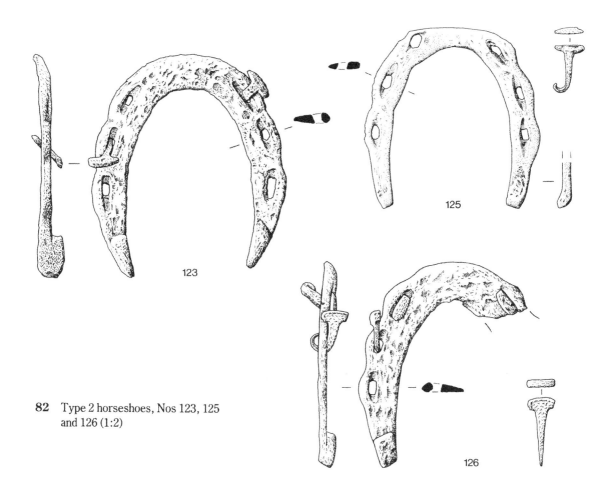

82 Type 2 horseshoes, Nos 123, 125
and 126 (1:2)

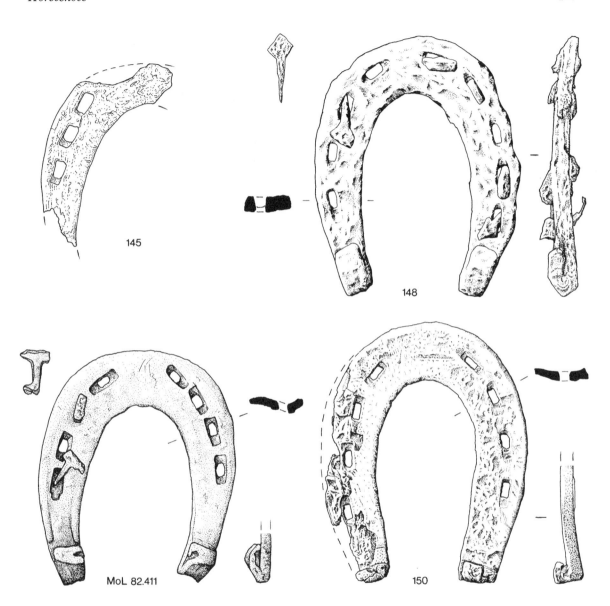

145

148

MoL 82.411

150

83 Type 3 horseshoes, Nos 145, 148, 150 and MoL
acc no 82.411 (from Thames foreshore at
Queenhithe) (1:2)

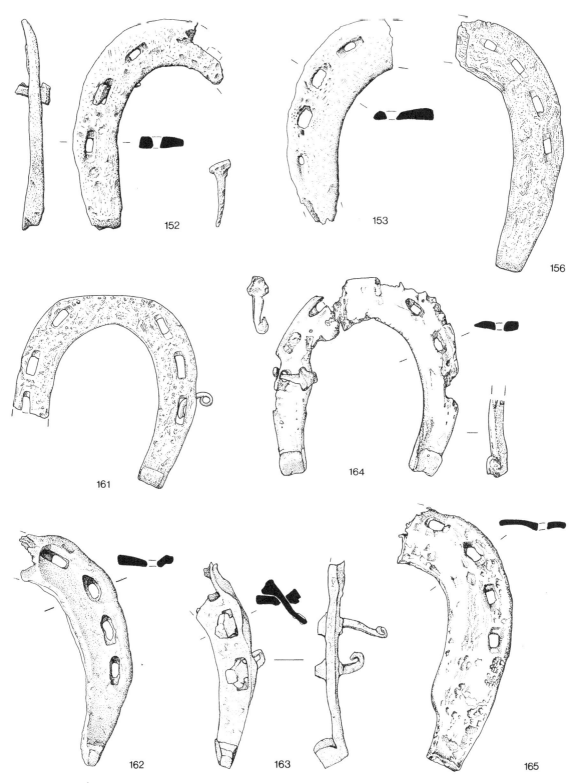

152

153

156

161

164

162

163

165

84 Type 3 horseshoes, Nos 152, 153, 156 and 161–5 (1:2)

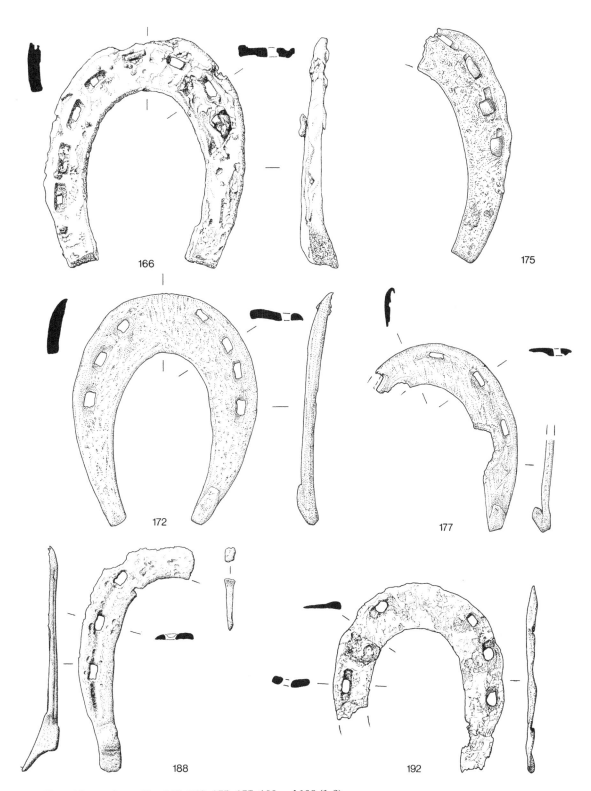

85 Type 3 horseshoes, Nos 166, 172, 175, 177, 188 and 192 (1:2)

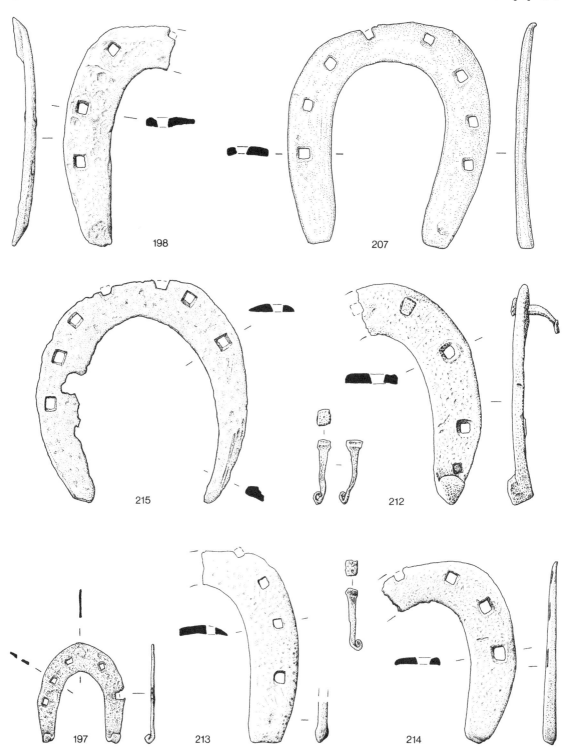

86   Type 4 horseshoes, Nos 198, 207 and 212–5; miniature horseshoe, No 197 (1:2)

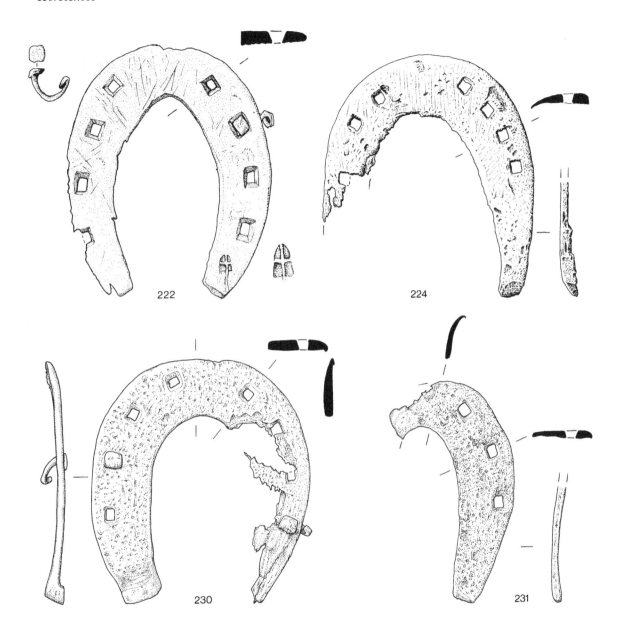

87 Type 4 horseshoes, Nos 222, 224, 230 and 231 (1:2; mark on No 222 1:1)

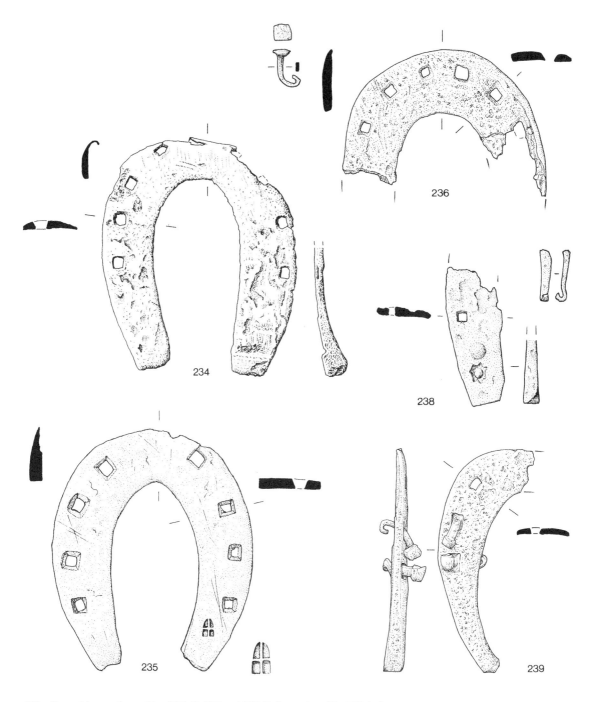

88   Type 4 horseshoes, Nos 234–6, 238 and 239 (1:2; mark on No 235 1:1)

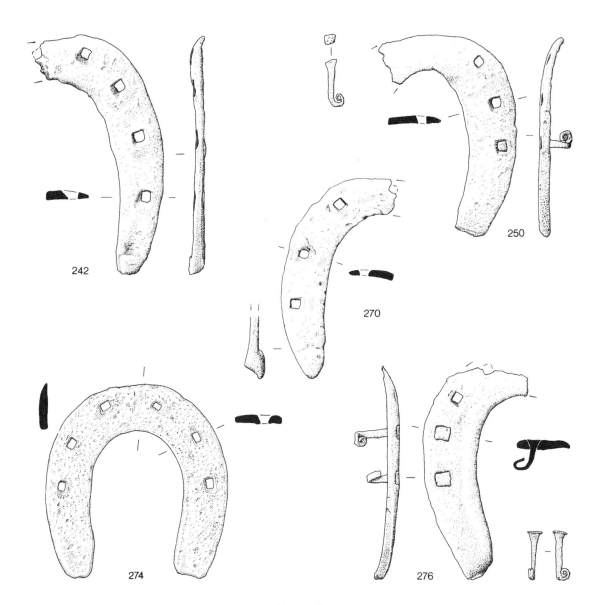

89 Type 4 horseshoes, Nos 242, 250, 270, 274 and 276 (1:2)

Spurs and spur fittings

BLANCHE M A ELLIS

with contributions by Geoff Egan

Introduction

FUNCTION AND FASHION

As well as being functional objects for riders, spurs had a fashionable importance (at least for men) and were the status symbol of the horseman, while gilded spurs generally denoted knighthood. Women wore them only when necessary for riding; spurs would have been a nuisance with long skirts, and since such skirts would have concealed them, spurs would have had no fashionable interest to women. When Chaucer's Wife of Bath set out for Canterbury, 'Up-on an amblere easily she sat, . . . And on hir feet a paire of spores sharpe' (Skeat 1895, 424–5): the poet suggests a much-travelled woman, comfortably riding astride (Fig 8). Boys were taught to ride as soon as they were old enough to learn, and there have been occasional finds of very small spurs made for children, including a little spur from Salisbury (Ellis 1991, no 36, fig 20) and probably No 353 below from the Thames at London Bridge.

Jousting spurs are mentioned in a number of medieval records, including an *Inventory of gds of Simon de Burley Kt at Mews & Baynards Castle in London*, dated 9 November 1387 (PRO E 154 Exchequer K.R. Inventories bundle 1 No 19). Listed under '2 Armour pur les Joustes' is 'Item iiij pair esperons pur les ioustes s'dorez'. It has not been possible to identify any particular spurs in this collection as jousting spurs, and it is not certain whether such spurs were different from other military spurs. Doubtless, participants in the sport would have wished to be well turned out and are likely to have made sure that their spurs were fashionable and bright, purchasing new ones if necessary for an important tournament. An exceptionally fine, large, tinned iron long spur in the Royal Armouries collection, recovered from the Thames foreshore at Queenhithe in 1977, may have been a jousting spur. Its curved sides have an upper flange forming a pointed crest, a neck 150mm long with a star rowel of six points (diameter 92–4mm) and an elaborate buckle and attachments (Royal Armouries VI–434). Giltspur Street in the City of London, known in the Middle Ages as 'Gyltesporstrete' and sometimes called 'Knyghtryders strete', is adjacent to Smithfield where tournaments were held.

Gilded spurs were buckled on to a man's heels as part of the formal ceremony of making him a knight, and gilt spurs were considered to be the prerogative of knights. By the late 14th century there were complaints that many mercenary soldiers, some of whom called themselves 'knights', wore golden spurs without ever having been knighted (Jones 1980, 18–19, 240, n 7). There are not, in fact, any gilded spurs in the group under discussion, but a gilded copper-alloy spur of very similar form to No 328, now in a private collection, was a London find from Walbrook (Alexander & Binski 1987, 259, no 166).

Most of the spurs in this catalogue were found in or near the River Thames. Horses were taken to the river to be watered and were exercised along the banks or even in the water. A worn spur leather might break unnoticed and the spur be lost. One of a pair of spurs left in a stable might have fallen into the straw and been included among the sweepings from London's multitude of stables at the riverside dumps, along with odd or damaged spurs which had been thrown away.

LONDON SPURRIERS

None of the spurs in this catalogue can be identified as the work of a particular maker, although most were probably made in London. Fourteenth-century records show a concentration of spurriers on the west side of the City near the River Fleet, including Spurrier Row, the medieval name for Creed Lane near Ludgate (Ekwall 1954, 169). Iron spurs were forged and the Museum of London has an unfinished one, acc no A2425 (London Museum 1940, 108–9, no 8 fig 34). Copper-alloy spurs were cast and No 364 is an unfinished copper-alloy rowel.

As at all times, medieval records were often about those who were in trouble or troublesome. The *Articles of the Spurriers* of 1345 are no exception (Riley 1868, 226–8):

Be it remembered, that on Tuesday, the morrow of St Peter's Chains [1 August], in the 19th year of the reign of King Edward the Third etc, the Articles underwritten were read before John Hamond, Mayor, Roger de Depham, Recorder and the other Aldermen; and seeing that the same were deemed befitting, they were accepted and enrolled in these words.

In the first place, – that no one of the trade of Spurriers shall work longer than from the beginning of the day until curfew rung at the Church of St Sepulchre, without Newgate; by reason that no man can work so neatly by night as by day. And many persons of the said trade, who compass how to practise deception in their work, desire to work by night rather than by day: and then they introduce false iron, and iron that has been cracked, for tin, and also they put gilt on false copper, and cracked. And further, – many of the said trade are wandering about all day, without working at their trade; and then, when they have become drunk and frantic, they take to their work, to the annoyance of the sick and of all their neighbourhood, as well as by reason of the broils that arise between them and the strange [not of their trade] folks who are dwelling among them. And then they blow up their fires so vigorously, that their forges begin all at once to blaze; to the great peril of themselves and of all the neighbourhood around. And then too, all the neighbours are much in dread of the sparks, which so vigorously issue forth in all directions from the mouths of their forges. By reason whereof, it seems unto them that working by night [should be put an end to,] in order such false work and such perils to avoid; and therefore, the Mayor and Aldermen do will, by assent of the good folks of the said trade, and for the common profit, that from henceforth such time for working, and such false work made in the trade, shall be forbidden. And if

any person shall be found in the said trade to do the contrary hereof, let him be amerced, for the first time in 40*d.*, one half thereof to go to the use of the Chamber of the Guildhall of London, and the other half to go to the use of the said trade; the second time, in half a mark, and the third time, in 10*s.*, to the use of the same Chamber and trade; and the fourth time, let him forswear the trade for ever.

Also, – that no one of the said trade shall hang his spurs out on Sunday, or on other days that are Double Feasts; but only a sign indicating his business: and such spurs as they shall so sell, they are to shew and sell within their shops, without exposing them without, or opening the doors and windows of their shops, on the pain aforesaid.

Also, – that no one of the said trade shall keep a house or shop to carry on his business, unless he is free of the City; and that no one shall cause to be sold, or exposed for sale, any manner of old spurs for new ones; or shall garnish them, or change them for new ones.

Also, – that no one of the said trade shall take an apprentice for a less term than seven years; and such apprentice shall be enrolled, according to the usages of the said city.

Also, – that if anyone of the said trade, who is not a freeman, shall take an apprentice for a term of years, he shall be amerced, as aforesaid.

Also, – that no one of the said trade shall receive the apprentice, serving-man, or journeyman, of another in the same trade, during the term agreed upon between his master and him; on the pain aforesaid.

Also, – no alien of another country, or foreigner of this country, shall follow or use the said trade, unless he is enfranchised before the Mayor, Aldermen, and Chamberlain; and that, by witness and surety of the good folks of the said trade, who will undertake for him as to his loyalty and his good behaviour.

Also, – that no one of the said trade shall work on Saturdays after None has been rung out in the City; and not from that hour until the Monday morning following.

Not all the spurriers of London were irresponsible citizens. Two of those sworn to keep the *Articles* were Nicholas le Sporiere and Thomas atte Crouche, whose names were frequently recorded among sureties for guardianship, witnesses, etc. Both were included among 'many of the wealthier and wiser Commoners of the City' called upon to raise money towards the repair of two vessels for the war with France at a congregation in the Guildhall on 25 March 1356 (Sharpe 1905, 58–9). Thomas atte Crouche 'sporiere' was elected to keep the keys of Ludgate in 1343 (Sharpe 1904, 92) and in 1356 received Ordinances regarding charges for carts using it to pay for repairs (Sharpe 1905, 81). His active involvement in local affairs continued until 12 July 1371, when a Royal Writ to the mayor and sheriffs forbade them to put Thomas atte Crouche upon assizes, juries etc., should he be proved to be over 70 years of age (ibid. 285).

The names and activities of many more medieval spurriers survive in the records of the City of London but their details are beyond the scope of this volume.

TERMINOLOGY

Spurs with single-pointed goads have been worn in Britain from at least as early as the Roman occupation (Shortt 1959, 61–76). Before the introduction of the rowel in the 13th century it was unnecessary for spurs to be defined by goad type. The term *prick spur* has long been used (Holme 1688, II, 325/1) to describe the earliest form of spur with a single goad. *Spurs*, *rowels* and *buckles* are medieval terms. They appear among a list of goods of John Frenssh, spurrier of London, valued when an action for debt was brought against him in 1421 (Thomas 1943, 93–4). This includes '5 pairs of rowels, 1½*d*.; 7 pairs of double bocles, and one bocle 10*d*., and '20 pairs of whole and broken spurs called *roghe spurs*, 3*s*. 4*d*.' (roghe or rough spurs seem likely to have been scrap for re-forging). Also '24 pairs of spurs called hangers', the meaning of which is unknown. *Long spurs* are the spurs with very long necks, fashionable in the 15th and the early 16th century. They are so described in contemporary inventories, which also list as *short spurs* the more practical spurs of similar form, but with shorter necks, preferred by the less fashion-conscious riders of the period. Both long and short spurs were in the King's Great Wardrobe in 1483 (see below). Medieval *spur leathers* are relatively rare, but the London waterfront excavations have provided an unusually large quantity of well-

preserved spur leathers including that on spur No 323, No 399 and also the group of 16, found together, from Baynard's Castle Dock, all made of leather with tinned iron studs and mounts (Nos 379–95). After the death of King Henry VIII, a 1547 inventory of his property at Westminster lists 'Itm v paier of Spurres three of them guilte and twoo paier silvered wt Lethers of vellet' (Dillon 1888, 270, f431a). This shows the use of the terms *leathers* for spur straps, even when they were not made of leather, soon after the end of the Middle Ages. Various woven and other fabrics were occasionally used to provide decorative coloured spur straps for ceremonial occasions in the medieval period when the term *tissues* was sometimes used. An inventory of the Royal Wardrobe in the Tower of London in 1345 includes 'esperouns dorez ov' les tissues de soie iij paire desperons dorez garnissey de quir noire' (PRO E 101/390/7).

Very few medieval spur leathers made of fabric have survived anywhere (Ellis 1991, 57; Egan & Pritchard 1991, 49). The Museum has three narrow silk tablet woven braids from 14th-century London which might have been part of either spur leathers or girdles (Crowfoot et al. 1992, 133, nos 143, 450–1, A, B & C, fig 100). In 1811 Stothard recorded cloth spur straps on the copper-covered wooden monumental effigy of William de Valance, Earl of Pembroke (died 1296) in Westminster Abbey (Stothard 1817, detail 5, pl 45). He wrote: 'In the spurs it is remarkable that they have been fastened with cloth, in the form of straps of an extraordinary thickness; of these as might be expected, but a small portion remains.'

The post-medieval terminology used in this catalogue is based mainly on the terms used in Walsall (Staffordshire), an important centre for the manufacture of spurs for at least four centuries. Robert Plot described the making of spurs on a visit to Walsall in 1686 (Plot 1686, 376–7, para 79). He mentioned the *body of the Spurr* and listed various forms of spur *neck*. The body of the spur is the spur itself without any moving parts. It includes the neck, which projects behind the wearer's heel to carry the goad. As an English spurmaker's term, neck is used in this catalogue in preference to the alternative 'shank', which is used by North American spurmakers and is favoured by some writers including J Ward Perkins (London Museum 1940). The spur *sides*, which flank the wearer's foot, were so called by Messrs J Rock & Co (Hardware) Ltd of Walsall in the 1950s. Modern terms include the *terminals* at the front ends of the spur sides, identified descriptively as rivet-terminals and figure-8 terminals. The single ring and figure-8 terminals carry *attachments* for the spur leathers. They held the leathers either by rivets (No 323) or by a hook on the attachment which pierced the end of the leather and was then pressed to hold it securely (No 342). A *crest* is formed when the top edges of the spur sides are drawn up into a point where they join. Crests often curled decoratively over the spur necks, as on Nos 341 and 350.

The London Museum's early typology (London Museum 1940, 95, fig 28; 107, fig 33) is not used in this catalogue because, although correct in its detail, when used as a reference for subsequent archaeological finds it has occasionally been misunderstood, leading to error. The present writer prefers to consider each spur as a whole, with all its parts. The note ending catalogue entry No 340 shows that it would be unwise to consider the separate parts rather than the whole spur for dating purposes, while the uncommon post-medieval prick spurs mentioned below are sometimes mistakenly identified solely by their goads as medieval, despite the rest of their form being clearly later.

CHRONOLOGY AND DEVELOPMENT

The spurs of the late Saxon period had long, slim necks ending with tiny goad points (No 316). Larger, quadrangular goads succeeded them during the second half of the 11th century; No 317 from the Thames near London Bridge is an early example. The broad base of the goad was intended to give resistance, preventing too much damage to the horse. Spurs, when used sensibly as aids to ride properly trained horses, do not actually 'prick' them and are not cruel. Medieval horse owners would have avoided damage to their valuable animals by themselves and their servants. Nevertheless, spurs sometimes were used cruelly by careless or impatient riders and by those under stress or in haste in emergency, flight or battle. Manuscript illustrations of horses bleeding from spur wounds include several battle

scenes in the Maciejowski Bible, French *c*.1250 (Pierpoint Morgan Library, New York, MS 638 f33r etc; see Cockerell nd). Chaucer wrote, in the 'Tale of Sir Thopas': 'His faire stede in his prikinge / So swatte that men mighte him wringe, / His sydes were al blood.' (Skeat 1895, 503)

During the 12th century, spurs with their necks formed almost entirely into large and quite heavy quadrangular lozenge-shaped goads were popular throughout England and western Europe (No 319). Some had sides which curved very slightly under the wearer's ankle, a trend which increased until, by the mid-13th century, most spur sides were deeply curved. This type of prick spur is not represented in the group under discussion, but see acc no A4986 in the Museum of London collection, also C1219 and A4987 (London Museum 1940, 102, nos 3, 6, fig 31).

Number 321 is one of several iron spurs with traces of non-ferrous plating. Iron spurs were often plated with tin which protected them from rust and brightened their appearance (Jope 1956; Ellis 1991, 54, 61). The tinning was usually only a thin coating and excavated spurs have often lost all but the slightest traces of it.

The earliest rowel spurs appeared during the 13th century, following the general form of the contemporary prick spurs which they were soon to replace. The type of terminal to which the spur leathers were directly attached by rivets (No 318) did not normally outlast the prick spurs, although an early rowel spur with rivet terminals from Castle Acre Castle is an extremely rare exception (Ellis 1982, 234–5, no 143, fig 41). Terminals pierced with holes to accommodate separate attachments for the leathers held to them by ring loops became usual, although some of the attachments were themselves riveted to the ends of the leathers (No 323).

Some late 13th-century prick spurs and early rowel spurs had one ring terminal, while the other was formed as a vertically pierced slot (Nos 322, 324, 326, 329). The ring terminal, worn to the outside of the foot, held an attachment for a long leather (see Nos 323, 399), which ran down and under the wearer's foot, then passed up through the slot terminal on the inner side of the foot and across it to the buckle. The latter was either a long buckle attached directly to the ring terminal or a buckle attached to the ring terminal by its own short leather (No 323). This arrangement continued to be popular until about the middle of the 14th century, making it generally difficult to date early rowel spurs very closely by type; the close archaeological dating of some of the spurs described here is therefore of particular value. By the mid-14th century most spurs had two spur leathers, one above and one below the foot, held to the terminals by hook attachments (Nos 337, 366, 370); buckles were also attached directly onto the terminals, an arrangement which remained general into the post-medieval period.

Many of the earliest illustrations of rowel spurs, which appeared more or less simultaneously in several parts of Europe, showed very small, slender spurs with deeply curved sides and small rowels. In Chartres Cathedral, France, one window shows them being worn by Pharaoh as he drowns in the Red Sea and they also appear on the Charlemagne window, *c.*1230. They are worn by the three riders painted on frescoes in the chapel of San Sylvestro, adjoining the Church dei Quattro Santi Coronati in Rome, which was consecrated in 1246 (Masson 1952, 188 and C Blair, per comm) and in England a rowel spur can be seen on the first Great Seal of King Henry III (1218) and on the heel of a mounted Canterbury pilgrim on one of the 'miracle' windows (*c.*1220–30) in Canterbury Cathedral. Slender early rowel spurs are well represented in the group catalogued here. The archaeological dating of Nos 324, 325, 327 and 328 from Swan Lane suggests that they were deposited at the end of the 13th century, when they would already have been some years old. Their fragile proportions seem more suitable for town and court wear than for hard use on long journeys and military campaigns, for which the equally elegant but more substantial No 329 could have been worn.

We have already mentioned the high quality of footwear found in 1972 in late 14th-century dump deposits at Baynard's Castle and drawn attention to the proximity of the King's Great Wardrobe (Grew & de Neergard 1988, 29), an official establishment which, from the 14th century, provided clothing and accoutrements to the royal household and to government offices (Spencer 1972, 20). The detached side of No 323 (Figs 91–3), decorated with roses and a tiny swan, is from an exceptionally attractive spur, which even

a wealthy owner must surely have been sorry to have broken. When excavated, its leathers were stiffened, buckled in position as during wear, despite the fact that there was no sign of the rest of the spur with the slot terminal through which the leather would have passed. The surviving side would have been worn with its buckle to the outside of the foot, displaying the roses and swan as the rider passed; the missing inner side must have been plain since such prominent decoration would have been inconvenient on the inner side of the foot. It is reasonable to speculate upon the possibility that, when the broken spur was discarded, somebody might have kept the decorated fragment and buckled the leathers in order to hang it up, perhaps as a pattern to be copied for a replacement, for sentiment or simply because it was pretty. The swan and roses were probably heraldic. At the time when the spur was worn, a cult of the swan was developing in England. The families of Tony and de Bohun proudly claimed to be Knights of the Swan by descent from Godfrey de Bouillon, Count of Boulogne, to whom the old European legend of the Swan Knight had become attached. The Bohuns displayed the swan as their badge. Other families also used the device and King Edward I, who encouraged the cult, held a Feast of the Swans at Westminster in 1306 at which Prince Edward of Wales was knighted before swans (Wagner 1959; Cherry 1969).

The decoration of spurs by the application of complete motifs in the manner of No 323 is extremely rare. The gilded copper-alloy spurs of Bertrand de Goth (died 1342) have very much larger, six-petalled flowers. (These French spurs are acc no 26.80.1 & 2 in the Metropolitan Museum of Art, New York; Dean 1926, 129–30). Similar large flowers decorate a contemporary rowel spur excavated at the castle of Saint-Vaast-sur-Seulles, Normandy, which was destroyed following a siege in 1356 (Blangy 1889, pl 30, no 1). A strange, large, bronze prick spur with a buckle similar to those of the de Goth spurs has four heraldic lions on its inner side and small, four-petalled flowers on its outer side, all between claw settings for missing jewels (Museo Civico, Bologna, Italy, acc no 343; Boccia 1991, 102, no 189, col pl VII). In England, the prick spurs worn by Sir Robert de Bures on his monumental brass (*c.*1331) in Acton Church, Suffolk, have smaller flowers along their sides

(Binski 1987, 95, fig 88). It is possible that these were a whim of the engraver of this London-made brass and not representative of the decoration seen on actual spurs, but while spur leathers and terminals on brasses sometimes have flowers, the sides of spurs on other brasses are shown plain.

By the second quarter of the 14th century most spurs had rowels and, although they did not disappear completely, prick spurs became very rare during the later Middle Ages. They were to have a brief fashionable revival in England during the mid-17th century, when they were some-times called 'scotch' spurs. The gold prick spurs made in 1660 and used in the coronation cere-monies of English monarchs are kept in the Tower of London. These and other late prick spurs are of similar form, except for their goads, to the rowel spurs of the period. Despite this, survivors are occasionally mistaken for much earlier medieval prick spurs.

In use, spurs must often have been wet, and the corroding together of similar metals would have restricted free movement, especially of rowels. This may have been one reason for the combination of iron with copper alloy for different parts of some spurs, although the copper-alloy spur No 329 has both the rowel and rowel pin made of iron.

A gilded copper-alloy rowel spur from Ludger-shall Castle (Wiltshire), now in Devizes Museum, has an iron rowel pin with a copper-alloy rowel (Fig 100; Ellis forthcoming, no 7). Apart from its metal, it is extremely similar to the iron spur No 338 with which it is discussed below. The similar-ity of these two spurs is of particular interest because, while No 338 lacks its rowel, the Ludgershall spur is one of a very small group dating from 1350–1400 which have rather curious rowels of only four points. They seem certain to have been products of the same place, although they have been found in England and France and one (British Museum acc no WT 942), probably comes from Italy. The iron 3-point rowel in the damaged rowel box of 15th-century spur acc no 7430 in the Museum of London collection (Guild-hall Museum 1908, 269, no 98) may perhaps be associated with this group. It is unfortunately impossible to be certain of the type of rowel now missing from No 338.

No 333 has a rowel of ten points, diameter 39mm. Large rowels had become fashionable by the mid-14th century, and later in that century some rowels were huge with many points, as seen on the detached rowels Nos 361 and 362 and in Fig 107 (the Calveley spur).

By 1400 the necks of spurs were becoming longer, and as the 15th century progressed spurs with very long necks complemented the fashion-able trend towards lengthening and pointing everything that could be so treated, not least the long, pointed toes of boots and shoes. The development of this popular fashion is unlikely to have resulted from the development of horse armour, which only relatively few of the richest knights could afford. The large numbers of sur-viving long spurs from mainly non-military sites, such as London (in the Museum of London's collection) and Salisbury (Ellis 1991, nos 23–33, 35–6, 39–43), testify to their popularity with riders of all kinds, civilians as well as soldiers. The *Vision of St Eustace* (National Gallery no 1436), painted by Pisanello (Antonio Pisano, died *c*.1455) in the first half of the 15th century, shows the saint on horseback wearing long spurs with hunting dress. Documents listed both long spurs and short spurs. A letter sent under the signet of King Richard III to Piers Curteys, Keeper of the King's Great Wardrobe in 1483, asked for the delivery of rich clothing including 'iij pair of spurres short all gilt' and 'ij pair of spurres long whyte parcell gilt' (British Library MS Harley 433, f126). Long spurs were popular with those who followed fashion, but they must have been a considerable nuisance at times, especially when the rider dismounted. Short spurs continued to be worn when it was more practical to do so and by those who preferred convenience to the ex-tremes of fashion.

The armoured figure of Sir John Harpedon on his monumental brass in Westminster Abbey (1438; Fig 102), wears spurs of a form which was popular in the first half of the 15th century and which appear on a number of memorial brasses made in the London workshops of that period. The sides of these spurs arc more or less hori-zontally around the back of the wearer's heel and only their front parts curve deeply under the ankle. Damaged spurs from Trig Lane, Nos 344–6, show this feature, as does the spur from the battlefield of Towton (1461), which is acc no 127 in the collection of the Society of Antiquaries

(London Museum 1940, 111–12, no 1, fig 35). Spur No 347 from Cutler Street also appears to belong to this group.

Apart from these, most spur sides continued simply to be curved, sometimes quite strongly, until the middle of the 15th century (see Nos 350–2). After about 1450 the sides of spurs gradually became less strongly curved, so that by the last quarter of the century many of them were horizontally fairly straight, although their front ends often turned upwards to the terminals. These are not represented in this group. Spur No 355 is probably the latest, dating from the second half of the century. Its broken sides still project downwards into a moderate curve under the wearer's ankle – but less strongly than those of, for example, No 351. In *The Adoration of the Kings*, one of the last works of the Milanese painter Vincenzo Foppa (died 1515), a page is removing a pair of gilded spurs with almost straight sides from a king's heels following a journey to visit the Divine Child (Fig 105; National Gallery No 729). The leathers of these spurs are decorated with a row of small studs, in the same way as several of the spur leathers from the London excavations.

Catalogue

Each spur is described as worn, with its goad at the back of the wearer's foot and the terminals of its sides at the front. The overall length measurement is that of the spur body without its moving parts, taken along the neck to a point mid-way between the terminals. The rowel diameter is given separately, and the span is the maximum width between the terminals. All spurs are of iron except where stated otherwise. As usual in this volume, a date for the archaeological context, where available, is quoted in the form of a ceramic phase or spot date. In addition, the description of each spur is followed by a date assigned by the author on the basis of its type or form.

PRICK SPURS

316 BWB83 acc no 616 (context 308) ceramic phase 6–12 Fig 90
l of neck 44mm
The front ends of both slender, round-section sides are missing but they were originally straight. Straight neck

with encircling double mouldings next to its junction with the sides, beyond which it swells into a long faceted cylinder, ending in a small pointed goad. (Probably early 11th century)

Compare London Museum 1940, 97–8, nos 1, 2, fig 29, also no 3 from the early 11th-century Cherwell deposit (Ashmolean Museum, Oxford acc no 1886. 1232), which has been identified with near certainty as a late Viking burial of a warrior with his horse (Blair 1994, 169–70, fig 98; Blair & Crawford forthcoming). A similar detached spur neck came from a mid-11th-century context at Winchester (Ellis 1990, 1037–8, fig 331, no 3860, pl LXIV).

317 ER1279A 14 – Fig 90
overall l 120mm, l of neck 55mm (including the 31mm goad)
D-section sides, now distorted but probably originally straight; terminals missing. Straight neck with long quadrangular goad supported on a short round stem, the latter with a group of three lines across it, with a V flanking its junction with the sides, also possible traces of non-ferrous plating. From Thames at London Bridge (Marsden 1971, 12). (Late 11th–early 12th century)

A similar but more complete spur, also from London (British Museum 56, 7–1, 2518), has incised line decoration on its neck, traces of tinning and lozenge-shaped 2-rivet terminals. Spurs of this type are worn by Rudolph of Swabia on his monument in Merseburg Cathedral, Germany, c.1080 (Busche & Lohse 1962, x, pl 20).

318 SH74 393 (627) – Fig 90
overall l 93mm
Side fragment. Iron with applied copper-alloy (probably brass or latten) sheet decoration. The thin, slightly tapered side is horizontally straight, of round section and nearly complete, having broken within the arc behind the wearer's heel. The terminal broadens to accommodate two rivets, one above the other, and has a straight front edge. The missing leather was held by these rivets between the inner surface of the terminal and a small, thin retaining plate which survives. A narrow strip of copper alloy, incised along its length with a pattern of diagonal lines, is applied along the upper surface of the side, where it could be seen when the spur was worn. The outer surface of the terminal and both rivet heads are plated with copper alloy. (Probably 11th or early 12th century)

This type of terminal was common on the late prick spurs but disappeared when the rowel spur was introduced.

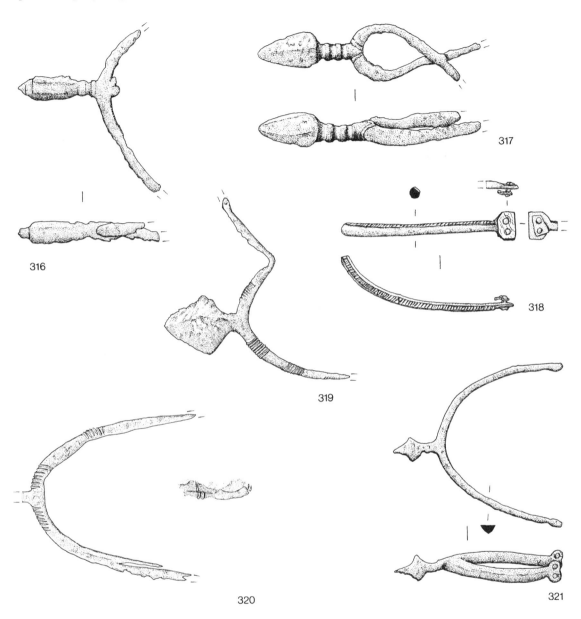

90 Prick spurs, Nos 316–21 (1:2)

319 OPT81 444 (69) 5 Fig 90
l of neck including goad (from X-ray) *c.*35mm
The slender sides project from a mass of soil, one distorted; terminals missing. Details obtained from the radiograph confirm that the neck is short, consisting almost entirely of a very large quadrangular, lozenge-shaped goad. The sides are decorated with groups of vertical lines or ridges alternating with plain surfaces; traces of non-ferrous plating. (Mid–late 12th century (from 12th-century ditch fill))

Museum of London acc no A1967 is similar, undistorted and retains its 2-rivet terminals (London Museum 1940, 102, no 2, fig 31).

The type is worn by a knight depicted on the

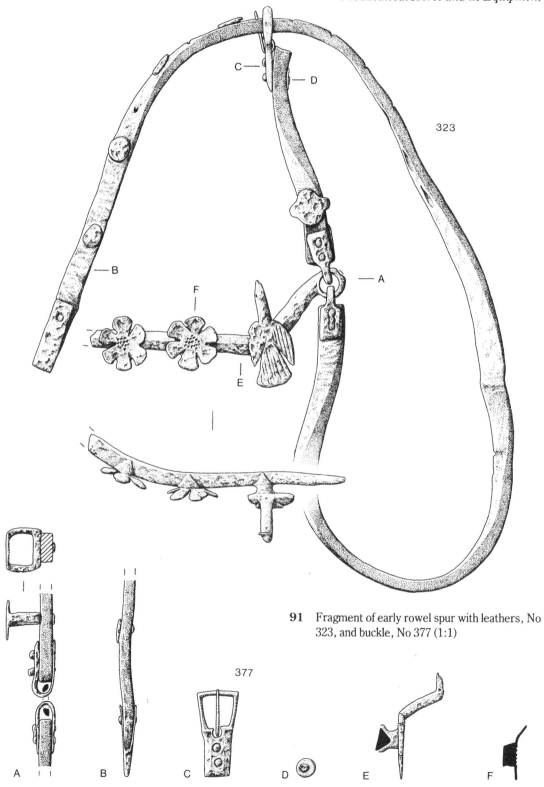

323

91 Fragment of early rowel spur with leathers, No
323, and buckle, No 377 (1:1)

377

A   B   C   D   E   F

12th-century Baldishol tapestry, Museum of Applied Arts, Oslo (Thordeman 1943, 92, fig 8; Royal Scottish Museum & Victoria & Albert Museum 1959, no 3, pl 17; Verlet 1965, 39 (illustration)).

320 MC73 1 (72) – Fig 90
overall l of the sides *c*.90mm, span *c*.75mm, l of smaller fragment 52mm

Two fragments, consisting of an iron arc and a separate short straight piece, both heavily encrusted. The former appears to be both straight sides of a spur, lacking the terminals. An X-ray shows a slight stump in the position of the spur neck and line decoration similar to that on No 319. The short piece may have been the spur neck or the end of one side and also has decorative lines. During conservation these lines were recorded as being radiographically denser than the corroded iron, suggesting inlay; an unidentifiable fine white powder was noticed in the corrosion. (Late Saxon – 12th century)

Found with late Saxon material, but decoration perhaps similar to No 319, which is 12th century (Marsden et al. 1975, 206 and no 142, fig 12).

321 POM79 535 (1431) spot date 1250–1350 Fig 90
overall l *c*.100mm, l of neck (with goad) *c*.25mm, span *c*.70mm

Heavily encrusted except for a small area of one short, D-section, straight side. The radiograph confirms a small, slender spur with 2-rivet terminals, at least one rivet remaining. The short neck swells into a conical pointed goad; traces of non-ferrous plating. (1160–1220)

ROWEL SPURS

322 BC72 3689 (109) – Fig 95
overall l (sides slightly twisted) 112mm, l of neck 27mm, maximum d of rowel 25mm

Early rowel spur for the left foot. The very slender square section sides plunge from their junction with the neck to bend at an angle under the wearer's ankle. One rectangular terminal is pierced with a slot for the leather to pass through vertically, the other is a single ring carrying a small rivet attachment for a narrow leather. The straight neck projects at a downward angle forming a point above its junction with the plunging sides of the spur. It is of slightly rounded square section, flattened alongside the rowel with squared ends to the rowel box. Star rowel of six round-section, sharp points, one tip damaged. (1250–1300)

Similar early rowel spurs include examples from London (London Museum 1940 100, no 6, fig 30); Beeston Castle, Cheshire (Ellis 1993, 165, no 1, microfiche M2: E14–59, 166, fig 112) and Rhuddlan, Clwyd (Ellis 1994, 188, no 137, fig 17:7). These are all iron but the Rhuddlan spur has a buckle and two rivet attachments made of copper alloy.

323 BC72 3664 (250) 10 Figs 91–3
overall l of side fragment 71mm, l of main leather as excavated, still buckled and stiffened into a curve, *c*.400mm, w of leathers varies, *c*.8mm

Detached spur side decorated with roses and a swan, with its complete leathers. Of the same type as No 322, it is of extremely slender triangular section, the front end bending up towards a single ring terminal. The side is decorated with two six-petalled flowers (Fig 91 F) riveted on to it. The centres of the flowers are textured with dots so that they appear to be roses. At the bend of the side a tiny figure of a swan (Fig 91 E) has been riveted to stand proud with its tail and wings spread and its neck raised, the head facing upwards.

92 Fragment of rowel spur with leathers, No 323

93 Close-up of side of
spur No 323, showing
decoration of bird
and roses

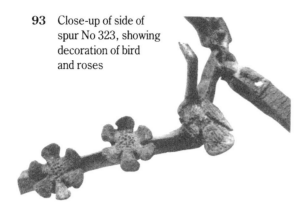

The terminal ring has two small rivet attachments
holding the leathers (Fig 91 A), which are very narrow,
but relatively thick, dark brown leather. The shorter
leather has a small iron buckle fixed to its end by two
rivets, one above the other, the lower one having a
small washer against the inner surface (Fig 91 D) below
the fairly square buckle frame with its long pin (Fig 91

C). The shorter leather also carries a small upright
square loop – with a quadrangular disc rather like a
signet ring – riveted to stand proud of it (Fig 91 A).
This would have held the pendent end of the longer
leather after it had passed through the buckle. This
main leather ran downwards from the lower part of the
terminal ring, passing under the wearer's foot to rise
through a slot terminal (like that of No 322) on the inner
side of the foot towards the buckle (Fig 91 D) for which
it is pierced. Beyond the buckle the leather bears four
flat circular plaques and its end is riveted between the
two sides of a narrow iron strap-end mount (Fig 91 B).
The position of the buckle and ring terminal show that
the fragment is the outer side of a spur worn on the
right foot. It is probable that the missing inner side
would have been plain. (1250–1325).

For comparisons and discussion of the decoration of
this spur, see section titled 'Chronology and development', above.

324 SWA81 725 (20/66) 9 Figs 94, 95
overall l 117mm, l of neck 29mm, span 74mm, maximum d of rowel (points vary) 27mm, l of attachments

94   Rowel spur and fittings, No 324

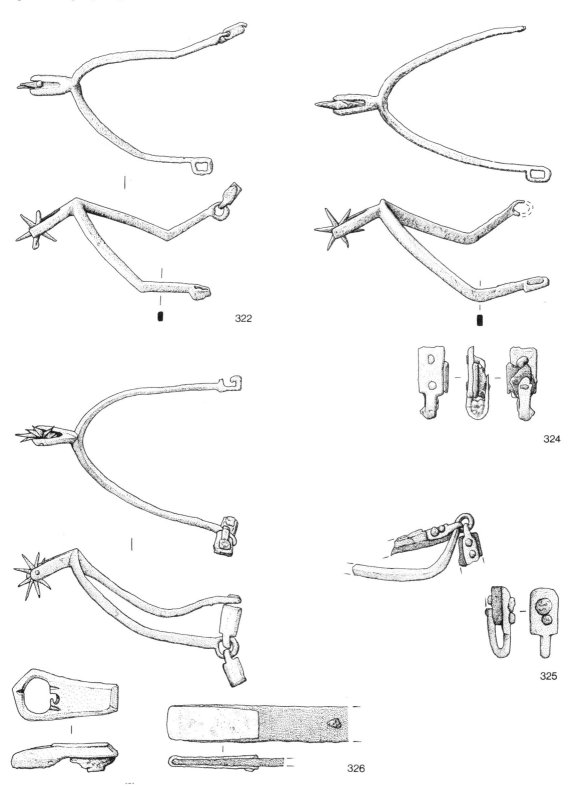

322

324

325

326

95 Rowel spurs, Nos 322 and 324–6 (1:2; fittings on Nos 324–6 shown 1:1)

96   Rowel spur and fittings, No 326

19 and 20mm, max l of leather fragments *c.*110mm, max w 8mm

Spur with much non-ferrous plating, probably tin, all over it; of slender proportions and similar to No 322, with tapered sides of rectangular section. One broken single-ring terminal and a slot terminal show it to have been worn on a left foot. The sides join in a rounded junction, from below which the straight neck swells a little before dividing into a rowel box with squared ends. Star rowel of six round-section, sharp points. Two rectangular iron rivet attachments for the leathers, now detached, are similar to those of No 323 with two rivets each and non-ferrous plating. The rivets, which may be copper alloy, remain, one still holding a scrap of leather. The spur is accompanied by four fragments of its leathers (not illustrated), pierced with holes for the buckle pin. (Mid-13th–early 14th century)

325   SWA81   785   (2051)   9   Fig 95
l of broken side 60.8mm, l of longest leather fragment 30mm

The triangular section side, which is tinned, bends strongly under the wearer's ankle and tapers to extreme slenderness as it rises towards the single-ring terminal. Two tinned iron attachments remain, each with two copper alloy rivets holding fragments of the leathers. (Typologically 1250–1300)

Similar to the sides of Nos 322 and 323.

326   SWA81   891   (2141)   9   Figs 95, 96
l 120mm, l of neck 27mm, span (slight distortion) now 77mm, d of rowel *c.*21mm, l of buckle 28mm, l of fragments of leathers *c.*150mm and 52mm, w *c.*8mm

Traces of non-ferrous plating, probably tin. The extremely slender sides, of rounded-square section, curve moderately under the wearer's ankle. The single-ring terminal worn to the outside of the foot and the inner slot terminal show that the spur was worn on the right foot. The straight, round-section neck projects strongly downwards carrying a small star rowel of nine needle-like points. Two attachments on the ring terminal each have one rivet retaining a scrap of broken leather. One of these leathers would have been short – for a long tapered buckle, now detached, with a D-shaped frame at its broadest end; pin lost. Its narrow end was attached to the leather by one rivet. The long leather which originally encircled the foot survives in three separate fragments, with a flat metal strap-end mount doubled over at one end and held by a single rivet. (1250–1300)

327 SWA81 2120 (2070) 9 Fig 97
l (distorted) 120mm, l of neck 27mm, d of rowel 26mm, l of attachment 17mm
Non-ferrous plating, tinning, which remains on the outer surfaces and terminals was probably worn away from the inner surfaces of the sides by use. Similar to No 326 but with triangular section sides, as No 323, which have become distorted during burial. Both neck and sides taper slightly towards their extremities, the neck divided for most of its length by the rowel box which has a squared end, pierced by the rowel pin; star rowel of six narrow sharp points, one missing. The arrangement of a single-ring terminal and a slot terminal indicates a spur for a left foot. One small attachment for a leather has become separated from the partly broken ring terminal. It consists of a narrow iron strip, doubled to form a loop through the terminal and clasping the remaining fragment of leather between its ends. These expand, one into a square and one into a disc shape, and a copper alloy rivet holds everything together. The square end, which would have been visible in use, has a narrow edge border of parallel lines. (1250–1300)

328 SWA81 2119 (2070) 9 Fig 97
l 80mm, span approximately 66mm, l of neck 11mm, d of rowel (points vary) 16mm, w of leather fragment 7mm
A very small tinned spur. The D-section sides curve evenly under the wearer's ankle and join in a small pointed crest above the short straight neck, which is divided for most of its length by the rowel box. Star rowel of six round-section sharp points. One terminal is a vertically pierced slot, the other, which is missing, would almost certainly have been a single ring (cf. Nos 322, 324, 326, 327, 329) – suggesting that this spur was for a right foot. It is accompanied by a scrap of its

missing leather narrow enough to pass freely through the terminal slot. (Probably 1260–1320)

329 SUN86 1075 (814) – Fig 97
overall l 103mm, l of neck 30mm, d of rowel 30mm (l of longest point 15mm), span now compressed
Copper alloy with iron rowel pin and rowel. The tapered sides, which are of triangular section, have become compressed, reducing their original span. They plunge forwards into deep curves under the wearer's ankle, and the front ends then rise and bend gracefully forwards to the terminals. One terminal is a single ring, the other a vertically pierced slot with its outer surface formed as a disc. The ring terminal would have been worn to the outside of a left foot; two attachments for the missing leathers remain on it, with square bodies to which the short leather for a buckle and the long encircling leather were attached by two rivets each; three rivets survive. Behind the wearer's heel the top edges of the spur sides extend into a flange which becomes a pointed crest above their junction. The straight, round-section neck projects slightly downwards and the rowel box divides most of its length. Star rowel of six round-section points (two broken). (1300–40)

330 TL74 594 (415) 11 Fig 97
l 120mm, l of neck 33mm, d of rowel (points vary slightly) 31mm, l of buckle 45mm
The surviving side, of D-section, plunges strongly down; its front end bends at almost 90 degrees under the wearer's ankle, rising towards a two-hole terminal with an oval outline. Both neck and side of this spur taper towards their extremities and form a thick, triangular-pointed junction together with the stump of the missing side. The sturdy neck has a straight bottom edge, while its top edge tapers down towards the oval disc-shaped rowel bosses. Both sides of the neck are decorated with two vertical ridges, each incised with a line. The thick rowel box edges are finished with a suggestion of rough faceting. The rowel has eight thick points. The long buckle attached to the uppermost hole of the terminal on the surviving side shows that the spur was worn on the left foot (buckles were worn on the outside). Below the pin, the body of the buckle projects down, then broadens into an oval area with the remains of a rivet at its centre. Beneath this is the ring hook fastening it to the spur terminal. The missing rivet probably held a D-shaped loop to retain the loose end of the leather, like a similar spur buckle from Salisbury (Ellis 1991, 74, no 17 a & b, fig 18). (1325–70)

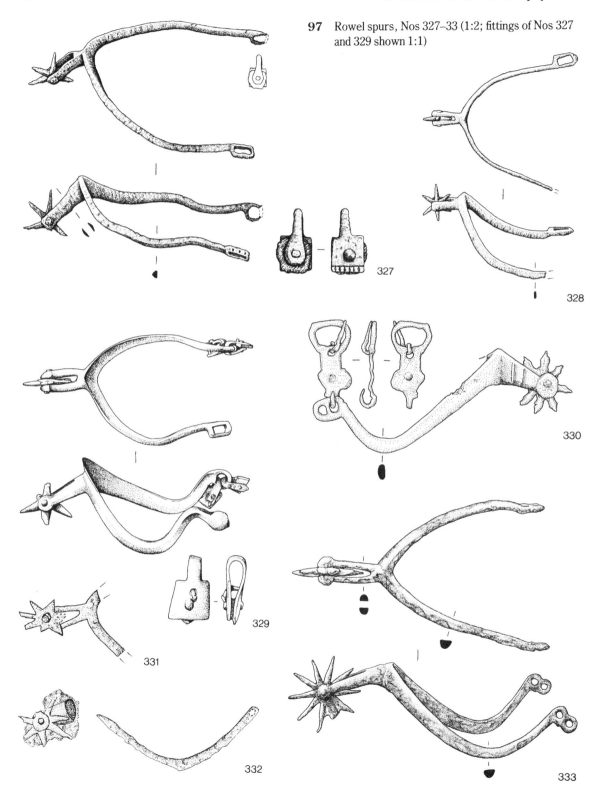

97 Rowel spurs, Nos 327–33 (1:2; fittings of Nos 327 and 329 shown 1:1)

327

328

329

330

331

332

333

331 SH74 75 (280) 15th-century dump Fig 97
l (including rowel) 60mm, l of neck 30mm, d of rowel
35mm
Fragment, described from a radiograph, which shows
traces of non-ferrous plating on the rowel. The remaining stumps of the broken spur sides project downwards
from their junction. The short straight neck is divided
for most of its length by the rowel box, which appears
to have fairly prominent conical rowel bosses; star
rowel of seven points. (Mid-14th century)

332 SH74 482 (291) 8 Fig 97
d of rowel (estimated from the longest point on the
actual size X-ray) originally 38mm
Fragments consisting of the core of a severely rusted,
curved spur side and a detached star rowel, heavily
encrusted, and shown by radiograph to have seven
points. (Probably 14th century; rowel too large to have
been earlier)

333 BC72 2438 (118) 10–11 Fig 97
l 122mm, l of neck 35mm, span 72mm, d of rowel,
points vary, 39mm
Traces of non-ferrous plating, probably tin. The slender D-section sides plunge into deep curves under the
wearer's ankle and rise towards figure-8 terminals at
the front. The neck is of rounded section and is fairly
straight, with a hint of a downward curve along its
length. It tapers towards the bold conical rowel bosses.
Large star rowel of ten round-section points (one
broken). (1350–1400)

Similar spurs are depicted on the monumental brasses of Sir Edward Cerne (1393) at Draycot Cerne,
Wiltshire, and Sir Morys Russell, (1401) at Dyrham,
Gloucestershire (Fig 98). The spurs worn by Edward
the Black Prince (died 1376) on his monumental effigy
in Canterbury Cathedral, Kent, are of the same basic
form although they have slight crests (Stothard 1817,
pl 86, details 4 & 5).

98 Spur shown on brass of Sir Morys Russell (d
1401), Dyrham, Gloucestershire – cf. No 333

334 BC72 1961 (55) 11 (not illustrated)
l of fragment 50mm, d of rowel originally 30mm; l of
part of spur side 37mm
Fragments, heavily encrusted, described from radiograph: (a) star rowel, probably of eight points, two still
complete, on a short (though perhaps incomplete)
straight neck; (b) part of slender spur side, its section
uncertain; (c) two further fragments of sides. (Probably
14th century, dated by context)

335 BC72 4369 (150) 11 Fig 99
overall l 115m, l of neck 31mm
Non-ferrous plating, probably tin. The slender, rounded D-section sides, both slightly distorted, curve
strongly under the wearer's ankle, ending in figure-8
terminals. The slightly tapered neck projects downwards; it is encircled by a moulding, decorated with a
row of parallel incised lines, next to its junction with the
spur sides; the remainder is divided by the rowel box.
The conical rowel bosses retain the pin but the rowel is
lost. (1340–1400)

336 ER1279A 13 – Fig 99
l now 92mm, l of neck 25mm
One severely rusted D-section side curves evenly
under the wearer's ankle; terminal lost. Only a stump
of the other side remains. The short straight neck is
encircled by a plain moulded ridge next to its junction
with the sides. The rowel is missing but at least part of
its pin remains. (1340–1400)

The spur is similar to and contemporary with Nos
333 and 335, although its side is more gently curved.
From Thames at London Bridge (Marsden 1971, 12).

337 BWB83 27 (142) 11 Fig 99 (from X-ray)
l 125mm, l of neck 45mm, l of rowel points 25mm
(original d estimated to have been 50mm)
Heavily encrusted, but traces of non-ferrous plating
appear on the X-ray. The D-section sides curve deeply
under the wearer's ankle then rise to what are probably
figure-8 terminals. The buckle, attachments for the
leathers, and possibly fragments of the leathers themselves, survive within the accretions. The neck, which
is straight or possibly slightly drooping, is divided for
most of its length by the rowel box. Three points (of
probably six to eight points) of a large star rowel
remain. The radiograph reveals a slender spur with a
small ridge round the neck next to its junction with the
sides (Nos 335, 336 also have this feature). The buckle
appears to be of the long type with a D-shaped frame at
one end (pin missing) and a small hook at the other end
to hold on to the spur terminal. Two attachments for
the leathers are quite long with narrow rectangular
bodies. (1340–1400)

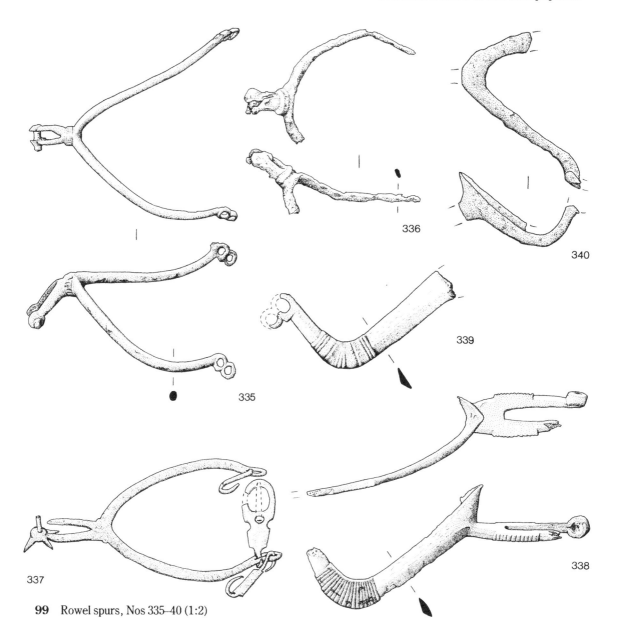

99   Rowel spurs, Nos 335–40 (1:2)

338   TL74   708   (415)   11   Fig 99
l 162mm, l of neck 61mm, including l of rowel box
43mm
Large rowel spur; one side missing; the other de-
scends forwards to bend at right angles under the
wearer's ankle. Its terminal has gone but compare No
339, a detached but almost identical side of a spur with
a figure-8 terminal. The side is of mainly triangular
section, but the area of the bend beneath the ankle is
flat, its outer surface decorated with fine vertical
ridges. The top edges of the sides rise into a high crest
where they join, and below it the straight neck projects, thick and flat in section. Both sides of the neck
are decorated with vertical ridges. One rowel boss is
missing, the other is a large thick disc; rowel and pin
are lost. (1340–90)

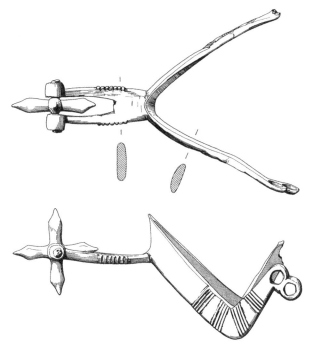

100 Rowel spur with iron rowel pin and copper-alloy rowel, Ludgershall Castle, Wiltshire (Devizes Museum – Ellis forthcoming, no 7) – cf. Nos 338 and 339

A gilded copper-alloy spur of extremely similar form, size and decoration came from the excavations at Ludgershall Castle and is now in Devizes Museum (Fig 100 – see Ellis forthcoming, no 7). It was found in two pieces, one in a courtyard outside the royal buildings erected 1341–3, the other in a post-medieval context. Its iron rowel pin holds a copper-alloy rowel of only four points. A few mid- to late 14th-century spurs with these unusual four-point rowels are known from sites in England and France. Most are of copper alloy. An iron spur – like No 338 except that it is undecorated and has a sagging curve along the length of its neck – is acc no 6689 in the Musée de l'Hôtel Sandelin, Saint Omer, France, where it was a local find. It has a four-point rowel, figure-8 terminals and large oval hook attachments for its leathers. The large rowel box of No 338 could have accommodated one of the large multi-point rowels fashionable in the late 14th century, but its similarity to the Ludgershall spur suggests that it may have been one of the small group with rowels of four points. (See section titled 'Chronology and development', above.)

339 BC72 4758 (255) 11 Fig 99
maximum l 102mm
Side of a spur, very similar to No 338, mainly of triangular section, with a strong bend under the ankle of flat section, decorated with a pattern of radiating vertical ridges on its outer surface. Both rings of the figure-8 terminal are broken. (From a large spur of 1340–90)

340 OPT81 132 (47) 9 Fig 99
maximum l of fragments 85 and 80mm
Two fragments, very heavily corroded. One spur side, probably of D-section, tapers as it plunges to where its front end curves strongly under the wearer's ankle before rising towards the missing terminal. It joins the stump of the other, broken, side in a high-pointed crest, below which the neck is missing. The second fragment (not illustrated) is the front end of the broken side, which on the radiograph appears to have a figure-8 terminal. (Mid-14th–mid-15th century)

Without the spur neck, it is impossible to date the fragments closely. As far as corrosion permits examination, the size and shape of the sides are similar to those of No 338, and a mid-14th-century date would not disagree with the context, but they are also like the sides of the 15th-century long spur No 348.

341 BC72 4168 (88) 11 Fig 101
l 144mm, l of neck 43mm, maximum d of rowel 35mm, l of small hook attachment 22mm, l of large attachment 62mm, w 14mm, d of rivet head 8mm (present measurements; spur distorted by burial)
Slender spur with unusual long attachment for a leather. The sides, which are of rectangular section, taper towards their figure-8 terminals while plunging forward into curves under the wearer's ankle; their span was compressed during burial. At their junction the top edges of the sides rise into a long thin crest which curls in a half circle, its tip touching the top of the spur neck. The area of the neck below the crest commences as square in section, defined by a slight ridge, then its top surface is scooped into a small hollow, only to regain its square section where it is touched by the crest tip. Behind this, the neck is divided by a long slender rowel box, which has disc rowel bosses with, between them, a star rowel of six points. The spur has two attachments for the leathers on one of its terminals. In its lower ring is a small hook attachment with a disc-shaped body, its size in proportion to that of the spur. The attachment in its upper ring is extremely unusual. Although it was present when excavated and therefore when the spur was used, it appears to be much too

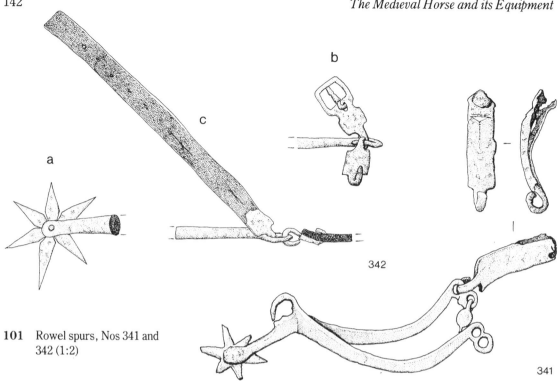

101 Rowel spurs, Nos 341 and
       342 (1:2)

large for such a slender spur with thin terminal rings.
The large attachment curves along its entire length to
lie comfortably along the top of the wearer's foot. It has
the usual form of bottom ring looped through the
terminal of the spur side, and above that it is divided
into a broad, double strip clasping what appears to be a
fragment of leather, secured at its uppermost end by a
large rivet. The outer surface slopes to a long central
ridge. The proportions of the spur anticipate the
fashion trend towards longer necks at the turn of the
century. The missing buckle must have been attached
to the empty terminal and, as buckles were worn on
the outside of the foot, this spur was for a right foot.
(1360–1400)

342 SWA81 4262 (2102) 12 Fig 101
d of rowel 50mm, l of neck fragment 45mm, l of buckle
40mm, l of attachments 25mm, w of spur leather varies
11–12mm
Three encrusted fragments joined by a spur leather;
non-ferrous plating revealed on X-ray. The fragments
comprise (a) a rowel of six lozenge-shaped points with
part, possibly most, of a straight neck; (b) the end of
one spur side with a single-ring terminal – a buckle with
a small square frame at one end, spreading into a
square area below the frame and pin, has a ring hook
looped through the terminal, which also holds a small,

square-bodied hook attachment for a leather; (c) the
end of the other spur side, also with a single-ring
terminal. It has two square-bodied hook attachments,
one holding the end of the spur leather, which is made
of leather. (Probably *c*.1400)

Typologically it is impossible to date the spur in its
present condition with certainty, but rowels with
lozenge-shaped points on spurs with single-ring terminals were popular early in the period of its archaeological
context.

343 SWA81 2707 (2117) 12 Fig 103
l 61mm
Front end of a spur side of D-section, curved and rising
to a single-ring terminal. (14th or early 15th century,
see note for No 342)

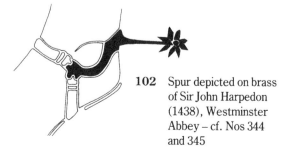

102 Spur depicted on brass
       of Sir John Harpedon
       (1438), Westminster
       Abbey – cf. Nos 344
       and 345

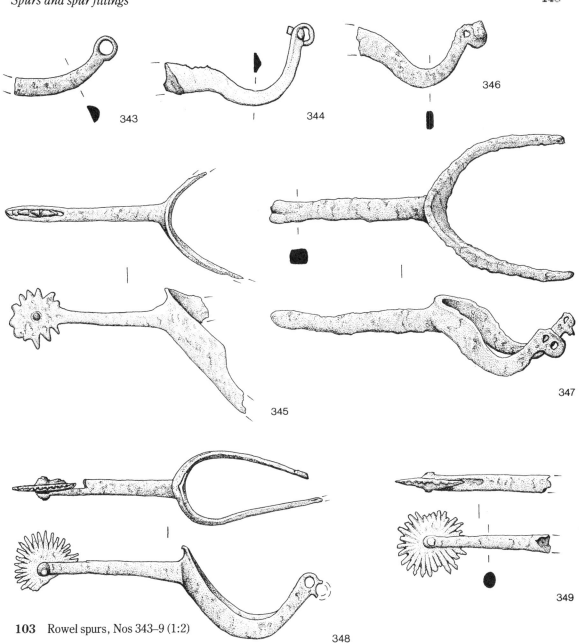

103 Rowel spurs, Nos 343–9 (1:2)

344 TL74 1201 (368) 12 Fig 103
l 88mm
Spur side of triangular section, with considerable traces of non-ferrous plating, probably tin, on its outer surface. It is gracefully formed with a small flange along the top edge, at the back of the wearer's foot, where it rises into a small crest point next to the break. From the rear, the side projects forwards and only slightly downwards, tapering as the flange disappears smoothly into the front part, which plunges into a deep curve under the ankle, rising again to its single-ring terminal. The upper and lower areas of this terminal are worn thin by the attachments for the leathers. Only half a ring hook of one attachment remains, rusted to the terminal. (1400–50)

Fig 103, unusually, shows the inner surface of the

spur side. This side is similar to those on the spurs of
Sir John Harpedon on his monumental brass of 1438 in
Westminster Abbey (Fig 102), compare also No 345.

345 TL74 2728 (368) 12 Fig 103
l 140mm, l of neck with rowel 80mm, d of rowel
originally 30mm

Long spur, heavily rusted; traces of non-ferrous plating
visible on radiograph. The top edge of the more
complete side rises into a slightly crested flange around
the back of the wearer's heel, while its front part
narrows as it plunges into a curve under his ankle (cf.
No 344 and the spur from the Harpedon brass of 1438 –
Fig 102). The long, straight, round-section neck is
slightly tapered and carries a (rusted) multi-point rowel
of 14 points, similar to the rowels of Nos 348 and 349.
(1400–50)

346 TL74 1204 (275) – Fig 103
l 70mm

Side of flat section and serpentine form, its front end
plunging into a strong curve under the wearer's ankle.
It tapers towards the small, two-hole terminal, which
has a small fragment of an attachment rusted on to it.
(Probably 1400–50)

Compare Nos 344, 345 and 347.

347 CUT78 47 (473) 1550+ Fig 103
l 166mm, span 69mm, l of neck 90mm, l of rowel box
(from X-ray) 38mm

Long spur; the D-section sides arc around the back of
the wearer's heel while only their front ends plunge
into strong curves under the ankle, rising to figure-8
terminals; the lower ring of one terminal is broken. It
appears probable that the top edges of the sides rose
into a very slight flange or crest above their junction
with the neck; details unclear even on X-ray. The neck,
which projects from the lower part of the junction of the
sides, is round and slightly tapered towards a very long
rowel box; rowel missing. The long rowel box could
have held quite a large rowel. (Probably 1400–50)

Compare Nos 345 and 346 from contexts of 1400–50
and also the spurs on the monumental brass at Kidder-
minster (Worcestershire) of Walter Cooksey, died
1415 (London Museum 1940, 104, no 7, fig 32). This
suggests the probable date for this spur, despite its
post-medieval archaeological context.

348 TL74 1106 (368) 12 Fig 103
l 152mm, l of neck 75mm, d of rowel, varies, c.35mm

Long spur with traces of non-ferrous plating, probably
tin. The flat section sides have been compressed, but
retain their strong even curve under the wearer's
ankle, rising towards damaged figure-8 terminals. A

pointed crest at the junction of the sides curls towards
the long, round-section neck, which tapers towards the
rowel box, one side of which is damaged although both
small conical rowel bosses survive. The multi-point
rowel is incomplete, leaving 19 of originally about 30
points (cf. No 349 below). (1400–60)

349 TL74 1179 (275) 12 Fig 103
l of incomplete neck 65mm, maximum d of rowel
39mm, l of whole fragment 85mm

Fragment comprising the rowel and broken neck of a
long spur, similar to No 348. The multi-point rowel has
29 points, several partly broken. (1400–60)

350 BC72 3877 (265) – Fig 104
l 156mm, l of neck 80mm, d of rowel originally c.40mm

Long spur, very severely rusted and flaking; possible
traces of non-ferrous plating visible on X-ray. One side,
possibly of D-section, plunges forwards into a strong
curve under the wearer's ankle. Its front end rises to a
terminal, which appears to be of single-ring form, and
retains the broken ring loop from an attachment. Little
remains of the other side. The top edges of the sides
are drawn up into a bold crest, which curls over their
junction with the long straight neck. Prominent rowel
bosses flank a star rowel of eight points, their tips
damaged. (1400–60)

351 ER872 184 – Fig 104
l 140mm, span 77mm, l of neck 72mm, l of rowel box
23mm

Long spur with slight traces of probable non-ferrous
plating, of small proportions but of sufficiently wide
span for wear by an adult. The square-section sides
taper forwards and plunge into strong curves under the
wearer's ankle, their front ends rising to figure-8
terminals. The sides join beneath what must have been
a moderate crest point, now broken. The slender,
round neck has a slight drooped curve along its length
and small rowel bosses but the rowel is lost. From
Thames foreshore. (1400–50)

The square section of the sides is fairly unusual for
spurs in general later than the exceptionally slender,
early rowel spurs such as No 322. The gentle curve
along the length of the spur neck is almost certainly
original. Other long spurs with this feature in the
Museum of London collection include acc no A2422
(London Museum 1940, 111, no 4, fig 35, and 7431
(Guildhall Museum 1908, 267, no 99 and pl LXXXII,
11).

352 ER1279A 15 – Fig 104
l (extremities missing) 120mm

Long spur; front ends of both D-section sides missing,

104 Rowel spurs, Nos 350–56 (1:2)

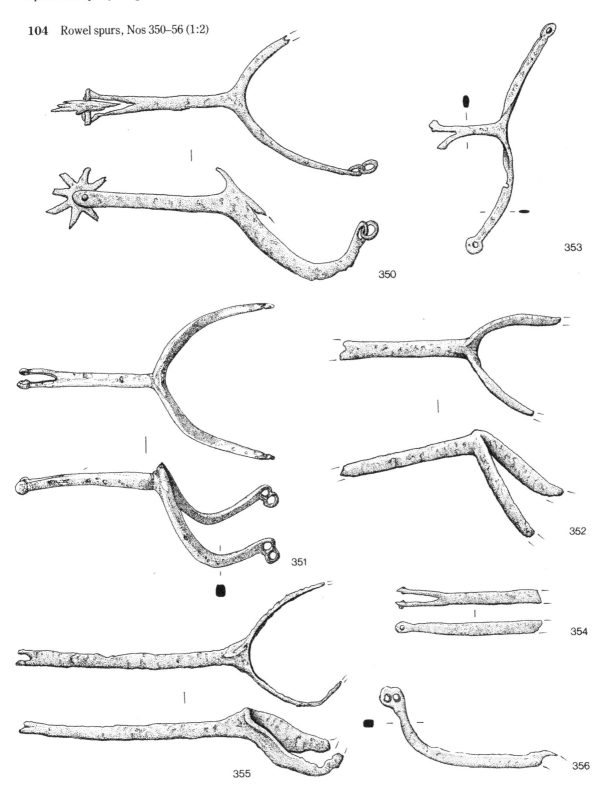

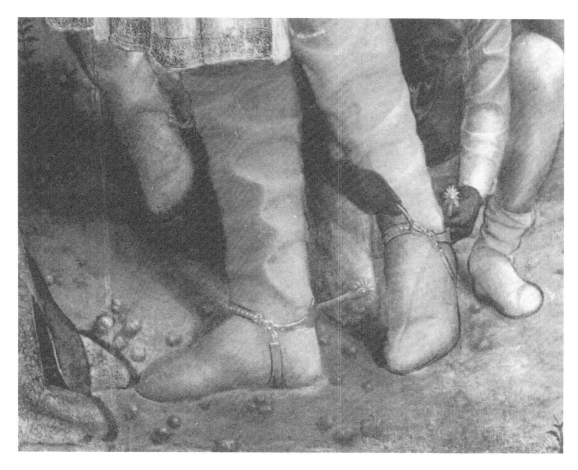

105   *The Adoration of the Kings* (detail): Vincenzo Foppa (d 1515) (National Gallery) – cf. No 355

but the sides project strongly downwards into what must have been a deep curve under the wearer's ankle (as do those of No 351). There appears to have been a crest point above the junction of the sides, which is now damaged. The long, round-section, straight neck is broken at the beginning of the rowel box division. From Thames at London Bridge (Marsden 1971, 12). (1400–50)

353   ER1279A   67   –   Fig 104
maximum l of distorted spur, terminal to terminal 132mm, l of neck 40mm
Delicately proportioned spur severely distorted, apparently under great weight. Its unusually short, thin sides are of flat section with very small single-ring terminals. It is no longer possible to tell whether the sides were horizontally straight or curved. The end of the very slender, oval neck has a small rowel box now

splayed open, so that its rowel and most of the rowel pin are lost. The proportions of this little spur, with its neck considerably longer than needed by the rowel box, suggest that it is a miniature long spur made for a child. From Thames at London Bridge (Marsden 1971, 12). (Probably early 15th century)

354   BYD81   49   (19)   12   Fig 104
l 81mm
Broken neck from a long spur, heavily coated with rust, which fills the rowel box; radiograph shows traces of non-ferrous plating, especially on one rowel boss. The slender, straight neck is of round section. The rowel box has small conical rowel bosses; rowel lost. (15th century)

355   ER1279A   66   –   Fig 104
l 175mm, l of (incomplete) neck 125mm
Long spur, badly rusted, the extremities gone. The

remaining parts of the sides are of flat section and project downwards less strongly than those of the long spurs described above. The long, straight, round-section neck has a broken rowel box so that the rowel and its pin are lost. From Thames at London Bridge (Marsden 1971, 12). (1450–1500)

Compare the spur shown on the slightly later painting, *The Adoration of the Kings* (see Fig 105), one of the last works by the Milanese painter Vincenzo Foppa (died 1515).

356 BYD81 50 (19) 12 Fig 104
l (from X-ray) 64mm
Side of a spur, almost complete, of extremely slender proportions. As the rest of the spur is missing, it is impossible to tell whether the side projected at a downward angle from behind the wearer's heel. It is in itself mainly straight, with only its front end of rectangular section turned up towards a figure-8 terminal. (Probably 1430–1500)

SPUR ROWELS

Star rowels have separate points joined only at the centre (as No 357); multi-point rowels have many points close to each other, often separated only at their tips (as No 361). Either description could be used for No 360. Simple star rowels with a varying number of points have been used on spurs from the introduction of rowels in the 13th century until modern times, so that typological dating of detached rowels is seldom possible; for example, No 357 from a context dated 1200–30 is similar to the rowel of spur No 341, context 1350–1400. The star rowels described below were probably made and used shortly before or during the period of their archaeological contexts.

Alongside the popular star rowels there have been a few recognisable rowel fashions. The rare group of 4-point rowels has been mentioned under catalogue No 338 above. Another 14th-century development throughout Britain and Europe was for increasingly large rowels of many points (Byrne 1959). The monumental brass made in London 1340–5 to commemorate Sir John de Creke in Westley Waterless Church (Cambridgeshire) shows his spurs with multi-point rowels which are not exceptionally large. A similar but larger rowel is depicted on the portrait of Sir Geoffrey Luttrell of Irnham (Lincolnshire) in the Luttrell Psalter, 1325–35 (Fig 17 – British Library Add MS 42130, f202b). The size of fashionable rowels steadily increased until by the last quarter of the century diameters such as the 60mm and 75mm of two detached rowels from Billingsgate (Nos 361, 362) were achieved. The former has 32 points and the latter, which is damaged, had more. Such a rowel was carved on the monumental effigy in Westminster Abbey of Sir Bernard Brocas (died 1400; Stothard 1817, pl 144). The rowel size can still be seen although the stone has worn smooth. Spurs with exceptionally large rowels are worn by Sir Hugh Calveley (died 1394) on his monumental effigy in Bunbury Church, Cheshire, which was probably carved between 1387 and 1394 (Fig 107 – Blair 1951, 1; Stothard 1817, pl 98, 99). The fashion for huge, multi-point rowels died out at the end of the 14th century with the advent of the long spurs, though smaller multi-point rowels were still sometimes used, as on the long spurs from Trig Lane (Nos 345, 348, 349). A few of the bigger long spurs had star rowels of large diameter, such as Museum of London acc no A4971 (London Museum 1940, 111, no 5, fig 35) and the spur from Queenhithe (Royal Armouries VI-434, above), but, in general, rowels became smaller during the 15th and early 16th centuries.

The rowel diameter measurement often varies slightly and the maximum diameter is given in the catalogue. When a rowel is no longer complete its diameter is estimated from its most complete surviving point. All rowels are of iron except where otherwise stated.

357 BIG82 acc no 2803 (context 4100) ceramic phase 7 Fig 106
d 33mm
Star rowel of six round-section points; traces of non-ferrous plating, probably tin. The context date (1200–30) is very early for a rowel when one allows for even a short period of use prior to its loss. (13th century)

358 BIG82 3659 (3204) 7 Fig 106
d 45mm
Star rowel of six widely separated, round-section points; traces of non-ferrous plating, probably tin. The tips are now distorted and bent. It is extremely unlikely to be earlier than 1300 despite its context date of 1200–30, when rowels were much smaller.

359 BWB83 213 (298) 11 Fig 106
d 70mm
Star rowel; its six points were originally of elegant,

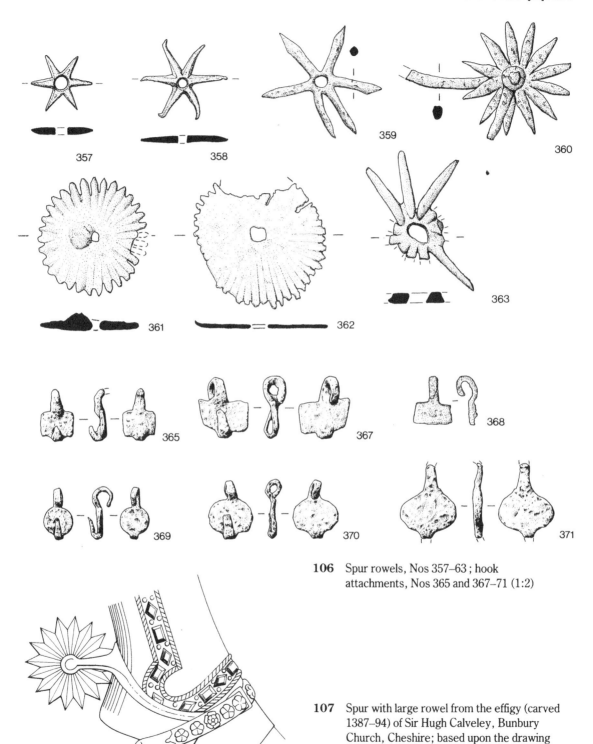

357   358   359   360

361   362   363

365   367   368

369   370   371

106 Spur rowels, Nos 357–63 ; hook
attachments, Nos 365 and 367–71 (1:2)

107 Spur with large rowel from the effigy (carved
1387–94) of Sir Hugh Calveley, Bunbury
Church, Cheshire; based upon the drawing
made by C A Stothard in 1813 (Blair 1951, 1;
Stothard 1817, pl 98, 99) – cf. Nos 361 and 362

elongated lozenge shape, but two are now distorted and there has been rust damage. The radiograph shows that the central hole has been worn into an oval shape by use. (1340–1400)

360 BWB83 152 (307) 11 Fig 106
d 62mm, l of longest box fragment 65mm
Star rowel with broken rowel box. Large rowel of 12 rounded lozenge-shaped points. It is flanked by the broken sides of a long rowel box which are slightly faceted, with disc-shaped bosses. The longest rowel box fragment has become curved. (1340–1400)

361 BWB83 534 (333) 11 Fig 106
d 60mm
Large multi-point rowel; non-ferrous plating visible on radiograph. Of the original 32 points, joined for most of their length, three are now broken. (1360–1400)

For a rowel of comparable size, see the effigy in Westminster Abbey of Sir Bernard Brocas (died 1400) and that of Sir Hugh Calveley (carved 1387–94) in Bunbury Church, Cheshire (Fig 107).

362 BWB83 2906 (286) 11 Fig 106
d 75mm
Large multi-point rowel; edges corroded. Originally about 47 points were joined together except at the tips, defined by incised radiating lines from the central hole. Similar to No 361. (1360–1400)

363 TL74 450 (415) – Fig 106
d originally 85mm
Star rowel; originally with 12 points of quadrangular section. The oval shape of the central hole suggests much wear during use, as if uneven weight had always caused it to return to the same position on its pin, perhaps because of a broken point. The rowel and its points were made in one piece; not, as damage appears to suggest, with separate points added to a central core. (1350–*c*.1380)

108 Unfinished copper-alloy casting of spur rowel, No 364

364 VRY89 (964) – Fig 108
d 57mm
Star rowel. Copper alloy, cast but unfinished, with surplus metal adhering, especially between two points

and joining the tips of two others. The eight points are elegantly formed, swelling into their greatest thickness at the base of the tips. Found during off-site recovery programme on spoil from site at Vintners Place, Upper Thames Street. (Probably 1340–1460)

HOOK ATTACHMENTS FOR SPUR LEATHERS

Hook attachments were in use from the 13th century into the post-medieval period, so that it is rarely possible to date separate attachments closely other than by their archaeological contexts. All are made of iron except for No 369.

365 BWB83 acc no 3437 (context 293) ceramic phase 11 Fig 106
w 18mm, maximum l 22mm
Non-ferrous surface plating shown on X-ray. A flat, rectangular body with a broken ring-loop rising from its top edge to attach it to the spur terminal; hook for the leather on its lower edge. (Typologically 13th–16th century, context late 14th century)

366 BWB83 3431 (307) 11 not illustrated
w 24mm, l 29mm
Similar to No 365, but complete; suggestion of non-ferrous plating on X-ray. (Context 1350–1400)

367 BWB83 4339 (110) 11 Fig 106
w 26mm, l 33mm
Similar to No 366. Its bold proportions and strong hook for the leather suggest that it came from a large spur, such as were popular during the context period 1350–1400.

368 BWB83 3791 (149) 11 Fig 106
w 19mm, l (now incomplete) 29mm
Similar to No 367 but broken; part of its body survives with a curved hook on one edge. (Context 1350–1400)

369 SWA81 788 (2983) 9 Fig 106
w 15mm, l 27mm
Copper alloy with gilding. Disc-shaped body, nicely detailed finish. (Late 13th–14th century)

370 BWB83 355 (157) 11 Fig 106
w 23mm, l 31mm
Oval body. Similar attachments are clearly shown on the long spurs worn by Richard Dixton Esq (died 1438) on his monumental brass in Cirencester Church (Gloucestershire). (Context 1350–1400)

371 BWB83 4315 (157) 11 Fig 106
w 29mm, l (incomplete) 37mm
Probable hook attachment. The roughly oval-shaped

body has extensions on opposite edges from which the hooks have broken off. (Context 1350–1400)

SPUR BUCKLES

Geoff Egan

Buckles with integral, bevelled plates

In all these buckles, the dimensions are for the complete object (frame and plate together). The plate has a single hole for the pin – all those that survive are of iron wire. Riveting arrangements are varied and often markedly crude – a possible pointer to reuse or a need for repair in the majority of these distinctive buckles (published as nos 482–7 in Egan & Pritchard 1991).

Only the last in this 13th–14th-century series is still in association with a spur (from a deposit possibly later than the other four). This provides a plausible interpretation for the category as a whole (see also Alexander & Binski 1987, 259–60 nos 166–7 for broadly comparable late 13th- and early 14th-century buckles with hooked ends still attached to spurs), but it remains to be seen whether the evidence holds true for future finds of other buckles of the series. The strength of the integral plates and frames relative to their size suggests that they were designed to stand up to fairly rough use, though the pins are not notably robust. Such spurs might have been more appropriate for use in towns rather than for long journeys or on military campaigns.

Copper alloy

372 SWA81 acc no 2261 (context 2279) ceramic phase 7 Fig 109
25 × 13mm
Gunmetal (AML); oval frame; notched lip; bilobed plate has integral rivet with irregular polygonal sheet rove; pin missing; leather from strap 8mm wide survives.

Iron

373 SWA81 acc no 3393 (context 2141) ceramic phase 9 Fig 109
32 × 12.5mm
Slightly trapezoidal frame; grooved sheet roller; plate has a transverse ridge and two rivets – one with a very large head and an (?) iron rove; tin coating on all these parts; pin incomplete; leather from strap survives.

374 SWA81 626 (2051) 9 Fig 109
25 × 13mm
Circular frame; plate has two dome-headed copper-alloy rivets, which share a rectangular copper-alloy rove; tin coating on frame, plate and rivet heads (MLC); leather from strap 9.5mm wide survives.

375 SWA81 780 (2051) 9 Fig 109
24 × 13mm
Trapezoidal frame; plate has transverse ridge and single rivet; pin is corroded and incomplete; tin-coating.

376 SWA81 2874 (2070) 9 Fig 109
26 × 13mm
Circular frame; pin notch; plate has transverse ridge and two dome-headed, bent tacks, one of which is of copper alloy and the other of lead/tin – these share an irregular-shaped rove; tin coating on plate and pin; on leather strap 36 × 10mm (torn off at other end).

377 BC72 3664 (250) 10 Fig 109
22 × 12mm
On a spur leather (see No 323); frame is slightly trapezoidal, and the sides are continuous with the plate (offset at the bevel); two dome-headed rivets with roves; tin coating; the pin has apparently broken or worn through the hole in the plate; on a short, thick strap *c.*57 × 8mm and 4mm thick.

Larger buckle with integral hook

378 BWB83 acc no 187 (context 301) ceramic phase 11 Fig 109
19 × 21mm
D-shaped buckle; iron; side projections; pin missing from broken hole; knop d 10mm; hook l 11mm; tin coating. Although this item seems too large for a spur, it may be compared with the much smaller buckles on the spurs (Alexander & Binski 1987, 259–60) cited in the introduction to this group.

SPUR STRAPS

Geoff Egan
incorporating comments by Blanche M A Ellis

The large group of late 14th-century upper spur leathers with decorative mounts (Nos 379–96) is a particularly welcome addition to the very few surviving examples of such leathers for spurs, formerly mainly known from medieval art. These distinctive leather straps have several common features: the mounts, usually of stamped sheet

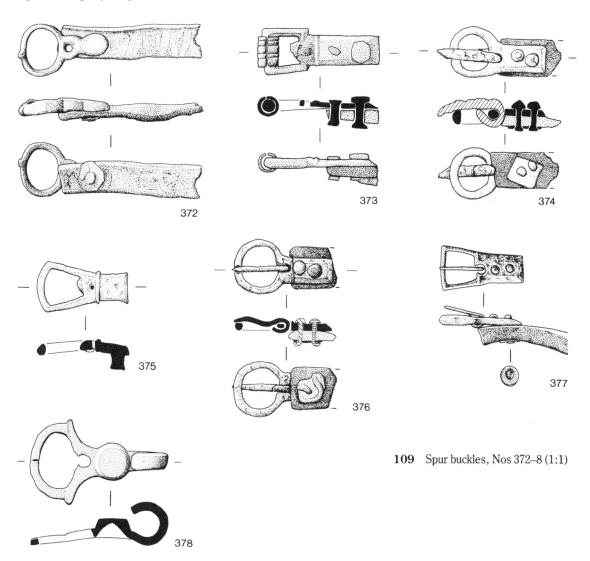

109   Spur buckles, Nos 372–8 (1:1)

iron, are set in two distinct groups towards each end, the strap between has a series of clumsily pierced holes along the centre and is often very abraded in this area; one end usually has a folded fitting like a strap-end, and the other has either a large, roughly cut hole (sometimes with the leather from its centre left attached at one point so as to form a crude tab) or another folded plate. The variety of the mounts on the 16 straps from a single dump at the BC72 site is extraordinary.

The length of the complete straps, the disposition of the mounts and the wear on some parts (e.g. on the plant mounts of No 396, Fig 112,

mount at right) are consistent with the function of the spur straps which pass over the instep of the foot (David Horn pers comm). The two groups of mounts would thus be set on each side of the foot. If there were more decorative ones at one end (as on No 396), these would probably be worn on the outer side, where they would be more visible. No matching pairs of straps were recovered at the BC72 site. (Although Nos 384 and 385 have similar mounts, there are differences in the sizes of the strap and other details.)

It is possible that in some places there was a ceremonial significance in the wearing of single spurs, as by a cup bearer in an illustration of a feast for the Duc de Berry (Longnon 1969, f2r – calendar illustration for January). There have been claims of burials in which the deceased wears only one spur; the only example in England of appropriate date was identified with a member of the Bro(u)gham family (Lacy 1911, 14–16) and the attribution has since been queried. It would be reading far too much into the present incomplete evidence to see any special significance in the absence of pairs in the BC72 group, this being almost certainly a result of the vagaries of deposition and recovery.

The degree of decoration on some of these items exceeds that on the small number of other identified spur straps from excavations. The present straps also include some that are wider than any others which have so far been identified with spurs. While these points do not invalidate the suggested identification, they reinforce the impression that these particular straps were not ordinary, workaday items but from some wealthier background in which ostentation was important.

The straps from the BC72 site are from dump deposits (contexts 55, 79, 83, 88, 88/1, 89, 150) that are notable because of indications that the assemblage of finds they produced is, in part, an unusually high-class one. This assemblage could represent items discarded from a store, perhaps from a well-endowed organisation such as the nearby King's Great Wardrobe (Grew & de Neergard 1988, 29). Presumably, very few institutions would have owned such showy equipment for so many riders. It is possible to speculate, therefore, that this group of materials may include parade items, bearing in mind the proximity of the storehouse of the extended royal household.

Narrow leathers with a single row of plain, domed circular mounts such as Nos 383 and 384 may be compared with those in *The Adoration of the Kings* by Vincenzo Foppa (Fig 105). The Milanese painter showed gilt spurs with red leathers. Single rows of circular mounts also decorate the leathers of the tiny spurs on a late 14th-century pewter badge from Salisbury (Spencer 1990, no 190, fig 250), while the surviving leather of an early 15th-century iron spur (Royal Armouries VI-424) has a row of domed mounts. The mounts on No 382 each have a central hole, though the position of the roves on

the back means that they could not have been used for the buckle pin; mounts in which the holes did accommodate the pin were found with a spur on a skeleton in the mass graves of the dead from the Battle of Visby (1361) on the island of Gotland, Sweden (Thordeman 1939, I, 122–3, fig 129), one of them still in place on the buckle pin.

Mounts in the form of simple flowers as on leathers Nos 388, 390 and 392 are commonly depicted on monumental effigies of knights, such as that of Sir Hugh Calveley in Bunbury Church, Cheshire (Fig 107; Stothard 1817, no 4, pl 99).

The corrugated mount on No 381 – paralleled by mounts on a purse from the same group of deposits, which may possibly have been an en-suite item (Egan & Pritchard 1991, no 1701) – is of a type clearly represented on the effigy carved in a London workshop in about 1340–50 for the tomb of a knight of the de Lucy family (formerly in Lesnes Abbey, Kent; now acc no A10–1912 in the Victoria & Albert Museum).

Variously patterned square mounts on spur leathers are also known (Byrne 1959, pl 30D) and those on the effigy of Sir Edmund de Thorpe (*c.*1417) in Ashwellthorpe Church, Norfolk (Stothard 1817, pl 112) have ridged mounts reminiscent of those on spur leather No 386.

Number 385 is rather wide for a spur leather but has evidence of having had rows of domed mounts similar to the copper-alloy ones on the spur leather from the mid 14th-century grave of Konrad von Heideck in Kloster Heilsbron, Bavaria, Germany (Hefner-Alteneck 1882, no I, pl 181), now in the Bayerisches Nationalmuseum, Munich. Number 394, with 25 domed mounts, is the widest of those catalogued below at 36mm. There is no strap of this size among other known spur leathers, though it shares several traits with the rest of the present group.

Leather No 399 is one of two long, slender versions probably from early rowel spurs. It is undecorated but is otherwise similar to that on spur No 323 and would have encircled the rider's foot, passing freely through a slot terminal on the inner side of the spur. The position of the holes show that beyond the buckle the strap-end was long enough to have trailed on the ground if the rider did not remove his spurs when dismounted. There is some evidence in contemporary art for very long upper spur leathers. Several riders illustrated on f24a and f24b of the Maciejowski

Bible (French, *c.*1250; Pierpoint Morgan Library, New York, MS 638) have the loose end of the upper spur leathers tucked neatly under their lower leathers. This would have kept them down and made them less likely to flap about or become unbuckled. An effigy of an unidentified knight in the Temple Church, London (Stothard 1817, pl 15) and that in Salisbury Cathedral of Sir William Longspee, who died in 1226 (ibid, 117), both include exceptionally long upper spur leathers; the latter also has them tucked under his lower leathers.

It is unfortunate that none of the spurs from the group of deposits at the BC72 site (Nos 334, 335, 341) can be associated with any of the individual decorated leathers, and that no buckle remained attached to any of these leathers. Among the catalogued spurs, only No 323 (from an earlier phase) has what might be claimed as a comparable decoration (in the sense that the bird and flower motifs might appear as mounts on straps of all kinds, not just on spurs and their leathers, like Nos 388, 390, 392), and in this it is unusual in the extreme. It is quite possible that the spurs and buckles were retained for use with other leathers when the BC72 group of leathers was discarded – perhaps a hint that these showy mounts were regarded as somewhat more readily disposable than the latter-day observer is at first inclined to think (cf. the discussion of spur buckles Nos 372–7).

The descriptions in Table 9 are set out according to the arrangement on a typical example of a strap of this kind (see Fig 110). The straps are all of leather, and the folded plates (presumably strap-ends) are all of tin-coated iron and have a single rivet. The straps are listed in order of increasing length of the surviving portion. (These items have been summarily published, primarily focusing on the mounts, as nos 1168–86 in Egan & Pritchard 1991).

INCOMPLETE STRAPS

Probably originally with two groups of mounts and from spurs, as Nos 379–96.

Note: For catalogue entries for Nos 379–96, see Table 9.

397 BC72 acc no 3524 (context 250) ceramic phase 10 Fig 112
strap 132 × 95mm, d of mounts *c.*65mm
Eight surviving circular mounts of tin (RAK, two analysed), in two groups on a leather strap (torn off at both ends; crude holes between the groups) (no 801 in Egan & Pritchard 1991).

398 BC72 1885 (83) 11 Fig 112
strap 95 × 12mm, d of mounts 8mm
Five surviving circular mounts of lead/tin (MLC, two tested), on a leather strap (torn off at both ends; holes for two other mounts now missing); further holes suggest the strap may have previously had other mounts set in a different configuration (no 829 in Egan & Pritchard 1991).

UNDECORATED STRAP

399 SWA81 acc no 4986 (context 2051) ceramic phase 9 Fig 112
400 × 8mm
Leather strap with a broken tinned iron attachment for the spur fastened by two copper-alloy rivets at one end, and, at the other, a narrow tinned iron strap-end (similar to that on the leather of spur No 323) with a single copper-alloy rivet. There is a small iron reinforcement(?) around the strap towards the attachment end, and the strap is pierced roughly by a group of holes to take the buckle pin two-thirds along its length. This long leather clearly functioned in an identical way to that surviving attached to spur No 323 from Baynard's Castle. Its ceramic phase date of *c.*1270–1350 echoes the date suggested above for the latter.

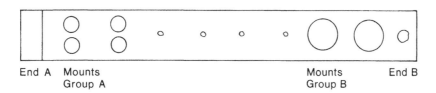

End A   Mounts   Mounts   End B
         Group A   Group B

110   Diagram of short spur strap showing position of mounts

Table 9: Catalogue of spur straps

Catalogue no	Site code and acc no	Context	Dimensions	End A	Mounts: shape	Mounts: group A	Mounts: group B	End B	Fig no
With stamped sheet-iron tin-coated mounts (ceramic phase 11)									
379 (probably part of following item)	BC72 2372	(89)	64+×10mm	plate	uncertain motifs 11×10mm	2 (?+1 lost)	(torn off)	(torn off)	Fig 111
380	BC72 2517	(89)	110+×11mm	(torn off)	(see preceding item)	1+	1	two holes	Fig 111
381	BC72 2622	(89)	115+×10mm	plate		1	(missing)	(torn off)	Fig 111
382	BC72 1605	(55)	120+×15mm		circular with central hole	4	(missing)	(torn off)	Fig 111
383	BC72 2310	(79)	122+×11mm		circular, domed, d 11mm	3 (+1 lost)	(hint of rivet hole)	(torn off)	Fig 111
384	BC72 2595	(79)	158+×10mm		circular, domed, d 9mm	2 (+1 lost)	(4 lost)	(?torn off)	Fig 111
385	BC72 2593	(79)	161+×25mm	plate with 2 circular mounts, d 9 mm	circular, domed, d 9mm	(?12 lost)	(1 rivet)	(?torn off)	Fig 111
386	BC72 2554	(83)	165×13mm	plate (lost)	rectangular with transverse central ridge, up to 11×10mm	3 (+1 lost)	(1 rivet)	hole	Fig 111
387	BC72 1676	(55)	175×12mm	plate	circular, domed, d 6.5mm	4 (+1 lost)	4	tab	Fig 111
388	BC72 2594	(79)	c.180×13mm	plate	domed cinquefoils with ridged lobes, d 12mm	3 (+1 lost)	1 (+2 lost)	hole	Fig 111
389	BC72 2412	(89)	182+×13mm	plate	(lost, rivets survive)	(3 lost)	(4 lost)	(torn off)	Fig 112
390	BC72 2549	(88/1)	186×13mm	plate (lost)	quatrefoils with domed lobes	4	1 (+3 lost)	hole	Fig 112
391	BC72 1715	(55)	192×12mm	plate	bar mounts with central lobe and trilobate sides, 8×12mm	3 (+1 lost)	(3 lost)	rough hole	
392	BC72 2596	(79)	c.195×11mm	plate	sexfoils with domed centre and lobes, d 11mm	4	1 (+1 lost)	rivet	Fig 112
393	BC72 2478	(79)	197×11mm	plate	bars with raised centre and bilobate sides, 7×11mm	2 (+3 lost)	3 (+1 lost)	hole	Fig 112
With lead/tin mounts (ceramic phase 11)									
394	BC72 2551	(83)	139×36mm	(torn off)	pairs of conjoined domed roundels, 5×11mm	10 (+5 lost)	2 (+8 lost)	?tab, among group of mounts	
395	BC72 3591	(150)	186×11mm	plate	circular, domed, d 4.5mm	9 (+3 lost)	14	rough holes	
396	TL74 1960	(275)	166×19mm	plate	A: circular, domed, d 5mm; B: plants	2	4	(torn off)	Fig 112

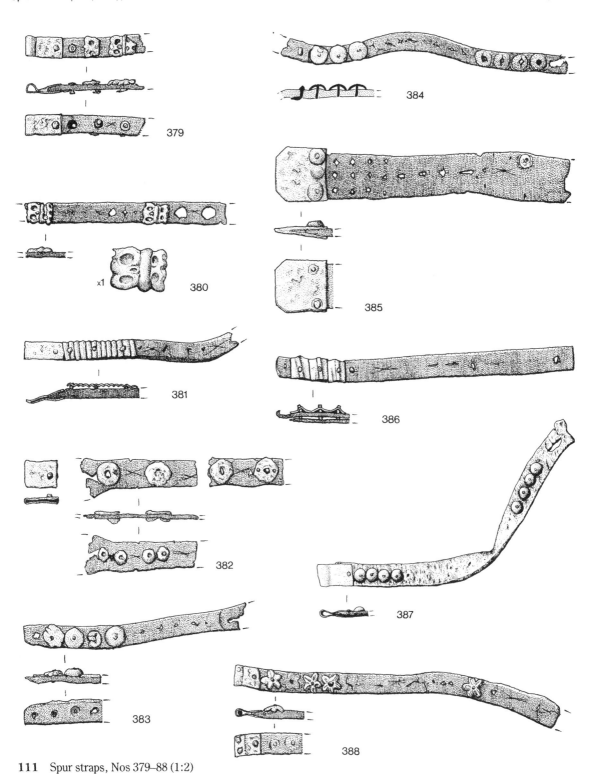

111 Spur straps, Nos 379–88 (1:2)

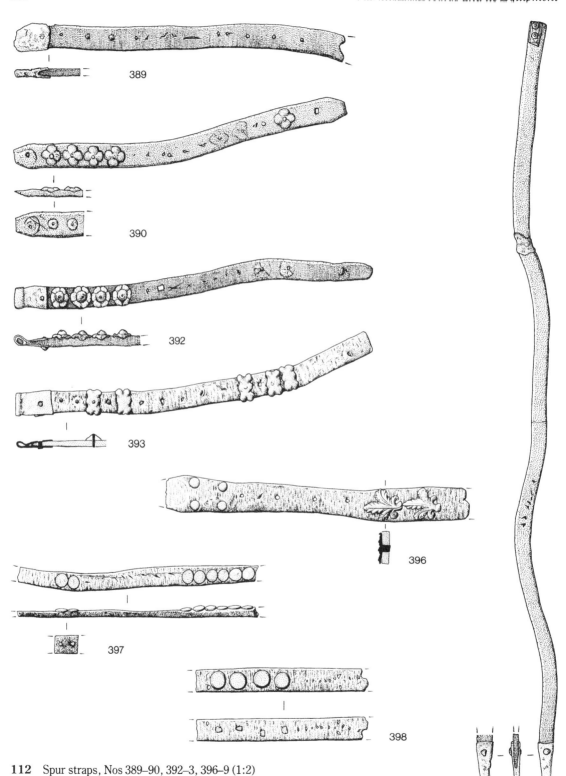

389

390

392

393

396

397

398

399

112   Spur straps, Nos 389–90, 392–3, 396–9 (1:2)

Curry combs

JOHN CLARK

Introduction

Curry or dress your Horse twice a day, that is, before water, and when he is curried, rub him with your hand, and with a Rubber: . . . and ever where the horses hair is thinnest, there curry the gentlest. (Markham 1662, 220)

The most durable of the implements used in the day-to-day care of the medieval horse, the iron curry comb or horse comb, is represented by a number of complete and fragmentary examples from the sites under review. In conjunction with finds from elsewhere, these allow an attempt to define a typological sequence for the item. I am grateful to my former colleague Michael Rhodes for the opportunity to consult his unpublished research notes on the medieval curry comb, which in many instances paralleled my own work.

The English word 'to curry' – from an Old French word meaning generally to put in order, prepare or arrange (*Oxford English Dictionary*) – was already being used by the late 12th century of the specific tasks of rubbing down or 'dressing' a horse – the current term for this process, 'grooming', is much later (ibid). Rubbing down the horse with brushes and/or curry comb before work and more fully on return to the stable after work is today regarded as essential to the horse's general health and condition as well as to its appearance. Caked mud, scurf and dried sweat is removed from the horse's coat, dead hair combed out, infestation by skin parasites discouraged, the underlying muscles massaged. This use of the curry comb is clearly shown in illustrations of about 1500 of the proverb 'to curry favour' (Fig 113 after Lemaître 1988 and Fig 114 – my thanks to Malcolm Jones for these references) and in a late 16th-century German work on horse care reproduced by Dent (1987, 168).

More recently there has been a change in the role played by the curry comb, foreshadowed by Youatt who, writing originally in 1831, recommended the use of the brush rather than the curry

113 'Currying favel'; French design for tapestry, *c.* 1500 (cf. Lemaître 1988)

114 Two men currying a horse, *c.* 1510–20 (British Library, MS Stowe 955, f11)

comb (1880, 128). In modern practice grooming is largely carried out using a series of brushes, with the occasional help of a plastic or rubber curry comb; the function of the metal curry comb, descendant of the medieval implement, is chiefly to clean the brush (Tuke 1973, 143, 147; British Horse Society 1988, 128–30). In 1908 it was reported that in the British Army 'the use of the curry comb on the skin is generally prohibited', though the authors of the *Animal Management* manual noted that outside the service it was used for the removal of caked dirt and 'with vanners and in commercial stables generally the animals are groomed all over with it' (War Office Veterinary Department 1908, 59). The United States Cavalry manual of 1941–2 states that 'the curry-comb is used to groom animals that have long, thick coats, to remove caked mud, to loosen matter scurf and dirt in the hair, and to clean the horse brush' (Devereux 1979, 125). Tuke comments: 'With the plastic and rubber curry combs on the market there is no real need to use a metal one to cut mud from the coat of a horse.' However, she also mentions the usefulness of the curry comb 'for the stripping out of dead coat from old horses and ponies'; this function of grooming, the removal of dead hairs that would otherwise become matted – particularly when the horse is moulting (Youatt 1880, 348) – should not be forgotten. The development of breeds with finer and thinner body hair may have encouraged gentler grooming methods; in the United States Cavalry 'the use of the currycomb should be prohibited in grooming animals recently clipped or that have a fine, thin coat of hair' (Devereux 1979, 125).

Hair fibres found in the same context at Baynard's Castle as the curry comb No 408 below – a fibrous organic layer which it was suggested represented stable sweepings – were investigated by Dr P L Armitage on the initiative of Michael Rhodes, then Finds Officer with the Department of Urban Archaeology. They were compared against a reference collection of mounted hairs and scanning electron microscope micrographs and found to compare favourably with the body hairs of domestic horse (Level III report, BYD81, 20 October 1981).

The word 'curry comb' itself, according to the *Oxford English Dictionary*, is not recorded before the 16th century – though it also quotes, from

115   Thirteenth-century groom, with curry comb in his belt, riding on a pack-horse – from a drawing by a follower of Matthew Paris of St Albans (cf. James 1920, pl 25)

1398, the phrase 'coryed wyth an horse combe'. The latter seems to be the normal designation for the object in medieval English; Kuhn & Reidy (1963, 954–5, sv 'hors-comb') give a number of instances of this word from about 1325 on, glossing the French *estril* and the Latin *strigilis*. A reference of *c.*1440 (ibid) gives us a choice of two English terms: 'Combe of curraynge or hors combe: *strigilis*'. The Latin *strigilis*, like the Old French word, is found in this sense considerably earlier than the English – in the 13th century and, in the form *strigilator*, 'curry-comber', in the late 12th century (Latham 1965, 455). It appears in such accounts as those of the manor of Cuxham: 'In ij strigilibus equorum emptis iijd' – for purchase of two horse strigils, 3 pence (in 1296–7; see Harvey 1976, 268); and in Royal Wardrobe accounts at about the same time: 'Item eidem pro tribus duodennis strigillorum emptis et liberatis marescallo. precium cuiuslibet iijd: vijs' – for three dozen strigils purchased and delivered to the marshal at 2 pence each: 7 [sic] shillings (*Liber Garderobe* of Eleanor of Castile, October 1289; see Parsons 1977, 68). For the price compare a *strilla* bought for 2*d.* in 1229 (*Calendar of Liberate Rolls* 1916, 144), two 'horscamb' for 4½*d.* in 1356–7 (Harvey 1976, 560) and 'paid fore a horscombe, iijd' in 1465 (Kuhn & Reidy 1963, loc cit). Twopence was also paid for a 'horscombe' purchased from the royal saddler John Hertyngton during preparations for the coronation of Richard III in 1483 (Sutton & Hammond 1983, 127).

Contemporary illustrations of identifiable curry combs are rare in English sources. An implement similar to those described here, with what seems to be a toothed blade and a handle set at right angles, is shown pushed through the belt of a figure in what is probably a mid-13th-century copy of a drawing by Matthew Paris (Fig 115; James 1920, 48 and pl 25; for date and attribution see Vaughan 1979, 221–2). The illustration shows a group of English bishops returning from Rome. An attendant, presumably a groom or horseman in the bishops' entourage, is riding perched on the back of a pack horse.

The curry comb may appear among tools in 15th-century wall-paintings of the 'warning to sabbath-breakers' or 'Christ of the Trades' type (Rouse 1991, 68); it occurs (perhaps) in the painting at St Just-in-Penwith (Cornwall); for a clear Austrian example dated to 1465 see Fig 116 (after Kühnel 1986, fig 274).

A 15th-century carving on a misericord at St Andrew's church, Greystoke (Cumbria) shows a horse being groomed (Remnant 1969, 31, pl 19c). One man holds the horse's head and another his tail or rear hoof; a third reaches across the horse's back from the far side with a curry comb

116 Curry combs, shown on a wall-painting of 1465 in Saak, Austria (above, cf. Kühnel 1986, fig 274) and a German woodcut of 1544 (below, cf. Dent 1987, 101)

117 Pewter badge in the form of a curry comb, inscribed 'fauel', 15th century, from the Thames foreshore (private collection) (1:1)

in his hand. Unfortunately its shape is not clear. The scene has been identified as a representation of the proverbial phrase 'to curry favel' or 'to curry favour', discussed below (Jones 1989a, 208).

Clearly related to the same phrase are a number of pendent badges of pewter in the form of a miniature curry comb, such as that found on the Thames foreshore at Cannon Street Station railway bridge and now in the Museum of London collections (acc no 86.59/1, illustrated in Spencer 1990, 111–12 fig 280). Another (now in a private collection) is shown here in Fig 117. Though none are from dated contexts, they are likely to be of 15th-century date. They carry the inscription 'fauel' – obviously a reference to the phrase 'to curry favel' or 'to curry favour'. That illustrated here and another recorded by the Museum of London seem to be from the same mould; the lettering on these examples is on the lower or inner side of the comb blade and would presumably normally be hidden from view.

The word 'favel' meant properly a *fallow-coloured* or tawny horse – a dun or possibly yellow dun (Davis 1989, 138; Dent & Goodall 1962, 107) – and was a popular horse name: 'Two stedes [steeds] found the kyng Richard / That on hight [one called] Favel, that other Lyarde' (1325: *Oxford English Dictionary* sv 'favel'). But during the 14th century the phrase 'to curry favel' came to signify the use of insincere flattery in hope of a reward from a superior (*Oxford English Dictionary* sv 'curry'); thus, c.1420: 'Lite may now with lordis duelle but thoo that kan conraye fawenelle' (Kurath & Kuhn 1952, 427 sv 'fauvel'). Kurath & Kuhn suggest the original meaning was no more than 'curry the master's horse' – presumably, to do dirty and menial work in order to get in the lord's good books.

However, 'Fauvel' is the name of the horse who is the anti-hero of Gervais de Bus's *Roman de Fauvel*, completed in 1314 (Jones 1989a, 207). Fauvel is a villainous lord surrounded by hangers-on like Pride, Flattery and Hatred, and his name, with its suggestion in several languages of some connection with 'falsity', seems to have ensured his popularity as a personification of falsehood, as in William Langland's *Vision of William concerning Piers the Plowman* (Kurath & Kuhn 1952, 427 sv 'favel'). Jones (1989a, 207–8) traces from this source the development of the French 'estriller fauvel', English 'curry favel' and Provencal 'saber de la falveta', all found in the 14th century with similar meanings – to groom (use soft soap on, butter up) the (horse-)lord to win his favour. The development of the English phrase to its present form 'to curry *favour*', a pardonable error, takes place in the 16th century (*Oxford English Dictionary*).

The act of 'currying favel' is illustrated in French books of designs for tapestries in the 15th century (Fig 113; cf. Lemaître 1988). Possibly in allusion to the phrase, two curry combs appear on the counter of a mercer's shop illustrated in a 15th-century manuscript of John Lydgate's English version of the French poem, *The Pilgrimage of the Life of Man* (Fig 118: British Library Cotton MS Tiberius A VII, f93 – see Basing 1990, 47, pl III). The shopkeeper is identified as 'Hagiography' or 'Holy Scripture'; her wares include 'Kombes [combs] (mo than nyne or ten,) / Bothe ffor horse and eke ffor men; / Merours [mirrors] also, large and brode . . .' (de Deguileville 1899–1904, 596, lines 22341–3). The presence of the combs is not immediately explained. However, when the Pilgrim picks up a mirror which flatters his looks, Hagiography tells him the mirror is called 'Adulacyoun' or 'Placebo' (flattery). She then embarks on a long disquisition on the evils of flattery, particularly the flattering of lords by their hangers-on (ibid. 597–600, lines 22411ff); the unexplained curry combs may relate to the same theme.

The significance of the curry comb badge to its

118   'Combs . . . both for horse and eke for men' displayed for sale in an enigmatic shop in a 15th-century manuscript of John Lydgate's *The Pilgrimage of the Life of Man* (British Library Cotton MS Tiberius A VII f93)

wearer is not immediately obvious – and given the positioning of the vital word 'favel' on the hidden side of some examples it may have been deliberately obscure. A badge that branded its wearer as a toady or lickspittle seems unlikely to have been popular! Malcolm Jones has suggested that the curry comb may be the badge of some English *societé joyeuse* or company of fools – though such companies are not well documented in England. At a festival held in Arras (in the north of France) in 1534 one of the companies in the procession to mass on the Monday of Carnival week was that of the *Prince de l'estrille* (Prince of the curry comb) from Douai, and a similar dignitary is recorded at Valenciennes in 1548 (Muchembled 1978, 147, 150 – I am grateful to Malcolm Jones for this suggestion and the reference).

Twentieth-century catalogues of stable equipment (like that of 1929 reproduced in Fig 119 – Harding 1929, 304) illustrate two distinct types of metal curry comb. In one, the normal type, a flat

119   'Stable requisites', including curry combs of various patterns, shown in a 1929 wholesale catalogue of ironmongery and hardware (Harding 1929, 304)

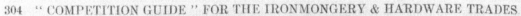

STABLE REQUISITES.

H 6726. CURRY COMBS.
8 Stamped Bars and 2 Knockers.
Japanned.
Common.   Strong.
16/-   17/- dozen.

H 6727. CURRY COMBS.
"Military Pattern"
7 Wrought Bars and 2 Double Knockers.
Japanned.   ...   22/- dozen.

H 6728. CURRY COMBS.
7 Wrought Bars and 2 Double Knockers.
Japanned.
Medium.   24/6 dozen.

H 6731. COW COMBS.
2 Bars and 2 Knockers.
18/- dozen.

H 6729. CURRY COMBS.
7 Wrought Bars and 4 Knockers
Extra Strong.   **Japanned.**
26/- dozen.

COW COMBS.
3 Bars and 2 Knockers.
H 6732. Common. *(Foreign).* 8/- dozen.
H 6732½. Best   ...   ... 19/- „

H 6733. HORSE MANE COMBS.
Japanned.
Cast.   ...   4/- dozen.

H 6730. CURRY COMBS.
8 Stamped Bars and 2 Knockers.
22/- dozen.

H 6734. *(Foreign).*
HORSE MANE COMBS.
Horn.   Elliptic Back.
4¾ inches.   12/- dozen.

H 6733. HORSE SINGERS.
Taper.   **Tin.**   Brass Filler Screw.
With Wick.
4   5   6 inches.
7/-   7/6   8/6 each.
H 6736.
Taper. **Japanned.** Brass Filler Screw.
With Wick.
4   5   6 inches.
7/6   8/-   9/- each.
For use with Naptha.

H 6738. HORSE SINGER HEADS.
Brass.   For Gas.
3   4   5 inches.
6/6   7/6   8/6 each.

H 6739.
COTTON OR WICK FOR SINGERS.
4 and 5 inches wide.
7/- lb.

H 6737. HORSE SINGERS.
"Albert" Pattern.
Japanned.   With Wick.
3   4   5   6 inches
8/-   9/-   10/-   12/- each.
With Tap,   5/- each extra.

For use with Naptha.

H 6740.   HORSE SCRAPERS.
Blued Spring Steel.
Straight.   ...   48/- dozen.

rectangular back is fitted with a series of serrated combs or 'bars'. A comb of this flat type is reported from a post-medieval (17th- or early 18th-century?) context at Ardingly (W Sussex) by Goodall (1976a, 63, no 43, fig 9b); compare two examples from Jamestown, Virginia (Cotter 1958, 176, pl 74). Another fragmentary example comes from London excavations, from a post-medieval context at Aldgate (AL74 376). An 18th-century French example appears in an illustration to Diderot's *Encyclopédie* (Diderot 1763–72 'Manège et équitation', 5 and pl XXVII, fig 9 'étrille'). In the second type the back itself is curved over to form a half cylinder with serrated edges, and it is sometimes fitted with an extra central bar. This type is almost identical to the late medieval form discussed below; even the additional central bar is recorded on one late medieval or 16th-century example (Goodall 1983b, 250, no 252, fig 10). The Museum of English Rural Life, Reading (Mrs J Betts pers comm) has not been able to explain the origin or significance of the term 'cow comb', adopted for this type of comb in the 1929 catalogue; the more normal designation in 19th- and 20th-century sources is a 'round' curry comb.

Two features of surviving early curry combs seem to reflect aspects of their use. The ends of the blades, whether of the semi-cylindrical form or the earlier angular shape (discussed below), are reinforced by doubling the metal back – usually on the inside. Although this serves the general purpose of stiffening the comb, it would also have a function in the light of the modern practice of knocking the comb sharply on the stable floor after use to dislodge the dirt from its teeth (Tuke 1973, 143). The modern combs shown in Fig 119 have 'knockers' to protect their edges; the 18th-century example illustrated by Diderot (above) has a similar projection labelled 'marteau'. On the 15th-century comb from Trig Lane (No 407) one end of the blade (though reinforced) is bent over, perhaps damage caused by just this sort of treatment.

Another feature is common to two of the combs described below (Nos 401 and 407), to a number of curry combs of medieval type in the Museum of London collections (MoL acc nos 7289, 7949, 13002, 16030, A605 – illustrated here in Fig 121 – and 84.408/2), and to 15th- and 16th-century examples from elsewhere (Goodall 1979a, 121, no 65, fig 63; Goodall 1990, 1054, no

3937, fig 338). In all these there are rings fitted loosely to one or more of the arms into which the handle tang is divided. In view of the incomplete condition of many surviving curry combs it is possible that this feature was much more widespread than appears at first sight. Its presence on both our earliest and latest examples proves a long life; it seems to have continued after the Middle Ages in a form in which the arms of the handle are extended beyond the point where they are riveted to the blade and then bent into loops to hold loose rings (cf. an unnumbered specimen in the Museum of London (Tudor & Stuart) collections). Another in the Museum of London (acc no 7290) has a series of five lugs riveted into its back and holding rings.

These rings serve no obvious practical function, apart, perhaps, from that of making a noise. There are obvious dangers in approaching a nervous horse from behind and touching its flank suddenly without alerting it to your presence; modern handbooks emphasise the need to 'always speak to the horse before approaching; speak before handling . . . The approach should always be to the shoulder' (British Horse Society 1988, 91–2). It is possible that the jingling rings, not found on modern curry combs, provided a useful adjunct to the groom's voice in calming the horse and warning it of the presence of the man's hand and the comb out of sight behind its head.

Common to the medieval curry combs from London and elsewhere is their construction from a sheet of iron bent or curved to bring the two long edges close together; these edges are serrated to form the functional part of the comb. A tang to take a wooden handle is fastened at right angles to this blade; it is riveted to the back of the blade and divided into two or three separately fixed arms for rigidity, which are clearly shown on the 'currying favel' badges.

Two and possibly three forms can be distinguished among the combs from London sites. Two combs, both from Swan Lane in contexts of ceramic phase 9 (*c.*1270–1350), have a blade that is not of the semi-cylindrical form seen in 15th- and 16th-century illustrations but of more angular shape, an open trapezium in section (Fig 120a). The tang, on leaving the handle, splits into two arms which run more or less parallel for some distance to the blade, then turn at right angles to extend along the back of the blade. They are

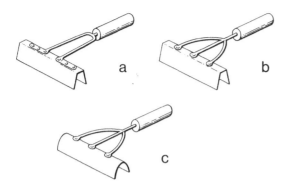

120 Types of medieval curry comb: **a** with angular blade and handle with two arms; **b** with angular blade and handle with three arms; **c** with semi-cylindrical blade

fastened by three rivets at each end (though this reconstruction of the handle of the incomplete comb No 400 is of course conjectural). This form can be paralleled by a complete example of similar date (*c.*1300–50) from Southampton (note by Ian Goodall in Harvey 1975, 282, no 2049, fig 254), though the latter has only one rivet at each end to fasten the handle, while unassociated tangs with two parallel arms (but without the extension at right angles along the back of the blade) come from Winchester from contexts of late 12th- and of 13th- to early 14th-century date (Goodall 1990, 1053–4, nos 3934, 3936, fig 338); the earlier of the Winchester objects seems to be the earliest published example of the form.

121 Curry comb from Westminster, MoL acc no A605, with angular blade and tripartite tang with loose rings

From phase 11 (1350–1400) at Baynard's Castle comes a curry comb blade of similar angular form to that described above, but with traces on the back of a different method of fastening the handle (No 402). The remains of the tang *in situ* and the spacing of the rivets indicate that the tang was divided into *three* arms (as often in the next group) rather than two (Fig 120b). A similar comb from the City of London Boys' School site is also included (No 406). A near-complete example, lacking only its wooden handle, is in the old Museum of London collections (acc no A605 – from Westminster; Fig 121). It is not clear, since so often all that remains is the detached handle tang, whether this combination of features – angular blade and tripartite tang – is recorded outside London.

What is surely a later development is the semi-cylindrical form of the blade of combs from phase 12 (1400–50) contexts at sites TL74 and BYD81, presumably the result of an improvement in smithing technique (Fig 120c). This is the form of blade represented in the 15th- and 16th-century French and German illustrations described above and in a German woodcut of 1544 reproduced by Dent (1987, 101 – see Fig 116), and by examples such as that from Wharram (late 15th- or early 16th-century: Goodall 1979a, 121, no 65, fig 63). The handle on the Wharram example is divided into two arms, but these are splayed rather than parallel as on the earlier SWA81 and Winchester examples. Comb No 407 has a handle with three arms, like the 'currying favel' badge and several of the incomplete combs reported elsewhere – as at Princes Risborough (14th- to early 15th-century: Pavry & Knocker 1957–8, 161, no 5, fig 12), Winchester (late 15th- to early 16th-century: Goodall 1990, 1054, no 3937, fig 338) and Waltham Abbey, Essex (16th century: Goodall 1973, 171, no 39, fig 12). In these later examples we may assume the blade was semi-cylindrical.

A similar three-armed tang is published by Manning (1985, 61–2, no G2, pl 26) from a Romano–British ironwork hoard from Sandy (Bedfordshire); given the dubious provenance of this hoard (ibid. 184) it is possible to question whether this object really belongs with the undoubtedly Romano–British material making up the bulk of the find. The more complete example to which Manning refers, from the Roman site at

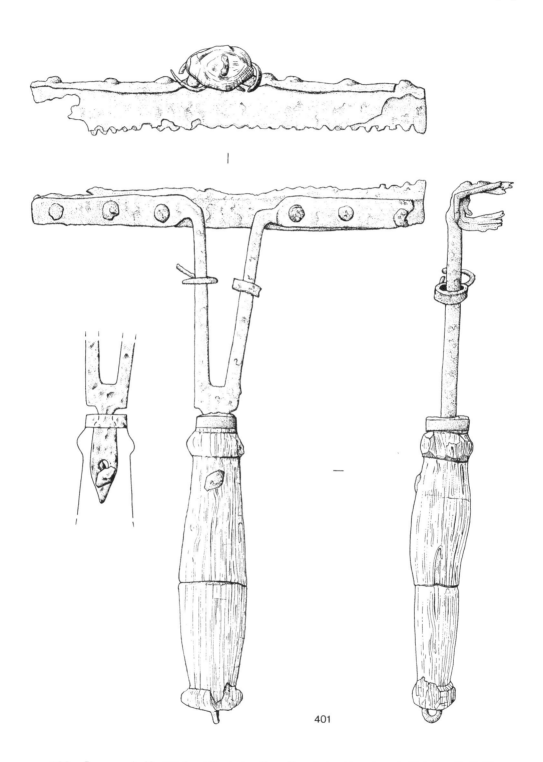

401

122   Curry comb, No 401; inset illustrates (from X-ray) short tang inserted into handle (1:2)

The Lunt, Warwickshire, was an unstratified find from the humus layer (Hobley 1969, 122, no 1, fig 25); taken in isolation it would most readily be related to our No 408 or the late medieval example from Wharram referred to above.

A reliable picture of the chronological development of an artefact cannot of course be derived from so few examples, yet its main features are clear. The earliest in Britain seems to be represented by the unassociated handle from Winchester in the late 12th century; the earliest complete combs surviving are those with angular blades, our No 401 and the Southampton example, of the late 13th or early 14th century. The type with a semi-cylindrical blade and a tang usually split into three arms seems to have been introduced at the beginning of the 15th century and continues into the 16th century – and given that the 'cow comb' of the 1929 catalogue matches this description, presumably much later! The flat-backed 'modern' form of curry comb is a post-medieval development.

In the following catalogue the combs are listed by the form of the blade – angular (as Figs 120a and b) or semi-cylindrical (Fig 120c); all are of iron.

Catalogue

Angular blades

400 SWA81 acc no 717 (context 2051) ceramic phase 9   Fig 124
blade l 226mm, w across teeth *c*.17mm
Blade only, the ends reinforced by folding inwards; the remains of the handle fastening extend along the back, held by three rivets at each end and folded over inside the blade.

401 SWA81 1302 (2146) 9 Figs 122, 123
blade l 213mm, w across teeth *c*.17mm, overall l 270mm
The blade is incomplete, but the ends can be seen to have been reinforced by folding inwards; the double-armed tang extends along the back of the blade and is held by three rivets at each end; it carries a loose iron ring (one formed of wire, the other of strip) on each arm. The tang is broken at the junction with the handle,

123   Curry comb, No 401

which is turned of alder wood and fitted with an iron ferrule; the tang extends only a short way into the handle and is pierced to take a nail to hold it in place – in this it differs from the Winchester examples, which have long pointed tangs. An iron loop for suspension is nailed into the end of the handle.

402 BC72 1764 (55) 11 Fig 124 (from X-ray)
blade l 187mm, w across teeth *c*.32mm
Blade only, incomplete, the ends reinforced by folding inwards; the pattern of rivets suggests a three-armed tang, the outer arms extending along the back and held by two rivets each, the central arm held by a single rivet.

403 BC72 4760 (255) 11 not illustrated
surviving l 80mm, h 43mm
Fragment of side of blade with serrated edge.

404 BC72 4887 (25) 11 not illustrated
blade l 145mm, w across teeth *c*.25mm
Blade only, heavily corroded; X-ray reveals the folded reinforcement of the ends, and the remains of a double-armed tang extending along the back held by two rivets at each end.

405 BC72 276 (24) – not illustrated
surviving l 110mm
Fragment of back of blade.

406 BOY86 801 (1131) – Fig 124
blade l 167mm, w across teeth *c*.30mm
Blade only, the ends reinforced by folding *outwards*; remains of a three-armed tang held by three rivets.

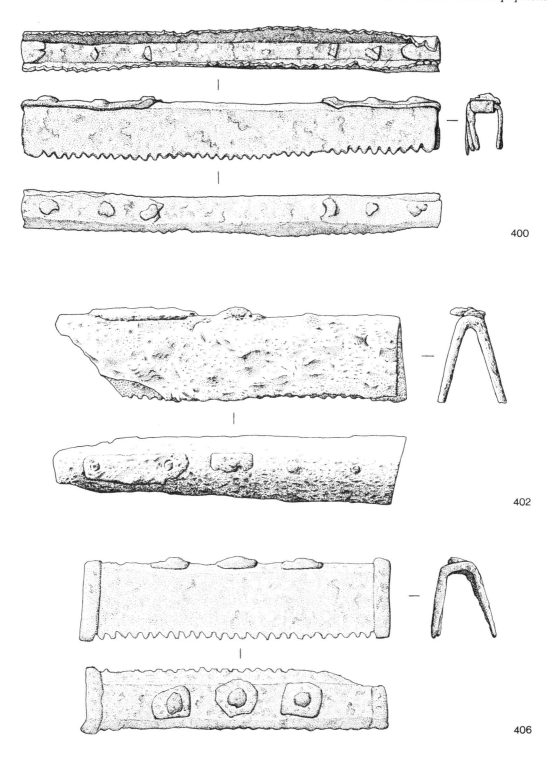

124   Angular curry comb blades, Nos 400, 402 and 406 (1:2)

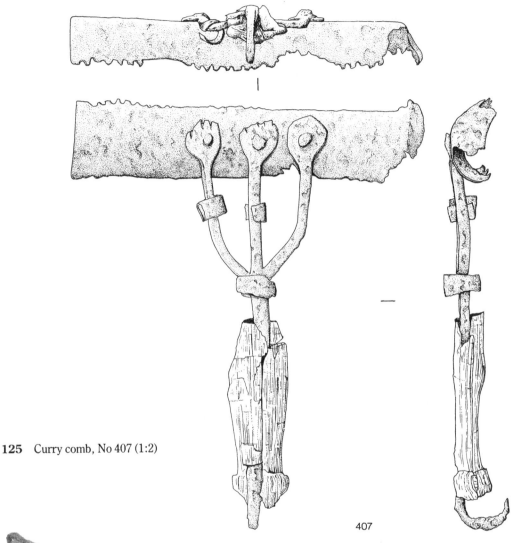

125 Curry comb, No 407 (1:2)

407

126 Curry comb, No 407

Semi-cylindrical blades

407 TL74 acc no 1643 (context 368) ceramic phase 12 Figs 125, 126

blade l 190mm, w across teeth *c.*35mm, overall l 221mm

The ends of the blade are reinforced by folding inwards – the right-hand end is bent and damaged; the tang has three arms, two of them carrying loose iron rings; the tang, fitted with an iron ferrule, extends through the wooden handle and is bent over at the top to form a hook; there were traces of unidentified matted fibre in this area.

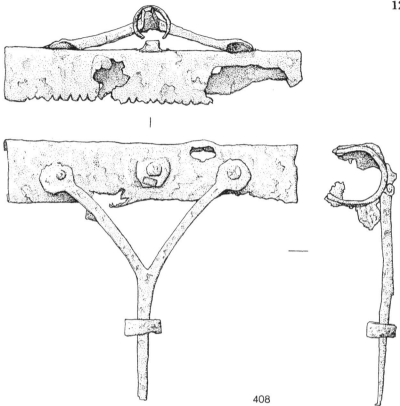

408

408   BYD81   45   (36)   12   Fig 127
blade l 158mm, w across teeth *c.*28mm, l over tang 130mm
The ends of the blade are reinforced by folding in-wards; the surviving tang has two arms, but there is also a third rivet in place on the centre of the back of the blade; the handle ferrule survives as a loose ring with traces of wood inside.

Appendix: skeletal evidence of medieval horses from London sites

D JAMES RACKHAM

(Note: In the English-speaking world today the height of a horse is measured at the withers (the highest point of the shoulders) in hands, each of four inches (approximately 10cm). However, this height is often quoted in the form 'hands.inches'; thus 14.2 hands (14.2hh) represents 14 hands 2 inches (58 inches or 1.48m). This usage may lead to confusion among an archaeological readership more accustomed to metric measurements and to interpreting the stop as a decimal point. We have therefore avoided the form where possible (with apologies to those to whom the usage comes naturally) and in this Appendix we normally quote typical heights of modern horses and estimated heights of early horses in hands and fractions of hands. – JC)

Physical character

The most frequent measure used to compare archaeological remains of horses is the withers height, the height between the shoulder blades. In 1888 Kiesewalter published a study of modern horses in which he produced a number of indices from which you could calculate the height of a horse at the withers during life, from a measurement of the lateral length of one of its long bones. The different bones required different indices. Almost all archaeological interpretations of horse size are based upon the results of Kiesewalter's work or that of Vitt (in von den Driesch & Boessneck 1974). Characteristically, since animal populations are subject to natural variation, withers height calculations from different bones of the same individual rarely agree precisely, although they generally correspond closely, and the work presumes a general conformity among horses with little relative variation in the skeleton. Unfortunately it is this relative variation which may reflect more specific differences in breed or function. This calculation produces a basic height estimate that can be interpreted in terms of 'hands'. One hand is equivalent to 101.6 mm (4 inches) – for instance a Shetland pony of the order of 10½ hands has a withers height of approximately 1.04 metres. The interpretation of the withers height for horses in London (using Kiesewalter) based on those bones where appropriate measurements have been taken is presented in Fig 128.

The data from the Roman, Saxon, medieval and post-medieval contexts can be compared against examples of modern breeds. The collection from Ludgate (LUD82, Wilkinson 1983) shows the greatest range and variability, including animals from 10¼ hands (about Shetland pony size) to nearly 16 hands. Nevertheless, none of these specimens match the size of horses used by the Metropolitan and City of London Police which are generally between 16 and 18 hands. The 18½-hand police horse plotted on Fig 128 was the largest in the City of London force until its retirement in 1992.

The few specimens from the Saxon period for which we have measurements from which we can calculate withers heights, all derive from one individual and illustrate the slight variability in calculations from different bones. This animal of 10th- to 11th-century date found at Ironmonger Lane (IRO80) was approximately 13¾ hands, a modern riding pony size. This appears typical of other finds of the period in Britain, for example Coppergate, York – 14 hands (O'Connor 1989); Flaxengate, Lincoln – 13½ hands (O'Connor 1982); Hamwih, Southampton – 13¼ hands (Bourdillon & Coy 1980).

The Roman specimens from London so far recovered have produced a maximum of 13¾ hands (LDW84), most specimens being over 12 hands except for one animal from late Roman deposits at Beddington Roman villa (BSF86) of

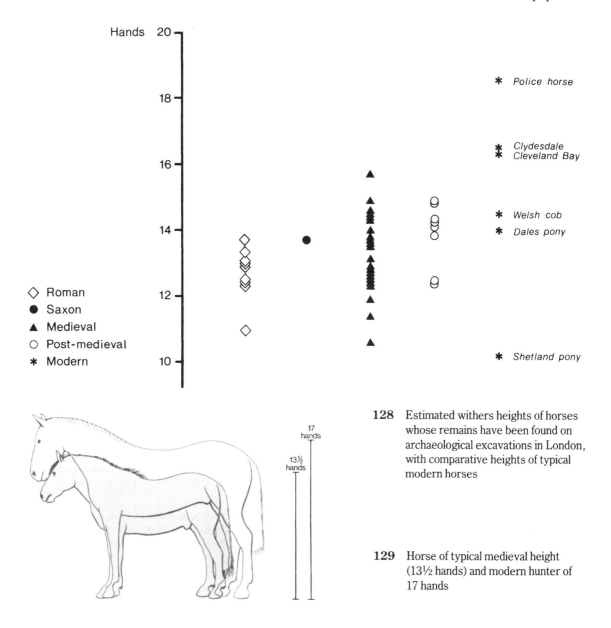

128   Estimated withers heights of horses whose remains have been found on archaeological excavations in London, with comparative heights of typical modern horses

129   Horse of typical medieval height (13½ hands) and modern hunter of 17 hands

just under 11 hands (Pipe & Rackham 1990).

Although the specimens from which the withers heights were calculated suggest a trend from small Roman horses to larger animals in the medieval period, other length measurements show a much wider range in the Roman period. Fig 130 illustrates that the range of Roman bones is as great as in later periods and Fig 128 should not be relied upon as representative of the size of

the animals in the horse populations of London.

Figs 130 and 131 illustrate robustness in relation to length in the metacarpus and metatarsus bones, and Fig 132 the breadth of the tibia. In Figs 130 and 131 the greatest length of the bone is plotted against its smallest shaft diameter. The relationship of these two measures is allometric (see for instance Prummel 1983), and as length increases so does shaft width at a proportional

130 Horse metacarpals from excavations in London: greatest length plotted against minimum shaft diameter

131 Horse metatarsals from excavations in London, compared with modern farm horse: greatest length plotted against minimum shaft diameter

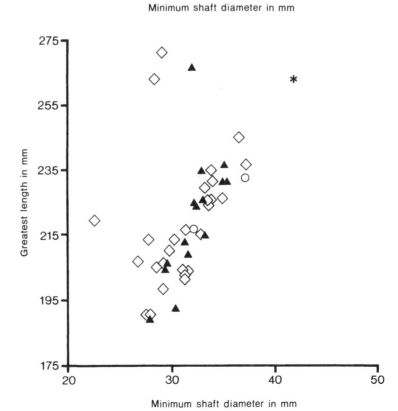

132 Horse tibiae from excavations in London: minimum shaft diameter plotted against distal breadth

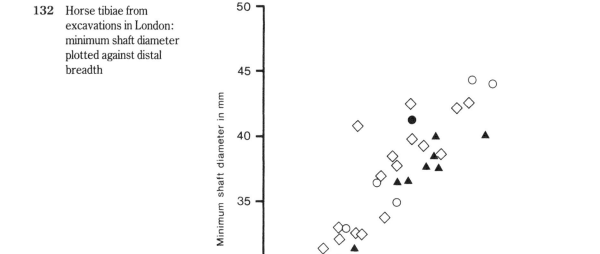

◇ Roman
● Saxon
▲ Medieval
○ Post-medieval

scale; the scatters are generally distributed along a straight line. Major changes or differences in conformity would be exhibited by a departure from this line, a point above it indicating gracility and one below it robustness.

It is apparent that three Roman and one medieval specimen are significantly more gracile, that is longer relative to shaft diameter, than the remainder of the sample. These are likely to be riding rather than working animals. A few individuals on Fig 130 may be a little more robust. The modern specimen plotted on Fig 131 is a farm horse burial of an animal of about 15¾ hands. This animal was clearly a heavy working horse. In Fig 131 one medieval example from LUD82 is clearly a very stocky and robust animal, likely to have been a small draught- or pack-animal. There is some suggestion in this figure that the medieval animals in the sample are more gracile than their Roman counterparts, a pattern also suggested by the tibial measurements (Fig 132). The medieval horses have a narrower shaft relative to their distal breadth, indicating less robust animals. The single late Saxon specimen

from IRO80 in Fig 132 lies in the Roman size range, and it is possible that these differences reflect the introduction of new breeding stock from the Continent or the more controlled breeding of native animals for riding stock. These data provide little evidence for the development in the medieval period of either a heavy war-horse or heavy farm animal.

Pathologies

Animals bred and used by man are generally claimed to exhibit both a greater diversity and a higher incidence of skeletal pathologies. For instance, in a study of over two hundred equids, Stecher & Goss (1961) found that the lateral facets on the transverse processes of consecutive lumbar vertebrae – present in both wild and domestic horses (Stecher 1962) – became ankylosed (fused) only in the domestic horses and mules in the sample. This condition, which may result in the fusion of the posterior spine in severe cases, has therefore been viewed as a result of the animals' use for riding or draught; Smythe (1962) suggests that it is caused by the additional stress incurred through these uses. Similar lesions may occur on the feet, where the bones of the ankle (hock) particularly have a tendency to become ankylosed in horses. The latter often develops as a result of arthritic irritation and inflammation. This can be very painful for the horse and is in fact alleviated by the complete fusion of adjacent bones, which reduces the joint movement without seriously affecting the animal's mobility. The increased stresses on the skeleton resulting from riding or harnessing to carts or ploughs are thought to be responsible for most of these pathologies, although they may be partially related to age.

Despite the recognition of the impact of these domestic uses on the skeleton they do not permit an identification of which uses an animal may have been put to. Certainly many of the lumbar vertebrae from sites in London show partial or severe ankylosis. The LUD82 samples show four individuals with severity varying from just the fifth and sixth vertebra fused at the lateral facets to four consecutive lumbar vertebrae fused together by ankylosis of the lateral facets, osteophytosis and fusion between the zygapophyseal articulations. A similar condition was observed on the Roman horse from ILA79. Other examples include Roman finds from Bishopgate (BOP82) and Hooper Street (HOO88) (in the latter of which the centra had fused), and a post-medieval example from 175 Borough High Street, Southwark (175BHS).

Incidence of fusion of the tarsals to the metatarsal bone, or lipping and pitting of the proximal articulation of the metapodials was found on six Roman specimens from Beddington Sewage Farm (BSF86), and post-medieval specimens from 175BHS and CH75 (Chaucer House, Tabard Street, Southwark). An inflammation (osteoporosis?) of the shaft of one metatarsus from a Roman context on OPT81 may indicate a contusion from striking something with the hock.

None of these pathologies is diagnostic, and all are found elsewhere at most periods.

One possibly diagnostic character which may at least identify an animal used for riding is exhibited by the Roman horse from ILA79 and three of the individuals from LUD82. All these specimens are jaws which show an abnormal wear on the anterior edge of the premolar 2. It has been suggested that this can be attributed to 'bit wear' (M Littauer cited in Clutton-Brock 1974, 93) and implies the use of a bit with a linked mouthpiece which could be drawn far enough back into the mouth for the animal to 'chew' (R A Harcourt cited in Armitage 1981b, 4–5).

Age and sex

In the present day a horse's reproductive life extends, on average, from about four years of age to 20 years (Jones 1971). Its functional life as a draught or riding animal can also be expected to last until the animal is between 18 or 20 years of age. Heavily used, overworked or maltreated animals may not survive so long, and since the keeping and feeding of a horse is expensive (see above), in an urban working environment animals are unlikely to be kept beyond their economic usefulness.

In view of this, the age distribution represented by the remains from London and other sites is surprisingly young. The ages of the animals in question have been estimated by comparison with bones of animals of known age in the Natural History Museum and from the wear of the incisor teeth (American Association of Equine Practitioners 1971). The six individuals from LUD82 varied in age from seven to 14½ years, and the late Saxon animal from IRO80 was between seven and eight years old. No other intact incisor groups have been found among the medieval horse bones. On the basis of postcranial bone development most animals represented on the medieval sites were adult – effectively older than four and probably older than seven. Only two bones indicating animals of less than four have been recognised in the whole collection of hundreds of bones, and these both derive from the middle Saxon site at Peabody Buildings, Westminster (PEA87). At a similarly dated site at Jubilee Hall (JUB85) and on postmedieval levels at 175BHS (Borough High Street) two further bones suggest animals over four but certainly younger than seven. There is no sign in any of the specimens of the level of tooth wear that one would expect on an animal of 18–20 years.

Evidence of the manner of death of any of the horses whose bones have been studied is absent except for one of the LUD82 specimens. The skull of this seven-year-old male showed evidence of having been pole-axed and carried a large depression in the top of the cranium. Such a blow is unlikely to have killed the animal outright; after being stunned, its throat would have been cut or it may have been decapitated. A second skull from Ludgate Hill (LH74) perhaps gives evidence of the latter since it carries a chop mark across the basal part of the occipital condyles, where the head joins the neck.

Slaughter of animals at this early age suggests maltreatment, accident or disease (the former had already developed ankylosing lesions on the posterior lumbar vertebrae). Certainly in the LUD82 individuals there is no evidence of the development of ankylosing lesions on the feet, which might have limited their usefulness. The general absence of aged animals may be a result of a combination of poor feeding and upkeep, hard work and a greater susceptibility to fatal disease and accident in a community not served by modern veterinary science.

The sex could be determined only for the partial skeletons; none of the other material was suf-ficiently intact. On the basis of the well-developed maxillary canine and features of the pelvis (Sisson 1953) all have been identified as male, although some or all may have been geldings.

Bearing in mind that we are looking at only eight individuals, hardly a statistical sample, the absence of females might reflect their importance for breeding, only the unwanted surplus of stallions being gelded and sold in town for riding and draught-animals. Unless past its breeding age – and then too old to work – a mare would have been a valuable animal and is likely to have been kept only by people in a position to look after it when in foal. This seems unlikely in the city; such animals were presumably kept on rural estates where they served as combined breeding and working stock (Langdon 1986, 86, 296; and remember William Fitz Stephen's reference to mares 'suitable for ploughs, sledges and carts' being sold in foal or with their foals at their sides at Smithfield in the 12th century – Kingsford 1908, 224). Only on a middle Saxon site (PEA87 – Peabody Buildings, Westminster) were juveniles present, perhaps reflecting a somewhat different character to the town at this period, when mares may have been stabled and foaled within the urban area.

Summaries

The medieval horse and its equipment

This volume is the fifth in a series devoted to the rich variety of finds of medieval date from excavations carried out in the City of London during the 1970s and early 1980s. Its subject is horse equipment: harness fittings such as bits and stirrups; horseshoes; spurs and spur fittings; and stable equipment, represented solely by curry combs. Unfortunately, no saddles or identifiable saddle fragments of medieval date have been recorded from these excavations.

After summarising the variety of material found, the introductory chapter draws on documentary and other evidence to set the historical background – particularly the significant part played by the horse in the life and economy of London: the horse market at Smithfield, the price of a horse and the costs of keeping it, the hiring of 'hackneys' for riding, the use of pack-horses and carts in and around London. The accounts of the London Bridgewardens provide information from a major public body which maintained its own transport department and fleet of carts, and the role of the London *marshal* or farrier is discussed. A survey of the significance of the skeletal remains of horses found in London follows. (This is further expanded in an Appendix.) Finally this and other evidence is drawn on in a discussion of the size and pulling power of the medieval horse.

A chapter on 'The excavations' provides a summary of information on each site. Most finds came from the deep series of riverside dump deposits south of Thames Street between Blackfriars (Baynard's Castle) and Custom House, an area reclaimed from the river between the 11th and the 15th century by the building of a sequence of new wharves and waterfronts. Close dating of the archaeological contexts, largely through dendrochronology, allowed the establishment of a series of 'ceramic phases' upon which the chronology of the published finds is based.

The catalogue of 408 finds follows, divided by type of object. Each section has an introduction in which the function of the object is discussed and, where appropriate, an overall typology and/or chronology is proposed; comparison is made with finds from elsewhere. Some previous finds in the older Museum of London collections are described and illustrated for comparison. Within each section, catalogue entries are arranged in the chronological order established by the ceramic phase to which they have been assigned, and within phase by site and context number.

In the cases of *horseshoes* and *spurs* the introductory essays are extensive, reflecting the large numbers and variety which were found. For *horseshoes* a series of four types is proposed, ranging in date from the 9th century to the mid-15th century; the significance of variation in size and weight is considered; documentary evidence for medieval horseshoeing practice is cited; the uncertainty of evidence for earlier horseshoes, particularly of Roman date, is briefly noted. The essay on *spurs* discusses the historical evidence for the work of the *spurriers* (spur-makers) of medieval London. Special attention is drawn to the survival of spur leathers (straps), particularly a group of 16 detached 14th-century straps with decorative mounts found in a single dumped deposit.

Le cheval et ses accessoires à l'époque médiévale

Ce volume est le cinquième d'une série dédiée à la riche variété des trouvailles médiévales provenant des fouilles effectuées dans la cité de Londres dans les années 1970 et au début des années 1980. Le sujet concerne les accessoires du cheval comme les garnitures de harnais tels que mors et étriers; les fers à chevaux; les éperons et les garnitures d'éperon; les accessoires propres à l'écurie étant uniquement représentés par des trilles. Malheureusement aucune selle ou fragment identifiable de selle de l'époque médiévale n'a été retrouvé durant ces fouilles.

Un chapitre d'introduction, après avoir résumé la gamme des objets trouvés, fait appel, entre autres, à l'évidence documentaire pour établir l'arrière-plan historique, particulièrement le rôle important joué par le cheval dans la vie et l'économie de Londres. Sont mentionnés le marché aux chevaux de Smithfield, le prix d'un cheval et les coûts d'entretien, la location de "hackneys" (chevaux de louage), l'utilisation de chevaux de somme et de charrettes à l'intérieur et aux alentours de Londres. Les comptes des gardiens de ponts londoniens nous fournissent des informations sur une institution publique majeure qui maintenait son propre département des transports et un parc de charrettes; le rôle du "marshal" londonien ou maréchal-ferrant est passé en revue. Une étude sur l'importance des restes de squelettes de chevaux trouvés dans Londres s'ensuit; celle-ci étant développée davantage dans un appendice. Pour finir, cette dernière et d'autres évidences forment la matière première d'une discussion quant à la taille et la puissance de traction du cheval médiéval.

Un chapitre sur les "Fouilles" nous fournit un résumé d'informations concernant chaque site. La plupart des trouvailles proviennent d'un ensemble de dépôts de détritus, situés dans les couches profondes, au sud de Thames Street entre Blackfriars (Baynard's Castle) et Custom House, un endroit gagné sur la rivière entre le 11ème et le 15ème siècle par la construction d'une série de quais et d'entrepôts. Une datation précise des contextes archéologiques, effectuée principalement grâce à la dendrochronologie, a permis l'établissement d'une série de "phases" établies par la datation des céramiques à partir desquelles la chronologie des trouvailles publiées est basée.

Le catalogue présentant les 408 objets trouvés s'ensuit, divisé par type d'objet. Chaque section a une introduction dans laquelle la fonction de l'objet est passée en revue et, si nécessaire, une typologie d'ensemble et/ou une chronologie est proposée; des comparaisons sont effectuées à partir des trouvailles émanant d'autres sites. Des objets provenant des collections anciennes du Musée de Londres sont décrits et illustrés en matière de comparaison. A l'intérieur de chaque section les notices du catalogue sont classées par ordre chronologique établi par leur appartenance

à telle ou telle "phase des céramiques", et à l'intérieur de chaque phase par site et numéro de contexte.

Dans le cas des fers à chevaux et des éperons qui furent découverts, les passages d'introduction sont assez longs, reflétant le grand nombre et la variété de ces trouvailles. On peut classer les fers à chevaux dans une série de quatre types différents datant du 9ème au 15ème siècle; la signification quant à la variation de la taille et du poids est prise en compte; l'évidence documentaire concernant le ferrage des chevaux est présentée; la fragilité du témoignage quant aux fers à chevaux antérieurs, notamment de l'époque romaine est mentionnée brièvement. L'essai sur les éperons passe en revue l'évidence historique concernant le travail des éperonniers du Londres médiéval. Une attention toute particulière a été portée aux courroies de cuir qui ont survécu et qui servaient à maintenir ces éperons; tout particulièrement un ensemble de 16 d'entre elles datant du 14ème siècle découvertes dans le même tas de détritus et qui présentent des ferrures décorées.

Das mittelalterliche Pferd und seine Ausstattung

Dieses ist der fünfte Band in einer Serie, die der großen Vielfalt mittelalterlicher Funde gewidmet ist, die bei Ausgrabungen während der 1970er und '80er Jahre in der Londoner City gemacht wurden. Das besondere Thema hier sind Gegenstände, die mit Pferden zu tun haben: Geschirrteile, wie Trensen und Steigbügel, Sporen samt Zubehör, und von den Stallgeräten allerdings nur Striegel. Leider gibt es keine mittelalterlichen Sättel oder identifizierbare Sattelteile.

Nach einem Überblick über die verschiedenen Fundstücke werden in der Einleitung auch dokumentarische und andere Quellen insbesondere zur bedeutenden, wirtschaftlichen Rolle des Pferdes in London, wie der Pferdemarkt in Smithfield, Pferdepreise, Unterhaltungskosten, Mietpreise für Reitpferde und die Verwendung von Packpferden und Wagen in und um London, herangezogen. Die Aufzeichnungen der Brückenaufseher geben Einblick in eine größere öffentliche Institution, die eine eigene Transportabteilung und einen Fuhrpark unterhielt. Wir erfahren auch etwas über die Rolle des Londoner 'marshal', des Hufschmieds. Danach folgt ein Überblick über die Bedeutung der Londoner Funde von Pferdeskeletten (weitere Ausführungen hierzu enthält der Anhang). Abschließend werden auf Grund dieses und anderen Materials Größe und Zugkraft des mittelalterlichen Pferdes erörtert.

Das Kapitel 'The excavations' faßt die Ergebnisse jeder einzelnen Ausgrabung zusammen. Die meisten Funde stammen aus einer Reihe stratigraphisch tiefer, am Fluß gelegener Müllschichten südlich der Thames Street zwischen Blackfriars (Baynard's Castle) und Custom House. Die Gegend wurde zwischen dem 11. und 15. Jh. durch den Bau einer Reihe neuer Werften und Uferbefestigungen der Themse abgewonnen. Relativ genaue Datierung, meist auf Grund von Dendrochronologie, ermöglichte die Begründung einer Reihe von 'keramischen Phasen', auf der die Zeitbestimmungen der Funde fußen.

Es folgt ein nach Arten aufgeteilter Katalog mit 408 Fundstücken. Jeder Abschnitt beginnt mit einer Einführung, in der die Funktion der Gegenstände erörtert und, wo möglich, eine allgemeinere Zuordnung und/oder Zeitbestimmung vorgeschlagen wird. Anderenorts gefundene Stücke werden verglichen. Auch werden einige frühere Funde aus den Beständen des Museum of London beschrieben und zum Vergleich bildlich dargestellt. Innerhalb jeden Abschnitts sind die Katalogartikel nach 'keramischen Phasen' zeitlich und im übrigen nach stratigraphischen Phasen der Ausgrabungsstätte und Kontextnummer geordnet.

Die Einführungen zu Hufeisen und Sporen sind entsprechend derer Menge und Verschiedenheit besonders ausführlich. Für die Hufeisen wird eine Klassifizierung in vier Grundtypen vorgeschlagen, deren Datierungen vom 9. bis zur Mitte des 15 Jhs. reichen. Ebenso wird die Bedeutung ihrer Verschiedenheit in Größe und Gewicht erörtert. Weiterhin werden schriftliche Quellen über die Praxis des Hufbeschlagens aufgeführt und auch die Ungewißheit früherer Quellen besonders aus römischer Zeit kurz gestreift. In der Abhandlung über Sporen werden die geschichtlichen Zeugnisse über die Arbeit der 'spurriers', der Sporenmacher, im mittelalterlichen London behandelt. Besonderes Augenmerk wird auf das Überdauern der ledernen Sporenriemchen gerichtet, insbesondere einer Gruppe von 16 separaten, mit Beschlägen verzierten Riemchen aus dem 14. Jh., die in ein und demselben Abfallhaufen gefunden wurden.

Bibliography

ALEXANDER, J & BINSKI, P (eds), 1987 *Age of Chivalry: Art in Plantagenet England 1200–1400*, Royal Academy of Arts, London

ALLEN, P, 1988 'The timber buildings catalogue – Cheapside study area' in Horsman, Milne & Milne, 52–65

AMERICAN ASSOCIATION OF EQUINE PRACTITIONERS, 1971 *Official Guide for Determining the Age of the Horse*, Colorado

ANDREWS, D D & MILNE, G (eds), 1979 *Wharram: A Study of Settlement in the Yorkshire Wolds 1*, Soc Medieval Archaeol Monogr Ser **8**, London

ARMITAGE, P L, 1981a 'Late Anglo-Saxon horse skeleton from Ironmonger Lane, City of London', unpublished archive report, Museum of London Department of Urban Archaeology

— 1981b 'Roman horse skeleton from Miles Lane, City of London', unpublished archive report, Museum of London Department of Urban Archaeology

— & CHAPMAN, H, 1979 'Roman mules', *London Archaeol* **3**(13), 339–46

AYTON, A, 1994 *Knights and Warhorses*, Woodbridge

AZZOLA, F K & BORMUTH, H, 1986 'Überregionale Entwicklungzüge historischer Handwerkszeichen der Hufschmiede', *Beiträge zur Erforschung des Odenwaldes und seiner Randlandschaften* **4**, Breuberg-Neustadt, 569–600

BARRÈRE, M, REY DELQUÉ, M & MILHAU, D, 1990 *Archéologie et vie quotidienne aux 13e–14e siècles en Midi-Pyrénées* (exhibition catalogue) Musée des Augustins, Toulouse

BASING, P, 1990 *Trades and Crafts in Medieval Manuscripts*, London

BENNETT, H S, 1968 *The Pastons and their England*, Cambridge

BERESFORD, G, 1975 *The Medieval Clay-Land Village: Excavations at Goltho and Barton Blount*, Soc Medieval Archaeol Monogr Ser **6**, London

BIDDLE, M (ed), 1990 *Artefacts from Medieval Winchester Parts i & ii: Object and Economy in Medieval Winchester*, Winchester Stud **7**, Oxford

BINSKI, P, 1987 'The stylistic sequence of London figure brasses' in Coales, J (ed) *The Earliest English Brasses*, London, 69–131

BLAIR, C, 1951 *The Effigy and Tomb of Sir Hugh Calveley*, The Bunbury Papers **4**, Bunbury

BLAIR, J, 1994 *Anglo-Saxon Oxfordshire*, London

— & CRAWFORD, B, forthcoming in *Oxoniensia*

BLANGY, COMTE DE, 1889 *Journal des fouilles de Saint-Vaast, siège de 1356*, Caen

BLUER, R, 1993 *Abbots Lane, London SE1 . . . An Assessment of the 1992 Archaeological Excavations*, Museum of London Archaeology Service, London

BOCCIA, L G, 1991 *L'Armeria del Museo Civico Medievale de Bologna*, Busto Arsizio, Italy

BOURDILLON, J E, 1993 'Animal bone' in Hawkes, J W & Heaton, M J (eds) *Jennings Yard, Windsor*, Wessex Archaeol Rep **3**, Salisbury, 67–79

— & COY, J, 1980 'The animal bone' in Holdsworth, P (ed) *Excavations in Melbourne Street, Southampton, 1971–76*, Council Brit Archaeol Res Rep **33**, London, 79–121

BOWIE, T (ed), 1959 *The Sketchbook of Villard de Honnecourt*, Indiana University Press, Bloomington & London

BRITISH HORSE SOCIETY, 1988 *The Manual of Horsemanship*, London, (9th edn)

BRITISH MUSEUM, 1958 *Guide to the Antiquities of Roman Britain*, London, (2nd edn)

BROWN, J, 1991 *The Horse in Husbandry*, Ipswich

BURKE-EASTON, J, 1982 'Excavations at the SE Tower of Baynard's Castle 1981', unpublished archive report, Museum of London Department of Urban Archaeology

BUSCHE, H & LOHSE, B (eds), 1962 *Romanesque Sculpture*, London

BYERLY, B F & BYERLY, C R (eds), 1977 *Records of the Wardrobe and Household 1285–1286*, London

BYRNE, B, 1959 'The spurs of King Casimir III and some other fourteenth century spurs', *J Arms Armour Soc* **3**(4), 106–15

CALENDAR OF LIBERATE ROLLS, 1916 *Calendar of Liberate Rolls Henry III Vol. I A.D. 1226–1240*, London

— 1930 *Calendar of Liberate Rolls Henry III Vol. II A.D. 1240–1245*, London

CALENDAR OF PATENT ROLLS, 1905 *Calendar of Patent Rolls Richard II Vol. V A.D. 1391–1396*, London

CAVE, C J P, 1948 *Roof Bosses in Medieval Churches*, Cambridge

CENTRE FOR METROPOLITAN HISTORY, 1991 *Annual Report 1990–91*, University of London, Institute of Historical Research, London

CHAPMAN, H, 1985 'Small finds' in Parnell, 60–67

CHAPPELL, E, 1973 'A study of horseshoes in the Department of Archaeology, Colonial Williamsburg' in Nöel-Hume, A, Abbitt, M W, McNulty, R H, Davies, I & Chappell, E *Five Artifact Studies*, Williamsburg, Virginia

CHERRY, J, 1969 'The Dunstable Swan Jewel', *J Brit Archaeol Ass* 3rd series **32**, 38–53

CHEW, H M & KELLAWAY, W, 1974 *London Assize of Nuisance 1301–1431*, London Rec Soc **10**, London

— & WEINBAUM, M, 1970 *The London Eyre of 1244*, London Rec Soc **6**, London

CLARK, J, 1984 'Richard Crips the Wheeler – a medieval craftsman and his tools', *Tools Trades* **2**, 13–28

— 1986 *Medieval Horseshoes*, Finds Research Group 700–1700 Datasheet **4**, Coventry

— 1988 'Some medieval smiths' marks', *Tools Trades* **5**, 10–22

CLUTTON-BROCK, J, 1974 'The Buhen horse', *J Archaeol Sci* **1**, 89–100

– 1992 *Horse Power*, London

COAD, J G & STREETEN, A D F, 1982 'Excavations at Castle Acre Castle, Norfolk 1972–77', *Archaeol J* **139**, 138–301

COCKERELL, S C (ed), nd *Old Testament Miniatures*, London

COTTER, J L, 1958 *Archeological Excavations at Jamestown, Virginia*, National Parks Service Archeol Res Ser **4**, Washington, DC

COWGILL, J, DE NEERGAARD, M & GRIFFITHS, N, 1987 *Medieval Finds from Excavations in London: 1 Knives and Scabbards*, London

CROWFOOT, E, PRITCHARD, F & STANILAND, K, 1992 *Medieval Finds from Excavations in London: 4 Textiles and Clothing* c.*1150–c.1450*, London

CUMMINS, J, 1988 *The Hound and the Hawk: The Art of Medieval Hunting*, London

CUNLIFFE, B, 1971 *Excavations at Fishbourne 1961–1969*, London

— 1975 *Excavations at Portchester Castle Vol I: Roman*, London

— 1976 *Excavations at Portchester Castle Vol II: Saxon*, London

DALTON, O M, 1912 *Catalogue of the Finger Rings, Early Christian, Byzantine, Teutonic, Mediaeval and Later*, London

DAVIS, R H C, 1989 *The Medieval Warhorse*, London

DE DEGUILEVILLE, G, 1899–1904 *The Pilgrimage of the Life of Man, Englisht by J Lydgate, A.D. 1426* (ed F J Furnivall), Early English Text Soc, Extra Ser **77, 83, 92**

DEAN, B, 1926 'Early Gothic spurs', *Bull Metropolitan Museum of Art*, New York, 129–130

DENT, A A, 1967 'The early horseshoe', *Antiquity* **41**, 61–3

— 1987 *Horses in Shakespeare's England*, London

— & GOODALL, D M, 1962 *The Foals of Epona*, London

DEVEREUX, F L, jr (ed), 1979 *The Cavalry Manual of Horse Management*, South Brunswick and New York (revision of United States Cavalry School, Fort Riley, Kansas *Animal Management*, 1941–2)

DHANENS, E, 1980 *Hubert and Jan van Eyck*, New York

DIDEROT, D, 1763–72 *Recueil de planches sur les sciences, les arts libéraux, et les arts méchaniques . . . 7 vols*, Paris

DILLON, H A, 1888 'Arms and armour at Westminster, the Tower, and Greenwich, 1547', *Archaeologia* **51**, 219–80

D'ONOFRIO, M (ed), 1994 *I Normanni, popolo d'Europa 1030–1200*, Rome

DYSON, T, 1989 *Documents & Archaeology: The Medieval London Waterfront* (Museum of London Annual Archaeology Lecture), London

EDGE, D & PADDOCK, J M, 1988 *Arms and Armour of the Medieval Knight*, London

EDWARDS, P, 1988 *The Horse Trade of Tudor and Stuart England*, Cambridge

EGAN, G, 1985/6 'Finds Recovery on Riverside Sites in London', *Popular Archaeol* **6**(14), 42–50

— & PRITCHARD, F, 1991 *Medieval Finds from Excavations in London: 3 Dress Accessories* c.*1150–c.1450*, London

EKWALL, E, 1954 *Street Names of the City of London*, Oxford

ELDRID, OTTAWAY & Co, nd (c.1910) *The "Whitecross" Illustrated Guide of Horse Equipment and Stable Requisites*, London

ELLIS, B, 1982 'Spurs' in Coad & Streeten, 230–5

— 1990 'Spurs' in Biddle, 1037–41

— 1991 'Spurs' in Saunders, P & Saunders, E (eds) *Salisbury Museum Medieval Catalogue Part 1*, Salisbury, 54–78

— 1993 'The spurs' in Ellis, P (ed) *Beeston Castle, Cheshire: A Report on the Excavations 1968–85 by Laurence Keen and Peter Hough*, London, 165–9

— 1994 'Spurs' in Quinnell, H & Blockley, M R with Berridge, P *Excavations at Rhuddlan, Clwyd: 1969–73 Mesolithic to Medieval*, Council Brit Archaeol Res Rep **95**, 187–8

—, forthcoming 'The spurs' in Ellis, P (ed) *Ludgershall Castle, Wiltshire: A Report on the Excavations by Peter Addyman, 1964–72*, London

EVANS, G E, 1960 *The Horse in the Furrow*, London

— 1970 *Where Beards Wag All*, London

FARLEY, M, 1976 'Saxon & medieval Walton, Aylesbury: excavations 1973–4', *Rec Buckinghamshire* **20**(2), 153–290

— 1982 'Excavations at Low Farm, Falmer, Bucks: II The medieval manor', *Rec Buckinghamshire* **24**, 46–72

FINGERLIN, I, 1971 *Gürtel des hohen und späten Mittelalters*, Munich & Berlin

FLEMING, G, 1869 *Horse-shoes and Horse-shoeing: Their Origin, History, Uses and Abuses*, London

FOX-DAVIES, A C, 1929 *A Complete Guide to Heraldry*, London

GAIMSTER, D R M, 1990 'A late medieval cast copper-alloy stirrup from Old Romney, Kent', *Medieval Archaeol* **34**, 157–60

GAIRDNER, J (ed), 1904 *Paston Letters*, London

GALLOWAY, J A & MURPHY, M 1991 'Feeding the City: Medieval London and its agrarian hinterland', *London J* **16**(1), 3–64

GAUTHIER, M M, 1972 *Émaux de Moyen Age*, Fribourg

GEDDES, J, 1983 'The blacksmith's life, wife and work 1250–1450', *Tools Trades* **1**, 15–37

— 1991 'Iron' in Blair, J & Ramsay, N (eds) *English Medieval Industries: Craftsmen, Techniques, Products*, London, 167–88

GILBEY, Sir W, 1976 *The Harness Horse*, Liss (5th edn, rev S Watney)

GOODALL, I H, 1973 'Appendix 6: iron objects' in Huggins & Huggins, 168–75

— 1975 'Metalwork from Goltho' in Beresford, 79–96

— 1976a 'The metalwork' in Bedwin, O 'The excavation of Ardingly fulling mill and forge, 1975–76', *Post-Medieval Archaeol* **10**, 60–4

— 1976b 'Iron objects' in Ketteringham, 55–60

— 1977 'Iron objects' in Durham, B 'Archaeological investigations in St Aldates, Oxford', *Oxoniensia* **42**, 142–8

— 1979a 'Iron objects' in Andrews & Milne, 115–23

— 1979b 'Iron objects' in Smith, G H 'The excavation of the Hospital of St Mary of Ospringe, commonly called Maison Dieu', *Archaeol Cantiana* **95**, 129–37

— 1979c 'Iron objects' in Rahtz, P *The Saxon and Medieval Palaces at Cheddar*, Brit Archaeol Rep **65**, Oxford, 263–74

— 1980 'Iron objects' in Palmer, N 'A Beaker burial and medieval tenements in The Hamel, Oxford', *Oxoniensia* **45**, 124–225

— 1982 'Iron objects' in Coad & Streeten, 227–35

— 1983a 'Iron objects' in Halpin, C 'Late Saxon evidence and excavation of Hinxey Hall, Queen Street, Oxford', *Oxoniensia* **48**, 41–69

— 1983b 'Iron objects' in Mayes & Butler, 240–53

— 1984a 'Iron objects' in Rogerson, A & Dallas, C *Excavations in Thetford 1948–59 and 1973–80*, E Anglian Archaeol Rep **22**, Gressenhall, 77–105

— 1984b 'Iron objects' in Allan, J P *Medieval and Post-Medieval Finds from Exeter 1971–1980*, Exeter, 337–8

— 1990 'Woodworking tools', 'Iron buckles and belt-fittings', 'Stirrups', 'Bridle bits and associated strap-fittings', 'Curry-combs' and 'Horseshoes' in Biddle, 273–7, 526–38, 1042–6 and 1053–67

— 1991 'The ironwork' in Armstrong, P, Tomlinson, D & Evans, D H *Excavations at Lurk Lane Beverley, 1979–82*, Sheffield Excavation Rep **1**, Sheffield, 131–46

— & OTTAWAY, P J, forthcoming 'Iron objects' in *Excavations at Wicken Bonhunt*, E Anglian Archaeol Rep, Gressenhall

GREEN, C, 1966 'The purpose of the early horseshoe', *Antiquity* **40**, 305–8

GREW, F & DE NEERGAARD, M, 1988 *Medieval Finds from Excavations in London: 2 Shoes and Pattens*, London

GRIFFITHS, N, 1986 *Horse Harness Pendants*, Finds Research Group 700–1700 Datasheet **5**, Coventry

— 1989 *Shield-Shaped Mounts*, Finds Research Group 700–1700 Datasheet **12**, Oxford

GUILDHALL MUSEUM, 1908 *Catalogue of the Collection of London Antiquities in the Guildhall Museum*, Corporation of London (2nd edn)

GUISSEPPI, M S, 1920 'The wardrobe and household accounts of Bogo de Clare, A.D. 1284–6', *Archaeologia* **70**, 1–56

HALBOUT, P, PILET, C & VAUDOUR, C (eds), 1987 *Corpus des objets domestiques et des armes en fer de Normandie: Du Ier au XVe siècle*, Cahier des Annales de Normandie **20**, Caen

HARDING, G & SONS LTD, 1929 *The 'Competition Guide' for the Ironmongery & Hardware Trades*, London

HARVEY, P D A (ed), 1976 *Manorial Records of Cuxham, Oxfordshire circa 1200–1359*, London

HARVEY, Y, 1975 'The small finds: Catalogue' in Platt, C & Coleman-Smith, R (eds) *Excavations in Medieval Southampton, 1953–1969*, vol II, Leicester, 254–93

HASLUCK, P N, 1904 *Saddlery and Harness-making*, London, (repr 1962)

HAWKES, C F C & HULL, M R, 1947 *Camulodunum, First Report on the Excavations at Colchester 1930–39*, Rep Res Comm Soc Antiq London **14**, Oxford

HAZLITT, W C, 1892 *The Livery Companies of the City of London*, London

HEFNER-ALTENECK, J H VON, 1882 *Trachten, Kunstwerke und Gerätschaften vom frühen Mittelalter bis Ende des Achtzehnten Jahrhunderts*, vol 3, Frankfurt am Main, (2nd edn)

HERRNBRODT, A, 1958 *Der Husterknupp*, Cologne & Graz

HEWITT, H J, 1983 *The Horse in Medieval England*, London

HEYMERING, H, 1990 *On the Horse's Foot, Shoes and Shoeing: The Bibliographic Record*, Cascade, Maryland

HICKMAN, J & HUMPHREY, M, 1988 *Hickman's Farriery* London, (2nd edn)

HOBLEY, B, 1969 'A Neronian-Vespasianic military site at "The Lunt", Baginton, Warwickshire', *Trans Birmingham Archaeol Soc* **83**, 65–129

HODGETT, G A J, 1971 *The Cartulary of Holy Trinity Aldgate*, London Rec Soc **7**, London

HOGG, G, 1964 *Hammer and Tongs*, London

HOLDEN, E W, 1963 'Excavation at the deserted medieval village of Hangleton, Part I', *Sussex Archaeol Collect* **101**, 54–181

HOLME, R, 1688 *Accademie of Armoury III*, London

HORSMAN, V, MILNE, C & MILNE, G, 1988 *Aspects of Saxo-Norman London: 1 Building and Street Development*, London Middlesex Archaeol Soc Spec Pap **11**, London

HUGGINS, P J, 1972 'Monastic Grange and Outer Close excavations, Waltham Abbey, Essex, 1970–72', *Essex Archaeol Hist* **4**, 30–127

— & HUGGINS, R M, 1973 'Excavations of monastic forge and Saxo-Norman enclosure, Waltham Abbey, Essex, 1972–73', *Essex Archaeol Hist* **5**, 127–84

HYLAND, A, 1990a *Equus: The Horse in the Roman World*, London

— 1990b 'The action of the Newstead cavalry bit', *J Roman Military Stud* **1**, 67–72

— 1991 'The action of the Newstead snaffle bit', *J Roman Military Stud* **2**, 27–33

— 1994 *The Medieval Warhorse from Byzantium to the Crusades*, Stroud

JAMES, M R (ed), 1920 *La Estoire de Seint Aedward le Rei*, Oxford

— (ed), 1933 *The Romance of Alexander – a Collotype Facsimile of MS Bodley 264*, Oxford

JENKINS, J G, 1962 *Agricultural Transport in Wales*, Cardiff

JEWITT, L, 1883 *The Ceramic Art of Great Britain*, New York (rev. edn)

JOHNSTON, D E, 1972 'A Roman building at Chalk, near Gravesend', *Britannia* **3**, 112–48

JONES, M, 1989a 'The depiction of proverbs in late medieval art' in Gréciano, G (ed) *Europhras 88: Phraséologie contrastive*, Collection Recherches Germanique **2**, Strasbourg, 205–23

— 1989b 'Folklore motifs in late medieval art I: Proverbial follies and impossibilities', *Folklore* **100**, 201–17

JONES, R A, 1971 'Horses' in *The UFAW Handbook on the Care and Management of Farm Animals*, Edinburgh, 177–88

JONES, T, 1980 *Chaucer's Knight: The Portrait of a Medieval Mercenary*, London

JOPE, E M, 1956 'The tinning of iron spurs: A continuous practice from the tenth to the seventeenth century', *Oxoniensia* **21**, 35–42

JUNKELMANN, M, 1990–2 *Die Reiter Roms*, 3 vols, Mainz am Rhein

JUSSERAND, J J, 1961 *English Wayfaring Life in the Middle Ages*, London (repr of 4th edn)

KERLING, N J M, 1973 *Cartulary of St Bartholomew's Hospital*, London

KETTERINGHAM, L L, 1976 *Alsted: Excavation of a Thirteenth–Fourteenth Century Sub-Manor House . . .*, Res Vol Surrey Archaeol Soc **2**, London

KINGSFORD, C L (ed), 1908 *A Survey of London by John Stow*, Oxford

KUBOVY, M, 1986 *The Psychology of Perspective and Renaissance Art*, Cambridge

KUHN, S M & REIDY, J (eds), 1963 *Middle English Dictionary: G–H*, University of Michigan, Ann Arbor

KÜHNEL, H (ed), 1986 *Alltag im Spätmittelalter*, Graz, Vienna & Cologne

KURATH, H & KUHN, S M (eds), 1952 *Middle English Dictionary: E–F*, University of Michigan, Ann Arbor

— 1959 *Middle English Dictionary: C–D*, University of Michigan, Ann Arbor

KURTH, W (ed), 1963 *The Complete Woodcuts of Albrecht Dürer*, New York (repr of 1927 edn)

LACY, C DE L, 1911 *The History of the Spur*, London

LAIRD, M, 1986 *English Misericords*, London

LAKING, SIR G F, 1920–2 *A Record of European Armour and Arms Through Seven Centuries*, 5 vols, London

LAMBERT, F, 1921 'Some recent excavations in London', *Archaeologia* **71**, 55–112

LANGDON, J, 1986 *Horses, Oxen and Technological Innovation*, Cambridge

LATHAM, R E (ed), 1965 *Revised Medieval Latin Word-list*, London

LEECH, R, 1981 'The excavation of a Romano-British farmstead and cemetery on Bradley Hill, Somerton, Somerset', *Britannia* **12**, 177–252

LEFEBVRE DES NOËTTES, R, 1931 *L'attelage et le cheval de selle à travers les âges*, Paris

LEIGHTON, A C, 1972 *Transport and Communication in Early Medieval Europe AD 500–1100*, Newton Abbot

LEMAÎTRE, J-L (ed), 1988 *Henri Baude Dictz moraulx pour faire tapisserie*, Ussel, France

LITTAUER, M A, 1968 'Early horseshoe problems again', *Antiquity* **42**, 221–5

LONDON MUSEUM, 1940 *Medieval Catalogue*, London

LONGNON, J, 1969 *The Très Riches Heures of Jean, Duc de Berry*, New York

McCARTHY, M R & BROOKS, C M, 1988 *Medieval Pottery in Britain AD 900–1600*, Leicester

MACDONALD, A D S & LAING, L R, 1974–5 'Excavations at Lochmaben Castle, Dumfriesshire', *Proc Soc Antiq Scotl* **106**, 124–57

MACGREGOR, A, 1982 *Anglo-Scandinavian Finds from Lloyds Bank, Pavement, and Other Sites (The Archaeology of York* **17**, fascicule 3), Council for British Archaeology, London

MANN, J G, 1938 'The lost armoury of the Gonzagas', *Archaeol J* **95**, 239–336

MANNING, W H, 1976 *Catalogue of Romano-British Ironwork in the Museum of Antiquities, Newcastle upon Tyne*, Newcastle upon Tyne

— 1985 *Catalogue of the Romano-British Iron Tools, Fittings and Weapons in the British Museum*, London

MARKHAM, G, 1662 *Markhams Maister-Peece*, 2 vols, London

MARSDEN, P, 1971 'Archaeological finds in the City of London 1967–70', *Trans London Middlesex Archaeol Soc* **23**, 1–14

— DYSON, T & RHODES, M, 1975 'Excavations at the site of St Mildred's church, Bread Street, London, 1973–4', *Trans London Middlesex Archaeol Soc* **26**, 171–208

MASSON, G, 1952 'Horse management in medieval renaissance Italy', *Country Life Annual*, 188–90

MAYES, P & BUTLER, L, 1983 *Sandal Castle Excavations*, Wakefield

MILLAR, E G (ed), 1932 *The Luttrell Psalter*, London

MILNE, G & MILNE, C, 1982 *Medieval Waterfront Development at Trig Lane*, London Middlesex Archaeol Soc Spec Pap **5**, London

MOORHOUSE, S & GOODALL, I H, 1971 'Metalwork – iron' in Moorhouse, S 'Finds from Basing House, Hampshire (c.1540–1645): Part Two', *Post-Medieval Archaeol* **5**, 36–52

MORGAN, J & SCHOFIELD, J, 1978 'Tree rings and the archaeology of the Thames waterfront in the City of London' in Fletcher, J (ed) *Dendrochronology in Europe*, Brit Archaeol Rep Int Ser **51**, 223–38

MUCHEMBLED, R, 1978 *Popular Culture and Elite Culture in France 1400–1700*, Baton Rouge, Louisiana & London

MURRAY, P & MURRAY, L, 1963 *The Art of the Renaissance*, London

MURRAY, P & DE VECCHI, P, 1970 *The Complete Paintings of Piero della Francesca*, London

MURRAY, R W, 1937a 'An enquiry regarding the date of some old English horseshoes', *J Brit Archaeol Ass* 3rd ser, **1**, 14–33

— 1937b 'Dating old English horseshoes', *J Brit Archaeol Ass* 3rd ser, **2**, 133–44

MUSTY, J & ALGAR, D, 1986 'Excavations at the deserted medieval village of Gomeldon, near Salisbury', *Wiltshire Archaeol Natur Hist Mag* **80**, 127–69

MYNARD, D C, 1969 'Excavations at Somerby, Lincs, 1957', *Lincolnshire Hist Archaeol* **4**, 63–91

NORTON, J, 1982 'Ironmonger Lane', *London Archaeol* **4**, 171–6

O'CONNOR, T P, 1982 *Animal bones from Flaxengate, Lincoln c.870–1500* (*The Archaeology of Lincoln* **18**(1)), Council for British Archaeology, London 1–52
— 1989 *Bones from Anglo-Scandinavian Levels at 16–22 Coppergate* (*The Archaeology of York* **15**, fascicule 3), Council for British Archaeology, London, 137–207

OPIE, I & TATEM, M (eds), 1989 *A Dictionary of Superstitions*, Oxford

OSCHINSKY, D, 1971 *Walter of Henley and other Treatises on Estate Management and Accounting*, Oxford

OTTAWAY, P, 1992 *Anglo-Scandinavian Ironwork from Coppergate* (*The Archaeology of York* **17**, fascicule 6), Council for British Archaeology, London

PARNELL, G, 1985 'The Roman and medieval defences and the later development of the Inmost Ward, Tower of London: Excavations 1955–77', *Trans London Middlesex Archaeol Soc* **36**, 1–79

PARSONS, J C (ed), 1977 *The Court and Household of Eleanor of Castile in 1290*, Toronto

PAVRY, F H & KNOCKER, G M, 1957–8 'The Mount, Princes Risborough', *Rec Buckinghamshire* **16**(3), 131–78

PIPE, A & RACKHAM, D J, 1990 'The animal bones from Beddington Roman Villa', unpublished archive report, Museum of London Department of Urban Archaeology

PLOT, R, 1686 *The Natural History of Staffordshire*, Oxford

POGNON, E (ed), 1978 *Boccaccio's Decameron*, Fribourg & Geneva
— 1979 *Les très riches heures du Duc de Berry*, Fribourg & Geneva

POPE HENNESSY, J (ed), 1985 *Italian Gothic Sculpture*, New York

POWELL, B, 1991 'Shoeing Downland oxen', *Weald & Downland Open Air Museum Magazine* **3**(6), 7–8

PRÉVOT, B (ed), 1991 *La Science du cheval au Moyen Age: Le traité d'hippatrie de Jordanus Rufus*, Paris

PRINCE, L B, 1980 *The Farrier and His Craft*, London

PRITCHARD, F, 1991 'Small finds' in Vince, 120–278

PRUMMEL, W, 1983 *Excavations at Dorestad 2: Early Medieval Dorestad, an Archaeozoological Study*, Rijksdienst voor het Oudheidkundig Bodemonderzoek, Amersfoort, Netherlands

R, E, gent, 1720 *The Experienc'd Farrier* (4th edn; first published 1678), London

RACKHAM, D J, 1989 'Animal remains' in Austin, D *The Deserted Medieval Village of Thrislington, County Durham, Excavations 1973–74*, Soc Medieval Archaeol Monogr Ser **12**, London 146–58

RANDALL, L M C, 1966 *Images in the Margins of Gothic Manuscripts*, University of California Press, Berkeley and Los Angeles

REMNANT, G L, 1969 *A Catalogue of Misericords in Great Britain*, Oxford

RIGOLD, S E, 1967 'Excavations at Dover Castle 1964–1966', *J Brit Archaeol Ass* **30**, 87–121
— 1971 'Eynsford Castle and its excavation', *Archaeol Cantiana* **86**, 109–71

RILEY, H T, 1861 *Liber Albus: The White Book of the City of London*, London
— 1868 *Memorials of London and London Life in the XIIIth, XIVth and XVth Centuries*, London

RIPPMANN, D, TAUBER, J, FRIEDERICI, A, LAVICKA, P & HARTMANN, F, 1991 *Eine Stadt um 1100*, Sigmaringen, Germany

RIVIÈRE, S, 1984 'Excavations at 27–9 Eastcheap', unpublished archive report, Museum of London Department of Urban Archaeology

ROBINSON, F N (ed), 1966 *The Works of Geoffrey Chaucer*, London

ROUSE, E C, 1991 *Medieval Wall Paintings*, Princes Risborough

ROYAL SCOTTISH MUSEUM & VICTORIA AND ALBERT MUSEUM, 1959 *Norwegian Art Treasures* (exhibition catalogue), Oslo

RUSSELL, J, 1939 'English medieval leatherwork', *Archaeol J* **96**, 132–41

SABINE, E L, 1937 'City cleaning in mediaeval London', *Speculum* **12**, 19–43

SALZMAN, L F, 1952 *Building in England down to 1540*, Oxford

SCHOFIELD, J, 1975 'Seal House', *Curr Archaol* **49**, 53–77
— ALLEN, P & TAYLOR, C, 1990 'Medieval buildings and property development in the area of Cheapside', *Trans London Middlesex Archaeol Soc* **41**, 39–237
— ROSKAMS, S & ALLEN, P, 1986 'Excavations at 1–6 Milk Street, EC2', unpublished archive report, Museum of London Department of Urban Archaeology

SCOTT, J H, & BRAY SYMONS, N B, 1964 *Introduction to Dental Anatomy*, London

SEABY, W A, 1950 'Late Dark Age finds from the Cherwell and Ray, 1876–86', *Oxoniensia* **15**, 29–43

— & WOODFIELD, P, 1980 'Viking Age stirrups from England and their background', *Medieval Archaeol* **24**, 87–122

SERJEANTSON, D, WALDRON, T & BRACEGIRDLE, M, 1992 'Medieval horses from Kingston-upon-Thames', *London Archaeol* **7**(1), 9–13

SHARPE, R R, 1901 *Calendar of Letter-Books: Letter-Book C. Circa A.D. 1291–1309*, London

— 1904 *Calendar of Letter-Books: Letter-Book F. Circa A.D. 1337–1352*, London

— 1905 *Calendar of Letter-Books: Letter-Book G. Circa A.D. 1352–1374*, London

— 1907 *Calendar of Letter-Books: Letter-Book H. Circa A.D. 1375–1399*, London

— 1911 *Calendar of Letter-Books: Letter-Book K. Temp. Henry VI*, London

— 1912 *Calendar of Letter-Books: Letter-Book L. Temp. Edward IV – Henry VII*, London

— 1913 *Calendar of Coroners' Rolls of the City of London A.D. 1300–1378*, London

SHEPPARD, F, 1991 *The Treasury of London's Past*, London

SHORTT, H DE S, 1959 'A provincial Roman spur from Longstock, Hants, and other spurs from Roman Britain', *Antiq J* **39**, 61–76

SINGER, C, HOLMYARD, E J, HALL, A R & WILLIAMS, T I (eds), 1957 *A History of Technology: Vol 3 From the Renaissance to the Industrial Revolution, c.1550–c.1750*, Oxford

SISSON, S, 1953 *The Anatomy of the Domestic Animals*, London (rev edn by J D Grossman)

SKEAT, REV W W (ed), 1895 *The Complete Works of Geoffrey Chaucer*, Oxford

SMITH, C R, 1855 *Catalogue of the Museum of London Antiquities*, London

SMITH, M Q, 1979 *The Roof Bosses and Vaults of Bristol Cathedral*, Friends of Bristol Cathedral, Bristol

SMITH, R, 1962 *Ceremonials of the Corporation of London*, London

SMYTHE, R H, 1962 'Ankylosis of the equine spine: Pathologic or biologic?', *Modern Veterinary Practice*, September 1962, 50–51

SPARKES, I G, 1976 *Old Horseshoes*, Aylesbury

SPENCER, B, 1972 *Chaucer's London*, London

— 1990 *Salisbury Museum Medieval Catalogue Part 2: Pilgrim Souvenirs and Secular Badges*, Salisbury

SPRUYTTE, J, 1983 *Early Harness Systems*, London (trans M Littauer)

STECHER, R M, 1962 'Lateral facets and lateral joints in the lumbar spine of the horse – a descriptive and statistical study', *Amer J Veterinary Res* **23**(96), 939–47

— & GOSS, L J, 1961 'Ankylosing lesions of the spine', *J Amer Veterinary Medical Ass* **138**(5), 248–55

STENTON, F M, 1934 *Norman London*, Historical Association Leaflets **93** & **94** (issued as one), London

— (ed), 1957 *The Bayeux Tapestry*, London

STEPHENS, W B (ed), 1969 *Victoria County History: A History of the County of Warwick: Vol 8 The City of Coventry and Borough of Warwick*, London

STOTHARD, C A, 1817 *The Monumental Effigies of Great Britain*, London

STOTT, P, 1991 'Saxon and Norman coins from London' in Vince, 279–325

STRAUSS, W L, 1972 *The Complete Engravings, Etchings, and Drypoints of Albrecht Dürer*, New York

SUTTON, A F, 1984 'John Hertyngton, supplier of saddlery to Richard III', *The Ricardian* **6**(86), 379–84

— & HAMMOND, P W, 1983 *The Coronation of Richard III: The Extant Documents*, Gloucester

TATTON-BROWN, T, 1974 'Excavations at the Custom House Site, City of London, 1973', *Trans London Middlesex Archaeol Soc*, **25**, 117–219

THOMAS, A H, 1924 *Calendar of Early Mayor's Court Rolls a.d. 1298–1307*, Cambridge

— 1929 *Calendar of Plea and Memoranda Rolls a.d. 1364–1381*, Cambridge

— 1943 *Calendar of Plea and Memoranda Rolls a.d. 1413–1437*, Cambridge

THOMPSON, A, 1979 'Excavations at 1–3 Tudor Street', unpublished archive report, Museum of London Department of Urban Archaeology

THOMPSON, N P, 1972 'Excavations on a medieval site at Huish, 1967–68', *Wiltshire Archaeol Natur Hist Mag* **67**, 112–31

THORDEMAN, B, 1939 *Armour from the Battle of Wisby, 1361*, vol I, Uppsala

— 1943 *Nordisk Kultur Vapen*, Stockholm

TREASE, G, 1970 *The Condottieri – Soldiers of Fortune*, London

TREUE, W, GOLDMANN, K, KELLERMANN, R et al., 1965 *Das Hausbuch der Mendelschen Zwölfbrüderstiftung zu Nürnberg*, plates volume, Munich

TRIBBICK, R, 1974 'Metal small finds' in Sheldon, H 'Excavations at Toppings and Sun Wharves, Southwark, 1970–2', *Trans London Middlesex Archaeol Soc* **25**, 90–99

TROW-SMITH, R, 1957 *A History of British Livestock Husbandry to 1700*, London

TUKE, D, 1965 *Bit by Bit*, London (repr. 1988)

— 1973 *Horse by Horse*, London

TYLDEN, G, 1965 *Horses and Saddlery*, London

UNWIN, G, 1908 *The Gilds and Companies of London*, London

USHER, A P, 1957 'Machines and mechanisms' in Singer et al., 324–46

VAUGHAN, R, 1979 *Matthew Paris*, Cambridge

VERLET, P, 1965 'Gothic tapestry' in Verlet, P, Florisoone, M, Hoffmeister, A & Tabard, F *The Art of Tapestry*, London, 9–76

VIGNERON, P, 1968 *Le cheval dans l'antiquité gréco-romaine* (2 vols), Nancy

VINCE, A, 1983 'The medieval pottery from Baynard's Castle 1981', unpublished archive report, Museum of London Department of Urban Archaeology

— 1985 'The Saxon and medieval pottery of London: A review', *Medieval Archaeol* **29**, 25–93

— (ed), 1991 *Aspects of Saxo-Norman London: 2 Finds and Environmental Evidence*, London Middlesex Archaeol Soc Spec Pap **12**, London

VON DEN DRIESCH, A & BOESSNECK, J, 1974 'Kritische Anmerkungen zu Widerristhohenberechnung aus Längenmassen vor- und frühgeschichtlicher Tierknochen', *Saugetierkundliche Mitteilungen* **22**, 325–48

WAGNER, A R, 1959 'The Swan Badge and the Swan Knight', *Archaeologia* **97**, 127–38

WAINWRIGHT, G J, 1967 *Coygan Camp: A Prehistoric, Romano-British and Dark Age Settlement in Carmarthenshire*, Cambrian Archaeological Association, Cardiff

WAR OFFICE VETERINARY DEPARTMENT, 1908 *Animal Management*, London

WARD, G R, 1939 'On dating old horseshoes', *Trans Lancashire Cheshire Antiq Soc* **53**, 140–75

— 1941a 'The Iron Age horseshoe and its derivatives', *Antiq J* **21**, 7–27

— 1941b 'The Iron Age horseshoe', *Antiq J* **21**, 238

WARD PERKINS, J B, 1941 'The Iron Age horseshoe', *Antiq J* **21**, 144–9

WARNER, G (ed), 1912 *Queen Mary's Psalter*, London

WATSON, B, 1992 'The excavation of a Norman fortress on Ludgate Hill', *London Archaeol* **6**(14), 371–7

WEBSTER, G, 1968 'The bronze handle of a Romano-British butteris', *Antiq J* **48**, 303–4

WEBSTER, L E & CHERRY, J, 1973 'Medieval Britain in 1972', *Medieval Archaeol* **17**, 138–88

WEINBAUM, M, 1976 *The London Eyre of 1276*, London Rec Soc **12**, London

WHEELER, R E M, 1943 *Maiden Castle, Dorset*, London

WHITE, L, jr, 1962 *Medieval Technology and Social Change*, Oxford

— 1978 *Medieval Religion and Technology*, University of California Press, Los Angeles

WHITE, W J, 1988 *The Cemetery of St Nicholas Shambles*, London Middlesex Archaeol Soc Spec Pap **9**, London

WILKINSON, R, 1825 *Londina Illustrata* **2**, London

WILKINSON, T S, 1983 'The equid bones from the medieval ditch at Ludgate (LUD82)', unpublished archive report, Museum of London Department of Urban Archaeology

WILLIAMS, F, 1977 *Excavations at Pleshey Castle*, Brit Archaeol Rep British Ser **42**, Oxford

WILMOTT, T, 1982 'A medieval armorial brooch or pendant from Baynard's Castle', *Trans London Middlesex Archaeol Soc* **33**, 299–302

WOODWARD, D, 1985 ' "Swords into ploughshares": Recycling in pre-industrial England', *Econ Hist Rev* **38**(2), 175–91

YOUATT, W, 1880 *The Horse*, London (4th edn)

YOUNGS, S M, CLARK, J & BARRY, T B, 1983 'Medieval Britain and Ireland in 1982', *Medieval Archaeol* **27**, 161–229

Printed and bound by CPI Group (UK) Ltd, Croydon, CR0 4YY

31/03/2025

01839049-0002